Theology and Feminism

Signposts in Theology

Theology and Feminism

DAPHNE HAMPSON

Basil Blackwell

Copyright © Daphne Hampson 1990

First published 1990

Basil Blackwell Ltd
108 Cowley Road, Oxford, OX4 1JF, UK

Basil Blackwell, Inc.
3 Cambridge Center
Cambridge, Massachusetts 02142, USA

British Library Cataloguing in Publication Data

A CIP catalogue record for this book is available from the British Library.

Library of Congress Cataloging in Publication Data
Hampson, Margaret Daphne.
    Theology and feminism/Daphne Hampson.
      p. cm. – (Signposts in theology)
    Includes bibliographical references.
    ISBN 0–631–14943–0   ISBN 0–631–14944–9 (pbk.)
    1. Feminist theology. I. Title. II. Series.
  BT83.55.H36 1990
  230'.082–dc20

                  89-28744
                  CIP

Typeset in 10 on 12pt Century Schoolbook
by Best-set Typesetter Ltd.
Printed in Great Britain by Billing & Sons Ltd, Worcester

ABOUT THE AUTHOR

Daphne Hampson started her career as a historian and wrote her Oxford doctoral thesis on the response in Britain to the church conflict in Germany during the Third Reich. She followed this by a Harvard doctorate in systematic theology. Since 1977 she has been a lecturer in systematic theology at the University of St Andrews. In the late 1970s she took a leading part in the campaign to allow women to be ordained in the Anglican churches in Britain. Now defining herself as post-Christian, she believes Christianity and feminism to be incompatible and the Christian myth to be untrue, while wishing to find a way to conceptualize God that is in continuity with the western tradition. Having spent many years in the United States, most recently in 1988/9 as a visiting scholar at Harvard Divinity School, she has engaged deeply with the development of feminist theological thought. Daphne Hampson was the first President of the European Society of Women for Theological Research.

For the members of the Quaker
Meeting, St Andrews, who have
during nine years cherished and
nourished me.

CONTENTS

PREFACE

My first editor for this book, Julia Mosse, gave me one instruction: it was to be user-friendly. I have accordingly divided the chapters into sections, each section being relatively self-contained. In some chapters, notably the Christology chapter, the middle sections could indeed have been placed in any order. But in general there is a progression of thought from one section to the next. The chapters likewise are reasonably self-contained, considering as they do different aspects of the interface between feminism and theology. But again there is a logical progression from one to the next. My hope is that a chapter, or a section, could be made the basis of a group or class discussion. My basic theme – namely that I do not think feminism and Christianity to be compatible – wends its way through the book. The last sections of the Methodology and Theology chapters discuss respectively the methodology of a post-Christian feminist position and what I believe the way forward to be.

I should at the outset clarify my use of the words 'female', 'feminist' and 'feminine'. 'Female' I use, as opposed to male, for the biological difference between men and women. 'Feminist' implies a certain set of views, which could be held by men but rarely are, about the equality of the sexes and the need for example for non-hierarchical relationships. Whether the fact that feminist views are likely to be held by people who are female owes solely to cultural conditioning, or there is a biological ground, is not something to which we can know the answer. The difference here between men and women would appear to be due in large part to cultural conditioning. But to state categorically that there can be no biological component would seem to be foolish. We do not know yet how male hormones (acting indeed before birth and the possibility of different socialization) may affect the male psyche. But that there might be a biological component does not lead me to conclude that men then should do what is 'natural' to them, for there must be a complementarity between the sexes. It makes me think that humanity is faced with a deeper problem than we knew. I use the word 'feminist', it should be noted, not as descriptive of how women always behave, but quite as much as prescriptive of a way in which I believe we all should behave. The word 'feminine' has for me wholly negative connotations. I use it to designate what it has been supposed by men, in a sexist society, that women should be. It is in this sense a cultural construct, and one which has been deeply harmful to women.

The bibliography is designed to help the reader to know where to turn for further reading. Therefore I have arranged the material under subject headings, rather than alphabetically. I list some works not mentioned in the text. A few works which happen to be mentioned in the text are omitted from the bibliography. I place the original date of publication in brackets at the end of a reference when this is of significance.

I have many people to thank for help and encouragement with this work. I must in particular make mention of my friends Helen Steven, Gillian Clark, Nicola Slee, Sarah Coakley and Patricia Richardson who have read the manuscript in whole or part. My mother, Joyce Hampson, has painstakingly read through the text and suggested many improvements. My editor at Basil Blackwell, Stephan Chambers, has taken a lively interest in the work. Kate Chapman, the desk editor at Blackwell, and Gillian Law, who copy-edited the book, have been unfailingly helpful. I dedicate the book to the group of my Quaker friends in St Andrews, Scotland. Though not a Quaker myself (and never likely to be) I have, in that meeting, found a source of inspiration and strength which has allowed me to move into a new world the other side of leaving the church and Christianity. Without them I do not know how I should manage.

Daphne Hampson
Harvard Divinity School
July 1989

ACKNOWLEDGEMENT

The author and publishers are grateful to Harcourt Brace Jovanovich, Inc. and to The Women's Press for permission to reproduce excerpts from *The Color Purple* by Alice Walker, copyright © 1982 by Alice Walker.

Introduction

Feminism represents a revolution. It is not in essence a demand that women should be allowed to join the male world on equal terms. It is a different view of the world. This must be of fundamental import for theology. For theology, as we have known it, has been the creation of men; indeed of men living within a patriarchal society. As women come into their own, theology will take a different shape.

In this introduction I shall consider the idea – which is likely to be held to be fantastic – that feminism represents the death-knell of Christianity as a viable religious option.[1] I do not say this lightly. I myself grew up within Christianity: it was fundamental to my whole outlook – so much so that I chose to study theology and wished, for twenty years, to be ordained. But I have in recent years had to extricate what it may mean to be a religious person from the particular expression of being religious which is Christianity, and to discard Christianity. It has not been easy. If one comes to conclude of Christianity, as I have, that it is neither true nor moral, one is faced with two alternatives. Either one becomes an atheist; which for me was not a serious possibility. Or one comes to reinterpret what one understands by being a religious person who loves God. It may be said by some that my problem was that I was a theologian. I should point out that it was in large part my training in theology which allowed me to find a way forward!

So it will be said that Christianity has weathered many a crisis: feminism is simply the latest. As the saying goes, Christianity is always adapting itself to something believable: it will do so again. It is conservative Christians who, together with more radical feminists, perceive that feminism represents not just one crisis among many. For the feminist challenge strikes at the heart of Christianity. Christianity, and Judaism, are religions which reflect a patriarchal world: God is represented as male, and in biblical religion men and women are often conceived to be differently placed both in relation to God and to one another. The religion of the Hebrew bible largely concerns the relation of a (male) God and His sons. In Christianity the basic symbol of the religion has been the trinity, the relation of Father and Son, through whom humanity is said to be taken up into God. Women may well not have much interest in this whole symbolic order.

So then it will be said that we cannot have such a sharp break with the past. We have to find a way to move forward from where we are. Human beings are social beings, shaped by their history. We cannot discard our Christian past. This is of course true if what is meant by such a statement is that our religion will be shaped by our western heritage. I myself certainly have no inclination to move outside that heritage; though, like others, I may find some things about other traditions helpful. But if what is meant is that we must needs go on living with the Christian myth, and interpreting the world through that pair of spectacles, then that is certainly not the case. That myth has rapidly been discarded by a large number of people, even in the last twenty years. Feminism will come to make it seem not only untrue but immoral. There have in our century been major discontinuities in other spheres of human thought and endeavour: in music, science or philosophy. There is no reason why there should not be discontinuity in religion.

Indeed it may well be the case that the revolutionary nature of our age makes a revolution in religion imperative if we are to remain in any sense religious. The need for a paradigm shift in religion has been with us for some time. Since the Enlightenment of the late eighteenth century it has been clear that there is a singularly ill fit between the basic axioms of Christianity and modern thought. Christianity proclaims a revelation in history, a revelation which makes for a particularity which is at odds with our knowledge of the constancy of nature or the fact that there are in history no interruptions from another order. It becomes difficult to believe that we are in God's particular providence, in the way in which this seemed feasible to those who drew maps of the world with Jerusalem at the centre, given that as we now know the world did not start in 4004 B.C. The scale has changed. Our knowledge today of other world religions has made the claims of Christianity increasingly untenable. The Christian religion becomes relativized. It comes to seem much more likely that the religious myth of the people of Israel, and the structure of

Christian theology, are simply the creation of one particular group of people, who interpreted the world from their perspective.

Now feminism has crowned the crisis. For feminists are saying that Christianity, and Judaism, have been patriarchal myths and that they have hurt women. Once there is a considerable group of people, born and bred within western religion, who turn upon it and declare it to be partial, then that myth is relativized with a vengeance. Feminists are of course making this challenge at a time when the truth of the myth is in any case disputed. Many cope with the crisis by saying that the myth of the religion is however, in its understanding of creation, sin, redemption and the eschaton, a 'true myth'. Those parts which seem non-essential, perhaps the virgin birth, they simply discard. But the feminist challenge makes it difficult to make the sideways move of saying that Christianity is symbolically true. For precisely the feminist contention is that symbols are powerful and may damage relationships.

The idea that Christianity may not be a force for good comes as a shock to many people. Surely, they say, women have only achieved the place which they occupy in society today in the west through the permeation of that society by Christianity. That may be true. Christianity, and Judaism also, have had a strong sense of the worth and dignity of each individual person – though we may note that women have not always been granted the status of those to whom such an ethic applied. But there is no reason why we should not retain these things: they are part of our western culture. The view however that Christian belief has been an unmitigated blessing has been shown by the feminist analysis of recent years to be far too simplistic. The fact that God has in the west been conceived as 'male', and the world of the bible has been considered to be normative for human relations, has served to legitimize the place which women have occupied in western culture and to thwart their striving for equality. To question the social order was to be disobedient to God.

Again it will be said that there have been previous occasions on which Christianity has had to come to terms with issues of human dignity and equality, and that it has done so successfully. The biblical message of love for the neighbour is fundamental, and passages seemingly hostile to women can come to be disregarded. Christianity will win through. Even in the more conservative churches women are beginning to play a greater role, even to be ordained. It will simply take time. To take a parallel example, in the nineteenth century the bible could be quoted to justify a use of slaves, provided humane. Now no one would do that. Indeed the principle of racial equality is increasingly coming to be recognized by everyone except a tiny minority in the Christian church. What is so different about the case of women?

But the challenge of feminism is not simply that women wish to gain an equal place with men in what is essentially a religion which is biased against them. The challenge of feminism is that women may want to express their understanding of God within a different thought structure. Certainly the masculine nature of Christianity, and equally of Judaism, is becoming increasingly problematic to a large number of women. Of course women want equality, and many still strive for equality within the Christian church. But the debate has moved on. While men (and some women) consider whether women can be full insiders within the church, women debate whether or not they want to be. Eleven years ago it was I who wrote the statement in favour of the ordination of women to the priesthood circulated to all members of the General Synod of the Church of England before the vote. Today finds me no longer Christian.

Many men will say that feminism is something which can be taken on board. Even conservatives will agree that, in the past, women have had a raw deal. But, say conservatives, Christianity allows for a dignified place for women. We must not confuse the masculine and the feminine: that would be to the detriment of each. What we desperately need in our world is the feminine. Women have an essential role to play. But women no longer (if they ever did) occupy the place which such men conceive the feminine to represent. Or else other men, of a more liberal disposition, say feminism is good, it will allow men in turn to discover a lost side of themselves. Men need to explore the ways in which they are loving and gentle, to allow themselves to cry or be weak. Our anima must complement our animus. But feminism is not in the first instance concerned with men discovering a lost side of themselves. It is about women coming into their own. This book is not essentially about men: it concerns women.

So it will be said that Christianity is a moral teaching for us to live by. We have in our present world the greatest need for the message which Christ proclaimed. Of course that is true. Nor is there any reason why we should discard that teaching, in so far as it is a part of our heritage and we continue to judge it to be good. But Christianity is not just a moral teaching. That would be humanism. Christianity is also a belief – if the salt is to retain its savour – in Christ.

Christianity proclaims the revelation of God in history, the belief in the uniqueness of Christ, and the inspiration of the literature which tells us of these things.

There lies the nub of the problem. For Christianity cannot discard this reference to a past period of human history. It must necessarily speak of God's act in Christ, and recite the literature which tells us of the tradition into which Jesus came. In other disciplines, philosophy, science or the social sciences, there is no necessary reference to the past. They may commence with the present, or where they believe truth to lie, drawing on the past only in so far as it still seems relevant. But Christianity is a religion of revelation with a necessary foot in history. It cannot lose that reference so long as it remains Christianity. And that reference is to a patriarchal history.

But, it will be asked, is there no way in which women and men can be enabled to go forward together? I would surely hope so. For this to be possible, however, it will be necessary that men should abandon a religion which reflects a patriarchal past, which gives them so much advantage and which in its symbol system is weighted against women. For how may women and men find a common spiritual future on the basis of a religion which reflects the lives of men and which leaves women distraught and angry outsiders? Whether men and women can find a common spiritual future depends on whether men are prepared to join women on the basis of equality. The decisive way in which men can do something to help at the moment is through giving up their power and being prepared to forgo the past. They cannot in any decisive way 'help' women. For women are not asking to be 'given' anything. They are asking to be allowed to determine their own lives. One gives people dignity and self-esteem by ceasing to dominate them and allowing them perfectly naturally to move into their future.

Religion may represent a last citadel for feminism. It is relatively easy to frame laws which declare woman to be an equal of man, or to give women the vote. It represents more of a disturbance to suggest that the laws or the political process may need to change if they are to accommodate women's needs and concerns as well as those of men. It constitutes a profound challenge to male thought that women should come to articulate how they view the world. Religion has represented that which encompasses our interpretation of our lives and our highest hopes. As women begin to name for themselves their ideals and aspirations, their understanding of what they mean by God and their beliefs about the nature of human relations, the religion of humanity may greatly shift. The revolution in religion will affect human society, for religion constitutes an underpinning of our lives.

Feminism is not going to disappear. That half of humanity should come into its own represents too deep a revolution. Feminism will come in time to shatter a picture of reality which came out of a patriarchal world. We find ourselves spiritually in a novel situation. The religion which we have known commences with Adam, the archetypal man, naming and thereby (in Hebrew thought) defining the essence of all living things – including the woman and her reality. The coming of age of women as feminists in theology consists in women beginning to undertake that process of naming for themselves. That, after four thousand years, constitutes a revolution.

NOTE

1 I am in this book specifically concerned with Christianity. Much that I say would also be true of Judaism, though my impression is that the way in which it is affected by feminism differs in some respects from the way in which Christianity is affected. I am moreover not qualified to comment on Judaism.

CHAPTER 1

Methodology

THE NATURE OF CHRISTIANITY

Christianity is a historical religion. By that I do not mean simply that Christianity arose at a certain time in history. Obviously that is true of all ideas and movements. Nor do I mean that it bears the imprint of the time when it arose. That too one may imagine must always be the case. I mean that Christianity proclaims there to have been a revelation of God in history. Therefore that time and that particular history in which the revelation is deemed to have taken place become integral to the religion. Christianity cannot lose its reference to that history.

It will be clear that human religion need not in this sense be historical. It could be believed that God, whatever was understood by God, was equally close to all times and places; that no particular period, and no particular events, were to be held to be more revelatory of God than others. Of course people in one time or place might be more aware of God, or more able to formulate their awareness in a way which persisted through further generations. But it would not be held that God revealed God's self to a particular people, or through a particular person, in a certain time in history. Religion then would be founded on religious experience in general. In conceptualizing what they meant by God, people in each age would be free to think again, starting from where they found themselves. Such a religion might also contain certain philosophical ideas, ideas which could be deduced from a priori reason. But history would be central to the religion in the way in which history is central to Christianity.

Of course Christians also want to start in the present in speaking of their awareness of God. Christianity has moreover incorporated philosophical ideas. But that is not the end of the matter. Christians, because of the type of religion which Christianity is, must always refer to certain historical events, above all to the person Jesus of Nazareth. Christianity has this necessary relation to history. Of a worship service in which no mention was made of Christ, the bible was not read, and no reference made to God's dealings with the people of Israel or of the early church, we might well say that it was theistic (if mention was made of God), but it could not rightly be called Christian.

Christians believe in particularity. That is to say they believe that God was in some sense differently related to particular events, or may be said in particular to have revealed God's self through those events, in a way in which this is not true of all other events or periods in history. Above all they believe that that must be said of Christ which is to be said of no other human being. However they may express his uniqueness, they must say of Jesus of Nazareth that there was a revelation of God through him in a way in which this is not true of you or me. God is bound up with peculiar events, a particular people, above all with the person Jesus of Nazareth. Therefore reference must needs always be made to this history and to this person.

Now I am not myself a Christian because I do not believe that there could be this particularity. I do not believe, whatever I may mean by God, that it could be said of God that God was differently related to one age or people than God is related to all ages or people. God is something which is always available, however much people in some ages, or some people in each age, may appear to be more aware of God. To put this differently and more technically, I do not believe that the causal nexus of history, or that of nature, could be broken. That is to say I do not believe that there could be peculiar events, such as a resurrection, or miracles, events which interrupt the normal causal relationships persisting in history and in nature. I do not believe in uniqueness.[1] Thus I do not for example think that there could be a human person (which Christians must proclaim) who stood in a different relationship to God than do all other human beings. True, Jesus of Nazareth may have been deeply aware of God; so have others been. But he was no more than that, I believe, a person deeply in tune with God. This is not a Christian position.

We turn then to the issue of the compatibility of feminism and Christianity. Clearly there can be no reason why one should not be a feminist and a religious person, in the sense in which I am myself a religious person. If one believes that God (whatever one may mean by God) is equally available to all times and places, then it is possible to start in the present in acquiring one's religious sensibilities and formulating what one may mean by God. Of course one may draw on the past as one will. There is no reason to think that people in the past may not have had a profound understanding of God, an understanding which will illuminate one's own. Again, people in other religions may likewise have had (though for myself as a westerner I find the most to be gained through looking at western religion). But no necessary reference is being made to history, to any particular literature, or any particular person. Presumably as a feminist one will only accept into one's formulation of one's religious position ideas which do not conflict with one's ethical position.

Christians however are not in this situation. For Christians believe there to have been a revelation of God in history. Therefore they must necessarily make reference to that history. In a Christian service the bible will be read, the story told of God's dealings with the people of Israel and of His coming in Christ, and above all the resurrection will be proclaimed. This history is not dispensable. In a subtle way, therefore, the history of a past age, the relationships between people which are embodied in the scriptures which tell of that revelation, and the teaching of Him who is believed to be the revelation of God will be made present. Moreover, these things will be brought into the present not as just any history or teaching, but as that through which God is supremely known.

Now that history is a patriarchal history. The relationships between persons of which the bible tells are relations between people existing in a patriarchal society. Women are either absent, or present fulfilling for the most part the roles which were assigned to women in that society. The figure of Christ is that of a male figure, and that is not to be evaded. God is conveyed through the use of metaphors which are male not female. And that history is not to be disposed of. It is necessarily present, and present as central to the religion. Even if at a conscious level people think that of course that was a patriarchal age, and we now live in certain respects in a more enlightened age, the metaphors and symbols which are present will be impressed on people's minds. The question then is not whether feminism and being a religious person are compatible. That is clearly the case. But whether feminism can be reconciled with Christianity is a very different question. For Christianity is a historical religion, one which necessarily relates to history. And the history to which it relates is a patriarchal history.

Moreover, that history and that revelation to which Christians necessarily make reference are in some sense normative for the religion. For it is that history, and that revelation, in which it is believed that God has made Himself known. Christians may hold very different positions as to how far it is normative. Some believe that it is normative in an absolute sense; that Christ revealed what is to be believed (for example about divorce) for all times. Others are of a more liberal disposition. They hold that the revelation was given through the cultural medium of one particular time, and that while the message may remain the same (for example that one should love one's neighbour) this may require a different expression in a different age. Likewise, they are prepared to make allowance for the fact that certain scientific facts about the world were not known, or for example that the biological relation of woman to man was misunderstood. But even Christians of a more liberal variety must necessarily make reference to a past age. (Thus in the current debate about the ordination of women, both sides ask what does Jesus' message suggest is the right thing to do, what difference does it make that Jesus was a male human being, or what kind of a community was the early church? Again they ask of what significance it is that the metaphors used for God in the Hebrew and Christian scriptures are overwhelmingly male?) Christianity, as long as it remains Christianity, cannot lose its historical reference.[2]

But suppose I am wrong in my basic presupposition that there cannot be particularity. Suppose – to take the clearest example, which would make what I believe to be the nature of the world fall to the ground like a pack of cards – that there was a resurrection. Not simply a resurrection in people's minds – I might well grant that – but a resurrection as an objective fact of history, so that it could be said that the causal nexus of history and that of nature were broken (for there are not resurrections). (Of course if there are resurrections, then my point is proved and there is again a regularity to nature; but then there is no particular reason for saying that Jesus is unique as Christians believe.) Suppose there was a resurrection. What follows? The resurrection, for people who believe it to have taken place, is presumably an objective fact of history; one which they cannot circumvent even if they would. Willy-nilly they are forced to concede that here is some fact or reality to which all else that they believe must necessarily conform.

So what of feminists, those who are convinced that Christian claims are true? Their feminism must in some way be fitted to the facts of Christianity. There was a resurrection. Christ is Lord, or in some sense unique. God is known through the people of Israel and the history of the church. The scriptures which tell of these events through which God is known become a unique book. They may be liberal, but there is a certain minimum reference to a particular history, above all to a certain person, which is not to be avoided if one is to call oneself Christian. But then there arises a theodicy question, a question to do with the justification of God. How can God be seen to be good when one considers what history has been, and what it has meant for women that God has been conceived in primarily male terms? True, it may well be that much good has come for women from Christian history and from Christ's moral teaching. But why, if God be good, has any harm come to women? For that God has been conceived as male, and that biblical teaching which arose out of a patriarchal society has been held to be the revelation of God, must surely be seen to be the underlying facts of western culture which have led to discrimination against women. There is then a theological question posed for one who takes the feminist agenda seriously and believes in human equality, as to how this revelation can be a revelation of God.

The question then as to whether feminism and Christianity are compatible is that of whether the equality of women is compatible with a religion which has come from a past patriarchal age. In this chapter I shall consider various answers given to that question. I shall first look at a conservative response to the gap which exists between the past in its understanding of women and the present. Basically conservatives see the past as normative and their view as to what women may aspire to is governed by that past. I shall then look at various Christian feminist and liberal responses which try to bridge the gap between past and present. Thirdly, I shall look at those Christian feminists who believe there to be no real gap, so that the problem is thereby solved. The situation which women face is, they say, essentially that which women have always faced under patriarchy, so that women have no difficulty in finding a solidarity with other women across the ages. Finally, I shall turn to a religious position such as my own which is not Christian, though religious and within the western tradition, in which the present is normative and the past is only drawn upon in so far as that seems to be appropriate. Such a religious position alone, I shall suggest, is compatible with feminism.

THE CONSERVATIVE RESPONSE

One response which can be made to the gap which exists between the world in which Christianity came into being and the present world is to allow what is to be held to be essentially normative for the religion to reside in the past. I shall call this response 'conservative'. There are different depths of conservatism possible. An extreme conservative position would be to believe that, through the fact that God chose to become incarnate within a particular society, indeed through the fact that God chose a particular tradition and people, all aspects of that society are to be conceived to accord with the will of God. In relation to the question of the position of women, it would follow that, since – it is thought – the new testament does not allow the headship of a woman, and through the fact that women did not exercise headship in that society, that a woman should be head of state is as wrong as that a woman should exercise headship within the church. A more moderate (though perhaps less consistent) conservative position would be to differentiate between what is God's will for His people, and what is allowable in the world at large. In relation to the example of the headship issue, it would follow that although a woman may not hold a position of authority in the church, she may be prime minister. An intermediate case would seem to be that of whether, and in what sense, a father should be the 'head' of the Christian family. But at least as far as the church is concerned, a conservative believes that what place a woman should hold was made known in the past and stands for all time.

The conservative outlook entails a particular conception of God (and of Christ), an understanding of which it cannot simply be said that it is held in common by all Christians: something I think often not recognized by conservatives themselves. For it is assumed that God, who is conceived in highly anthropomorphic terms, has given what amounts to a blueprint to humanity as to what His will may be. Listening on one occasion to a Greek Orthodox argue against the ordination of women, I had the distinct impression that his God, who seemed to reside immediately above the ceiling of the room in which we were gathered, had issued the most precise directions to humanity. God's plan is held to be comprehensive, and has been set for all time. God has given men and women differing roles within His creation, roles which do not change. Within Catholic thought these different positions of men and women tend to be thought 'natural', and it is contended that the same gender arrangements are to be found in all known human societies. To say this is, it should be noted, to make a theological point: since it is held that God is the creator, so that what is natural, and what is also found to be the case, must accord with what is God's intention.

These presuppositions are evident also in the way in which Christ is understood. Through Christ, who was and is God, it is considered to have been revealed to us what is God's will. Each of his actions acquires significance. Christ, as God, was omniscient, his outlook not limited by the time in which he lived. Thus Graham Leonard, a prominent English Anglican high church bishop, arguing against the ordination of women: 'The Lord of the Gospels whom I know, love and seek to obey is not one who was socially conditioned in what he said or did.'[3] Jesus was an essentially free agent. If then his actions simply accorded with what was the convention of his society, this was not because he had so to act, or failed to see that a certain convention was socially limited. He could, as God, have chosen to act otherwise. Thus the fact that he did not act otherwise is held to indicate that these social arrangements do indeed accord with the will of God. It is thought that Jesus was peculiarly open to women, breaking in this with custom. Since then, negatively, he did not number them among the twelve, it may be held to have been his intention not to do so. Thus the Vatican Declaration against the ordination of women: 'Jesus did not call any woman to become part of the Twelve. If he acted in this way, it was not in order to conform to the customs of his time, for his attitude towards women was quite different from that of his milieu, and he deliberately and courageously broke with it.'[4] It is believed moreover to be the case that, as God, Jesus had what may be called a trans-historical knowledge. His actions then (in this case in calling the twelve) did not simply relate to his immediate Jewish context, but are to be seen as a considered action undertaken in relation to his having founded the church. From what subsequently came about in history, one may say what was his intention. Thus it is sometimes said that, had Jesus intended that women should be priests in his church, he would have chosen his mother.[5]

Not only is it believed that God, through creation and revelation, has made known His will for humankind, a will revealed to us supremely through the words and actions of Jesus Christ, but He has continued to guide His church. A good reason then for thinking that it is not God's will that women be ordained is that the church has never done so. That this is the case stands, quite independently of the reasons which may have been given for not doing so in the past, reasons which may or may not appear cogent today. Thus the Vatican Declaration can freely admit that the former reasons for not ordaining women are now discredited, while at the same time pointing to the constancy of the tradition. In a matter as fundamental as that of the constitution of the church, God could not have allowed that error should have persisted over such a period of time.

Protestant conservatism has a different flavour from Catholic conservatism. For one of Karl Barth's disposition it could never be said that because something has been perceived to be natural by humankind, therefore it is the will of God. What is God's will is, for Barth, to be read out of the scriptures. (Though one must wonder how far Barth was influenced in his interpretation of scripture by the conservative Swiss background from which he came.) It therefore becomes imperative that the scriptures be interpreted so as to form a consistent whole. Barth believes that the scriptures from Genesis forward imply the headship of man and the subordination of woman. The order of salvation takes up the order of creation. Other evangelicals, perhaps particularly from an Anglo-Saxon tradition, may be less consistent, speaking also of what is found in 'nature'. But for all Protestants it is the record of scriptures which is crucial. They lack the Catholic sense that it is scriptures together with the unfolding tradition of the church in which authority lies.

I shall then turn to three examples which illustrate well the conservative mind-set. Conservatives believe revelation to have been given in the past, as do all Christians. But their understanding of revelation is that God has revealed what is to be the case, or what is truth, in very exact terms. The revelation is seen to have been essentially unaffected by surrounding circumstances, or indeed the historical circumstances of that time are believed to be revealed to be God's will for humankind. The revelation in that time, as it is believed to have been, is then transposed like a self-enclosed capsule into the present age. It is not to be affected, or not essentially affected, by the norms and outlook of another age. Likewise theological truth is held to exist in a sphere of its own, unaffected by scientific discoveries or knowledge which we now have which clashes with what is believed to be the biblical revelation. But such an outlook does not mean that the conservatives are not in trouble. For there is an inevitable clash between what they believe the place of women should be, and the beliefs of the surrounding world in which they are set, and which indeed they may themselves have to some extent appropriated.

The first example pertains to the failure, of Catholic Christians in particular, to contextualize the words and actions of Jesus in relation to the circumstances of the world in which he lived. Conservatives thus hold what must appear, to those who do not hold to a conservative position, to be a distorted conception of what he was about. Christians as a whole however may be said to have been slow to appropriate the results of textual criticism and historical research. That this is the case may be thought not to be chance. For Christians (inasmuch as Christians see a peculiar revelation to have taken place in Christ) tend to interpret Christ's words and actions in abstraction from any historical context, or, believing that God in Christ had a particular intention, they understand his words and actions in the light of later church history. In what I say here I may well not be followed in every respect by one or another scholar, and there are matters open to different interpretation. Nevertheless, the gist of what we need to know if we are to understand Jesus' words and actions will be evident. Jesus was a first-century Palestinian Jew. As a good Jew, it would seem highly unlikely that he had any intention of founding a new religion, let alone setting up a 'priesthood' for it. If (as he may well have done) he thought that he was the Messiah, then his choosing of the twelve would seem to have been a symbolic action, through which he should indicate to people who he was. The twelve represent the twelve tribes of Israel, which are in the last days to be gathered in. (Matthew says of them that they will sit on the twelve thrones of Israel, judging the twelve tribes.) By definition no woman could have been among the twelve, since a circumcised male alone could represent a patriarch of Israel. Furthermore, of the apostles it is said that they are to go out and bear witness to Jesus. Under Jewish law the word of a woman was not counted that of a witness. (Hence when the evangelist has the women discover the empty tomb, he does not have them witness to the resurrection but rather go and tell the men.) There is no indication that there was any direct connection between the twelve (of whom it is said in Acts that they stayed in Jerusalem) and the advent of ministry in the churches in the gentile world. Ministry seems to have grown up in a haphazard manner, basically in response to the need that various functions be performed. St Paul was not 'ordained' – and would not have known what the term connoted.

It is in the light of facts like these that Jesus' words and actions are to be understood. I repeat: what I have said here might well be qualified by one or another scholar in this or that regard. But the idea – current indeed in Anglican circles until the last century – that

Jesus 'ordained' twelve men (who became the first 'bishops'), who subsequently laid their hands on the heads of others, and so forth down to the present day, can certainly not be allowed to stand. One must interpret Jesus' actions in relation to his cultural context. To read them through a lens drawn from another context, for example that of later church history, is to impose a construction on the material for which there is no warrant. The result may be bizarre. Thus to those conservatives who, arguing against the ordination of women, contend that Jesus ordained no 'priestesses', it must be said that neither did he ordain any priests! Indeed the Levitical code was considered (for example by the author of the letter to the Hebrews) to have been both consummated and overcome in Christ. Finally, of the argument that Jesus treated women well (and thus it is of significance that he did not 'choose' women – to be part of a symbolic number of people who in any case had to be male!), it must be said that it is quite unwarranted. As we shall see later,[6] there is every evidence that Jesus (though kind to women) was deeply culturally conditioned. It would indeed be surprising were this not to be the case!

A second example of the conservative failure to consider cultural context and to relate theological belief to knowledge which we possess, is the contention that the church has never ordained women and cannot have been wrong. Let us consider this question. Why, one must ask, has the church not ordained women? It must in the first place be said that women in the past were not for example doctors or politicians, so it is hardly surprising that they should not have held public office in the church. (One holding my position might well want to say that, given the masculinist nature of the religion, no wonder women have been excluded from its ministry – but that is an argument as to why women should leave Christianity, not for ordaining them.) But further it must be said, in response to the conservative position, that it was not simply a matter of whim or chance that women were not in the past ordained. There were considered theological reasons, based on what was believed to be the case about the biological relationship of woman and man, as to why they could not be. Understandings of human reproduction have varied (and one cannot here consider all such understandings and their consequences for what the relation of man to woman was held to be). Moreover, it must be the case that biological beliefs have been intertwined with social reasons for not ordaining women. Nevertheless, it is instructive to look at why, for example, Thomas Aquinas thought that women could not be ordained (for his views have clearly been highly influential in the Catholic tradition). It is not that the question of the ordination of women is being considered for the first time in our day!

Thomas' thought on the matter is complex. It may or may not be that he would have thought it necessary for there to be a 'natural resemblance' (such as the Vatican Declaration believes to be necessary) between the male Christ and the male priest. This I shall consider below.[7] However, in the passage in which he specifically considers whether a woman can be ordained, his answering in the negative, it must be pointed out, is dependent on biological presuppositions which we now know to be false. Priesthood, he says, signifies authority.[8] (A statement with which it should be said not all Christians today would necessarily agree, but let us grant him that.) Now a woman is not such that she can signify authority; that is to say, she does not have the sign-quality[9] which could signify authority. For woman, he says, is in a state of subjection (*quia mulier statum subjectionis habet*). Thomas then proceeds to consider whether a slave (presumed male) could be ordained, giving the answer that obviously not while he remains a slave, for slavery cannot signify authority, but that slavery is a condition of external fortune, and if freed from his slavery, then he can be ordained. Woman's defect is by contrast by nature.

But why does Thomas consider a woman to be defective by nature? The answer is clear: it owes to the biological presuppositions which he takes from Aristotle. (Indeed in the same passage in the *Commentary* he puts forward an argument – which might well be used in favour of the ordination of women! – that order pertains to the soul, and the soul is without sex; a point, interestingly, to which he makes no response. Thus it is clear that it is owing to her *body* that a woman is defective.) Thomas' biology is apparent in his discussion in question 92 of the *Summa*.[10] Aristotle had argued that the male semen gave 'form' to the 'matter' provided by the woman; form here being a determining principle which shapes matter, such that in human beings the form is the rational soul, the particular characteristic which makes us human. Thomas modifies this. He wishes to assert that God gives the soul to the foetus. Thus for him the male has a lesser role, simply preparing the matter contributed by the female, so that it is ready to accept the soul. But it remains the case that the male is considered the superior. He takes it for granted that in human generation the female is the passive principle, the male the active. Further he comments that the male has the greater discretion of reason. Again he follows Aristotle in believing that each child ought to be male and that a female is the result of misadventure. He writes:

> Woman is defective and misbegotten, for the active force in the male seed tends to the production of a perfect likeness in the masculine sex; while the production of woman comes from defect in the active force or from some material indisposition, or even from some external influence; such as that of a south wind, which is moist, as the Philosopher [Aristotle] observes.[11]

He adds that it is nature's intention, for the purposes of generation, that some foetuses should turn out female. Yet this does not alter the fact that the female is essentially a misbegotten male, not another kind of human being.

We now know that, far from the male imposing form on female matter, making a human being what he or she is, foetuses come from an equal number of chromosomes from the male and from the female. Far from a male being the norm for a human being and the female a potentially male foetus which miscarried, female and male are two different kinds of human being. At least in relation to this argument of Thomas' against the ordination of women, it must be said that it does not hold water. His presumption that, through her body, a woman signifies inferiority, rests on a mistaken biology. One may think there to be very little point in simply reciting that 'the church has never ordained women' without enquiring into why this should have been. (Unless, that is, one is starting from an a priori stance that the church cannot, in such a fundamental matter, have erred.)

A third example of the way in which conservatives hold theological beliefs to exist in abstraction from the rest of human knowledge is the discussion about male headship. There are two passages in the new testament concerning male headship, one Pauline and one not.[12] Both argue directly from Genesis. Barth, considered by many the greatest theologian of the twentieth century, comments that, according to Genesis, woman was taken forth from man, and created in relation to the man's reality, and not vice versa. What sense, one must ask, the other side of Darwin, could this possibly make? We may not know exactly how evolution took place, but it is at least now clear that humanity evolved in some way from the higher apes; that there were female and male of other species on the earth before the appearance of women and men. It cannot then be that a man was present on earth before a woman, and the woman formed from him.

The two sexes evolved in relation the one to the other. To contend that Genesis is 'symbolically true' does not help the conservative case. It is not symbolically true: it is symbolically false. A 'true myth' would have to symbolize women and men evolving in relation to one another, neither sex being present before the other.

Considering these three examples one has to ask after the nature of the conservative mind-set. What is going on? For we are clearly concerned with intelligent human beings. It cannot be said of Barth that he did not know of evolution! It does however strike one of some of the conservative authors, particularly Catholic, that they have abstracted their theological beliefs from other knowledge of which they must be in possession. Perhaps it is the result of the almost exclusively 'arts' training which many theologians receive? I take two examples. The high church Anglican theologian Eric Mascall, writing in response to a report of a Lambeth subcommittee which commented that medieval understandings were based on false biological views, expressed himself thus:

> In the absence of any details it is difficult to assess the force of these references to biology and sociology ... (1) What, if any, were the false biological views in question? (2) How did it follow from them that women could not be ordained to the priesthood? (3) What are the views which have taken their place? ... (7) Have the views about women which have now come to be held proved to be true?[13]

This is clearly absurd. Given that we may have yet more to learn about human reproduction, it must be said that it is not a case of 'views' which may or may not be right. As we have seen, in the past false biological views led to false reasoning. We do at least now know that in the formation of the new foetus an equal number of chromosomes come from the male and from the female, and that a female is not a malformed male foetus: this is not a 'view'. Then take Leonard's speech to the General Synod of the Church of England before the crucial vote on the ordination of women to the priesthood in 1978. He said: 'If both our Lord and S. Paul were so conditioned, what about us? By what criteria do we judge that our conditioning in this century accords with the Divine will but that in the earlier generations does not?'[14] I find the remark significant for the assumption which is made that there was nothing harmful about the previous view of the relation between men and women; indeed the previous view may have accorded with the divine will and our present outlook not. But what I want to draw attention to here is the failure to understand that past social beliefs were formed within the context of false beliefs about the biological relation of woman and man. I see that I (who had written the statement in favour of the ordination of women to the priesthood which was circulated to all members of the Synod before the vote,[15] a statement to which Leonard may well in part have been responding) wrote in the margin of my copy of his speech: 'Have microscopes.'

The conservative outlook is then that of a peculiar kind of 'faith'. It is a faith that theology is God-given and self-enclosed, unaffected by humanity. Thus Barth continues to read what he does out of Genesis, setting aside all else that he must know, for the text alone counts. Thus the Catholic conservatives believe the church to be a God-given institution which cannot in major ways have gone astray. Jesus is held to be God, his actions God's actions in history, to be interpreted without reference to his actual historical circumstances. Taken in its own terms, the conservative position is unanswerable. One might however comment that it is possibly the case that those theologians whose views are now quoted as the word of God, or whose theological reasoning is taken over without question, may not have believed theology to exist independently of human knowledge or social conditions. Precisely they drew on what was common knowledge (that is to say what was believed to be knowledge) in their day. Might not St Paul or Thomas Aquinas raise an eyebrow at the idea that their views continue to be cited, given the knowledge which we now have about the origin of humankind or the biological relation of woman to man?[16]

One should not comment on how far the views which conservatives hold are a rationalization of a misogynist stance. That must vary from individual to individual and there is no need to say that simply to hold these views (if one believes them to be the revealed will of God) is in itself misogynist. What one should however point to is that the critique of western culture which in recent years has been mounted by feminists has not been understood or appropriated – and that in this there lies a certain blindness. Conservatives proceed as though the past relation between women and men has been satisfactory, as though no one has been wounded by it. As though it does not matter that half of humanity has been prohibited from realizing their potential. But such a blindness follows from the belief that women have a 'place' in God's scheme; one which is natural, or God's will for them, and in which therefore they should find themselves fulfilled. As Karl Barth expresses it, woman is to man as B is to A; why should woman mind?[17] The idea that western religion has itself been a cause of attitudes which have deeply harmed women obviously cannot be given entrance by them. For were this to be admitted to be the case, the belief that their religious position (in which women are subordinate, or hold a particular place) is of God would be undermined. Nor is there any recognition of the fact that relations of super- and sub-ordination are power relations which are in themselves wrong. In not believing such relations to be wrong, conservatives are going against the whole ethos of the modern world, in which it has increasingly come to be held that humans should be treated as equals. Conservatives may well believe that the abuse of their authority by men is wrong, but that relationships in which one sex is in such a position that it could so abuse the other are in themselves wrong cannot be admitted.

Yet it is the idea that men should have power over women, coupled with the belief that women have a particular 'role' – much more closely specified than is any corresponding male 'role', that is coming to be questioned. Thus conservatives – try as they may to isolate their theology in a cocoon separate from human knowledge, culture and society – are in trouble. Indeed the pressure for change is not something which batters the conservative position from outside, it is a worm which undermines it from within. For in that they are living in the modern world, and in so far (one must say) as they are good persons seeking to do what is right, conservatives must see much of the critique of past patriarchal relationships to be justified. A notable example of this is the decree of the Second Vatican Council 'Gaudium et Spes' which speaks of the dignity of persons, men and women alike. But when the church has spoken in these terms, saying in effect that women should not be discriminated against in the world, it becomes all the more problematical for it to appear suddenly to turn around and declare that women may not be ordained in the church!

The conservative stance then crumbles from within. Or else it becomes an increasingly embattled stance, out of touch with the world. It has been well said that to say the same thing in a different age is to say something different. At one time the beliefs held about woman in the church, that she might not be ordained, that she was placed subordinate to man, that she had her 'own' sphere of motherhood, were simply at one with the beliefs of the world in which the church was situated. There was nothing particularly remarkable about these views; though some brave women in each age may have tried to overstep the limits set for them. As we have seen, beliefs held about women were simply the logical corollary of biological views, or the understanding of the origin of humanity. But to continue to proclaim these things, to continue not to ordain women, in the world of today, sets the church apart. It leaves it in an indefensible position. Indeed the kinds of arguments that are mustered (Jesus did not ordain women and that is a fact, the church has not ordained women and that is a fact, women in all societies have been subordinate to men and that is a fact) become no arguments at all when we realize the context in which Jesus did what he did, when we know that the biological views on which Thomas Aquinas' views were founded were false, and live in a world in which (in our western societies at least) women are coming to take their place as the equals of men.

ATTEMPTS TO BRIDGE

Christians of a liberal disposition and Christian feminists attempt to throw a bridge between past and present. They must necessarily as Christians make reference to the past. But they seek also to have a religion which is in tune with the world in which we live. I shall here consider three such attempts to connect past and present: firstly, that which I shall call a 'kairos' approach, in which the past is basically normative but it is said that there can be development; secondly, that which I shall call the 'golden thread' approach, in which a leading motif is lifted out of the past and applied in another situation; thirdly, that which I shall call an 'a priori ethical' position, in which essentially authority is seen to lie in the present but there is not perceived to be any fundamental clash with the past. I shall describe these approaches as ideal types, but in each case illustrate them by reference to the work of one or another theologian. I shall suggest that there are fundamental problems with each.

The 'kairos' approach

I gave this approach this title following a pamphlet which reproduces a lecture given by the English Anglican bishop of high church disposition John Austin Baker to a conference of the Movement for the Ordination of Women.[18] I believe that it is (in less thought-out form) widely followed by proponents of the ordination of women, perhaps of a less radical variety, and certainly I would think that it appeals to many men. Having written a fairly scathing account of this approach in draft, I sent it to John Austin Baker (as I have also sent my account of their work to Christians feminists whom I discuss in this book for comment) only to receive a delightful letter from him which rescinded much that he had written, explained that he had been given the title, and essentially agreed with my criticism! I shall press on however, for this pamphlet is the best exposition of which I know of what I believe to be a widely held position.

Baker considers the biblical theme of 'kairos', the time (unlike normal linear time) in which action is demanded or a time which is opportune. The Israelites believed in a divine purpose in history, which unfolds stage by stage. 'That history, because it is God's history, is a purposeful line; but because it is human history as well, it is also a zig-zag one.' God is seen as one who can bring about such kairoi in history, and who has a will for humankind.

> It is not even a question of God inspiring people to exploit these opportunities when they arise. It is a matter of God actually creating the pregnant or opportune situation. ... And let us be quite clear that the fact that any particular system doesn't go on for ever doesn't mean it wasn't God's will when it came in. 'God fulfils himself in many ways' – because he does take history seriously. He made it.

Thus, in relation to the ordination of women, the question to be asked is: 'Is this the opportunity God has deliberately created for this new development in the life of Christ's Church?'

It is clear why this approach has appeal. It is a particularly neat fit with Christianity itself. Christianity is a historical religion; Christians believe that God is actively involved in history. The kairos approach allows people to say that God is indeed involved in history and continues to be involved, bringing about in time something new. Christianity is a religion in which there can be development precisely because it is a historical religion, tied to history. Such thinking may have a particular appeal to Catholic Christians, who tend to think in terms of an evolving revelation. At the same time the kairos approach apparently allows it to be said that the past has not been at fault; it is simply that God moves with humanity into a new age.

I believe this approach to be ethically incoherent. The fact that I should think this, and thought this at the time when I was one of the leaders of the movement campaigning for the ordination of women, brings it home to me how difficult it was for me to work within that movement. Consider what the kairos approach implies. It is being suggested, is it, that God saw nothing wrong with the past situation in which only men could be ordained? That God has waited until this late hour to create a situation in which it is right to ordain women also? That God has perhaps changed His mind? The kairos approach makes God both immoral (if God saw nothing wrong with the previous sexism of the church's stance) and fickle. The conservative position, in which God has created a fixed place for woman in an ordered universe, is actually not in the same way morally objectionable and is much more coherent. The kairos approach, whereby God in God's good time brings into being a new situation, can only be morally credible if one fails to see in sexism the evil which it is.

Of course the response which is likely to be made to such objections is that God works with human beings, so that only when human society has reached a certain stage of development does it become appropriate to ordain women. But this also is ethically incomprehensible. For according to the kairos approach, God is to be seen as deeply involved in the direction of human history! Now sexism is so fundamental an evil that it becomes very difficult for anyone who has grasped this to envisage that God could be said to have been involved with human history. Of such a God one may well say, with Alice Walker's Celie, that he 'just sit up there being deef'.[19] Moreover, the kairos approach cannot speak to the fact of an all-male priesthood (which God is supposed to have given to His church and to have been adequate in past ages) precisely having been one of the factors making for the secondary position of women in society. If men alone could represent God, then somehow they were the lords of women. If women could not represent God, that reflected upon women.

A kairos approach whitewashes the past. The Christian church, it implies, has not, through its sexism, been a cause of sexism in the world. (The fact that this might have been the case seems to be beyond the imagination of many even of liberal disposition in the church.) The church has nothing for which to apologize. Men are let off scot-free. They are now to admit women to orders, orders which they themselves have rightly filled over the centuries. Meanwhile a woman who adopts a kairos approach is to see herself as one whom God has now deigned to choose, and privileged at that. But if only now is it God's intention that they also be admitted to orders, women must necessarily see themselves as some kind of secondary citizens. At a time when my country had a woman in the highest office of state, women were still not admitted to the lowest order in the church, that of deacon.

The 'golden thread' approach

This approach has considerable theological ancestry, particularly Lutheran. It is a way of bringing some kind of order to the many diverse things which the scriptures could be said to be about. Luther imposed a coherence upon Christianity through concluding that justification by faith was the theme which unlocked the scriptures. He then proceeded to read them in terms of this motif. In the twentieth century we find the Lutheran theologian and new testament scholar Rudolf Bultmann reading the scriptures in terms of a very similar theme. Taking an existentialist approach, he says that it is God who delivers us into freedom, which is not something which we can accomplish for ourselves. Much liberation theology has implicitly worked with what I here call a 'golden thread' approach. The theme which interests such theologians is that of liberation: this is both read out of the scriptures and the scriptures are read in terms of this theme.

It is in the fact that a golden thread methodology may be a two-stage operation that its potential value lies in relation to the issue of women. Thus one may (first stage) read the meaning of scripture out of it, and then (second stage) apply what one holds to be the golden thread to another situation, not considered in the scriptures. Or (another possibility), one may judge one theme in scripture to be an organizing focus (first stage), and then (second stage) bring that criterion to scripture, judging other themes to be of lesser importance or frankly wanting. I shall consider each of these possibilities. In the first case one asks (stage one) what it is that the scriptures (or Christianity) are essentially about? One responds that Christianity is about the dignity and integrity of persons as children of God, and consequently their liberation from oppression. One then asks (stage two) what this implies for how women should be treated in the church in our day? The great advantage of this approach is that it gets away from picking out odd texts from the bible to 'prove' one thing or another and asks after the underlying message. Moreover, it allows us to adjudicate on a matter with which the bible does not concern itself (as it may be said not to concern itself with the question of the liberation of women). It can moreover, as in the second case, be used in order to produce coherence within the biblical material itself. Thus it may be said (stage one) that fundamental to the biblical outlook is that in Christ there is neither Jew nor Greek, nor bond nor free, no more male and female. Other biblical passages (stage two) may then be held to be less than adequate in terms of this criterion.

It is of interest to consider the issue of women in comparison with other issues in relation to which such a methodology has been applied. Luther himself knew well what methodologically he was doing and what was necessary: that he needed to order and adjudicate. For as he said – in inimitable words – 'the scriptures have a wax nose.' Thus, working in terms of what I have called a 'golden thread' approach (the golden thread being justification by faith) he names the Epistle to James (which appears to speak of justification by works) an 'epistle of straw'. An example in relation to which the opponents of the ordination of women might be expected to agree that they were making use of such a methodology is the case of slavery. The new testament implies that the use of slaves, provided it is humane, does not contravene the will of God. But in time Christian people came to ask after the fundamental values of Christianity; such that slavery then became an impossibility. Liberation theology does not, in the same sense, require a two-stage operation. For the call to liberate the poor, it may well be said, is to be read directly out of scripture. An argument that the equality of women is a necessary implication of Christianity must clearly employ a two-stage operation. But this is not necessarily a bad thing. For people are forced, as I suggested, to employ a more sophisticated hermeneutic than simply selecting odd biblical verses. It should be noted that what I have called a two-stage golden thread approach implies that human beings have some kind of control over what they will say is right. In this it begins to approach to what I shall call an 'ethical a priori' position.

I should like to consider momentarily the application of such an approach to the various (conflicting) new testament verses which have to do with the status of women. I certainly used to use a golden thread methodology, together with other kinds of considerations, when arguing for the ordination of women. It seemed to me axiomatic. But this is not surprising, since I basically held an a priori ethical position. Thus it seemed to me clear that the Galatians passage (that there is neither Jew nor Greek, nor bond nor free, there is no more male and female)[20] was of the essence of Christianity. Other passages were to be judged mistaken in terms of this criterion. How could one, should one wish, argue that it is the Galatians passage which is fundamental? (The fact that I found it offensive to have to make any such argument for human equality shows that I was working with an ethical a priori approach, but I believe that a case can be made.) In this passage, one may well argue, Paul broke through to the ultimate implications of the Christian message. It is a passage in which he is concerned with the nature of life in Christ (for it is a baptismal statement). Indeed it may well be intended as a statement as to what should be the case in the eschaton. By contrast, the Corinthians passage in which Paul speaks of male headship, and in which it is said that women should be silent (a verse which is probably an interpolation and does not owe to Paul), he is concerned with a practical situation which has arisen, a situation in which the church, still insecure in a pagan world, was likely to cause scandal if it departed too far from social convention – and his concern is that it should not unnecessarily put itself in jeopardy. One forgives him. One might further say that Paul would surely want to be judged in terms of the highest that he knew. Furthermore one may argue that the subordination of women in the church reflected the cultural conditioning of people in the first century. By contrast, the principle of human equality is a fundamental implication of the gospel. (Yet again it must be said – an argument which does not directly arise out of a golden thread approach but which is pertinent here – the two passages in the new testament which speak of women's subordination both rely on the Genesis account of creation and fall, an account no longer valid in a post-Darwinian age.)

The golden thread approach, coupled with considerations such as that post-Darwin certain past arguments no longer hold water, together with an element of an a priori ethical stance, seems to me to provide the best concerted argument for the ordination of women.[21] Yet there seems to be a dearth of people arguing consistently using a golden thread methodology. That this is the case is significant. Christians seem to believe themselves to be under a pressure to find texts in the bible which directly support their case. Those arguing for the ordination of women clutch at verses, or at historical evidence from the past, which seem to support 'their' side.[22] The fact that this is so indicates well that scripture is considered to be sacred literature. (Something that arises out of the fact that Christianity is a historical religion in which there is a belief in revelation, so that the literature which tells of this revelation is a literature apart.) Christians must have difficulty in using the bible to speak to contemporary issues so long as this belief persists. The joy of a golden thread approach is that it provides a way of moving between the past and the very different circumstances of the present. It allows a translation process to be undertaken, while the underlying theme (that for example of human liberation) remains constant.

The problem with such an approach is of course that if one's start-ing-point is 'what are the scriptures fundamentally about?' (and not 'what is a priori right?' – which would be an 'a priori ethical' position) it is perfectly possible for others to contend that they consider some quite other theme to be 'fundamental' to the scriptures. Thus oppo-nents of the ordination of women might plausibly say (as Barth would seem to) that fundamental to the scripture is male headship. A conservative could adduce, in support of this contention, the fact that in scripture God is overwhelmingly conceptualized by using male metaphors; that God came in Christ, a male human person; and that he chose men alone to head the church (if one thinks that the calling of the twelve bears a relation to the constitution of the church). At the end of the day it is a case of choosing what one's faith will be about – a point which Christians are reluctant to acknowledge. Once one has conceded that, then one has entered the arena of an 'a priori ethical' position.

Among Christian feminist theologians who may be said to have employed in part a 'golden thread' approach, although not specifically in relation to the question of ordaining women, is Rosemary Ruether. Ruether is a liberation theologian; indeed she has worked consis-tently from a liberation perspective in relation to such issues as third world poverty, anti-semitism and militarism. It is from this perspec-tive that she approaches the women's issue. Ruether speaks of 'claiming the prophetic-liberating tradition of Biblical faith as a norm through which to criticize the Bible'[23] – a golden thread ap-proach. As she herself comments, the theme of liberation is not marginal to the scriptures.[24] Elisabeth Schüssler Fiorenza has criti-cized Ruether here, asking how one should distinguish script from scripture.[25] But I find Ruether to be fully justified: one must, as a theologian, make some judgement as to what the scriptures are about, and Ruether is explicit as to how she reads.

But, proceeding further, I find Ruether's work to be less than sat-isfactory because muddled methodologically. Ruether, who is by training a historian, and politically of left-wing convictions, comes quickly simply to embark on a description of certain threads which she believes to have run through history. Thus we have the impres-sion of what we may call a 'sacred history', threaded through history: the history of the liberation of people. Indeed at times it appears that she thinks that this liberation progresses from age to age (though in correspondence she tells me that she thinks that the conclusion to history may well be that we annihilate ourselves).[26] If this is how her

work is to be read, then we are of course back with all the problems of
the kairos approach: why has history been what it has been and
given what history has been what may be said of God's intention in
relation to women? There is however one vital difference between
Ruether and the kairos approach as I described it. Ruether does not
think in terms of a God who is transcendent above history and acts as
an agent in history; and this we might say lets her off the hook as far
as the theodicy question is concerned. But in that this is the case, has
not another problem appeared? Has she in fact any concept of God at
all, or simply a 'transcendent life principle'?[27] What is that other
than simply a human conception? It seems to me questionable that
Ruether is herself theistic.

Ruether in fact seems reluctant to pursue what I have called a two-
stage approach. And that she does not do this is not accidental. For,
given her Marxist-Hegelian approach (as I should want to call it), all
reality tends to be collapsed into history. It becomes difficult then to
adduce abstract principles which should have a life of their own,
quite apart from whether they have been exemplified within history,
which may be used to judge history. Equally (as I have suggested) it
is difficult for her to have a God who is something other than a force
(perhaps a human idea) present within history. In the event one is
hard pressed to see how hers is a theology, as opposed to simply a
political agenda for the liberation of people. (In fact, if one reads her
work carefully, one notices that she never speaks of God, but rather
of people's concept of God, which may lead them on in their striving
for justice.)

An 'ethical a priori' position

In order to give a sense of an 'ethical a priori' position, I will at this
point in the book say something of my own odyssey. Such a recitation
may lead to the conclusion that one who consistently holds to this
position (as has been my experience) lands outside the church. By an
'ethical a priori' position I mean to indicate that certain principles
are held to be an a priori and not subject to qualification. One
considers oneself able to be a Christian while holding to these
principles because one believes that these very principles are fundamental to Christianity, or at least not incommensurate with it. The
theological justification behind such an approach (not that I had necessarily thought this out at the time when I was a member of the
church) must surely be that God's will must be held to be one with

what is good, and therefore what Christianity proclaims cannot differ from human ethical goods.

Consider then my own odyssey in relation to the Christian church. From aged twelve to fourteen I was on Sundays marched, crocodile-wise, from my girls' boarding school to the local Anglican church. Some time during those years I remember thinking it offensive that all the people 'up front' in black were male. This was the mid-fifties. Going to another church (of the Presbyterian Church of England) my love of God came to be the central factor in my life, and aged almost sixteen I told my headmistress with quiet confidence that I wished to be ordained. As an undergraduate, still thinking of ordination, I visited a woman minister, and returned discouraged, having grasped that women were normally relegated to minor churches. Upon receiving a degree which would allow me to undertake research, I turned down a place which I had been offered to study theology, and went to Oxford. During my years in Oxford, working as I was largely in the field of recent Anglican ecclesiastical history, I was increasingly drawn to Anglicanism. I have memories of asking permission to take communion. The rule was that as a member in good standing of another church (and I was a member of the Presbyterian Church of England) one might do so on a temporary basis; but that if one found oneself doing so for any extended length of time, one should ask oneself whether one should not be confirmed. I had asked myself, and the answer was no, not as long as that church refused to ordain women! This was in the late sixties. Writing a doctorate on the British response to the church conflict in Nazi Germany, I was well aware that Dietrich Bonhoeffer had refused to grant that the established national Protestant Church was in fact a Christian church so long as it refused to ordain people who were racially Jewish. I believed I should consider the Anglican Church not fully Christian in that it discriminated against women; though I wanted to worship there. I wrote as much in a letter to my bishop in Scotland in 1974 or 1975, at which time I was asking that he ordain me.

I in fact came to be confirmed by mistake! I finally asked that same bishop, who was a personal friend, for baptism. I was not sure that I had been baptized (having shrunk back from the outstretched hand with water in my late teens, believing baptism a piece of medieval nonsense), while wanting to be a member of the church. I now wanted desperately to belong to the Christian church in general (which to me, from my Free Church background, was what baptism implied) while not able to belong specifically to the Anglican Church (which was what confirmation implied) so long as that church discriminated against women. For the bishop, however, who knew his church history, it would not have made sense (as he subsequently told me) to baptize an adult without also confirming her, for the two ceremonies had originally been one. Some months later it dawned on me that he had put his hands on my head and what this implied!

Finding myself through a *fait accompli* an insider, I took it to be 'God's will'. Save for this fluke I could not have been in the position in which I now found myself. For three years from 1977 I worked all hours, sacrificing my career and my free time, for the cause of the ordination of women in the British Anglican churches. I had by this time spent some years in the States, including a year living in an Anglican theological college, and had watched my friends become ordained. I was in an ambiguous position. The ordination of women was something for which I was supposed to argue. Yet as far as I was concerned it was an a priori matter that the church should not discriminate. To be forced to argue that one is a full human being of equal dignity (for that is what it felt like) is quite extraordinarily undermining.

One moment which I recall vividly illuminates the problematic position in which I had placed myself. Having in Scotland lost the vote for the ordination of women to the priesthood, it seemed profitable to argue that women should be ordained to the deaconate (that is to say be made deacons, not simply deaconesses). We had an expert team, among us people with a first-rate knowledge of Greek and early church history. It was my task to put the material together. It seemed necessary to argue (that it was relevant both proponents and opponents seemed agreed) that Phoebe of Romans 16 might indeed be accounted a 'deacon' and not simply a 'deaconess'. I remember my feelings. What was I doing, in the late twentieth century, arguing that what happened in the first century was of relevance to whether or not I could be a deacon. I had never had to argue that as a woman I should have an education, become a theologian, own a house, or anything else. What did that do to me as a person, to my sense of myself in the Christian church? In 1980, coming back from a hospital in the States where I had been told that I ought to have an operation (interestingly on my throat – it was as though all the tension caused by what I could not say was caught up there), I saw that I had to be free of this. Back in Britain writing my last newsletter to the Group in Scotland I had loved and brought together, I said that I thought we had to be much bolder, taking an a priori stance on the fact that there could be no discrimination against women.

But the problem with taking such an a priori stance is that it

clashes with the nature of Christianity. For Christianity is a historical religion. Thus, in consideration of such an issue as to whether
women can be ordained, relevant factors for people come to be (as I
have said) questions such as what was the case in the early church,
what would Jesus have done, how is God envisaged in the religion of
the ancient Hebrews? Were we not concerned with a historical
religion we could settle such matters as to who might be the ministers in the religion (if indeed there were to be any) on a priori ethical
grounds. It is because of this historical dimension to the religion that
those arguing (for example) for the ordination of women apparently
find it so difficult to say, in the way in which it has been possible to
maintain in the sphere of politics, that we hold these truths to be self-
evident, that all human beings are created equal and must not be
discriminated against. There is always this reference to history, and
the reference is to a sexist history. Questions of human dignity and
equality are however not matters which one should have to argue
(which was what I was forced to do when I was in the church). To
entertain the idea that they are matters which are open to discussion
is in fact deeply offensive. It is owing to the fact that Christianity is
a historical religion, having a necessary reference to a past period of
human history, that such a discussion needs to proceed.

THE DENIAL OF DISCONTINUITY

In recent years there have been feminist theologians who, far from
believing there to be a gap to be bridged between past and present,
have emphasized rather the continuity to be found in the situation of
women. Thus there has grown up an interest in feminist 'herstory';
etymologically impossible, the word emphasizes that his-story has
been just that – the history of men. But the work which I want to
consider here is not simply historical, it is also theological in intent.
We are to read the stories of women as though they were our stories,
empathizing with them in their suffering and standing with them in
their courage in the face of patriarchy. I shall discuss the work of
Elisabeth Schüssler Fiorenza and of Phyllis Trible.[27] What I shall
want to argue is that their position is caught up in a circular
argument: the only reason one could have for wanting to stand in this
kind of relationship to biblical women is that one is Christian, but
these writers never tackle the prior question as to whether feminism
is in fact compatible with Christianity, such that one should want to
stand in relationship to biblical women.

I shall in considering the work of Schüssler Fiorenza look in particular at the essay 'Toward a Critical Theological Self-Understanding of Biblical Scholarship', in her collected essays *Bread Not Stone*,[28] as this represents a somewhat later and more refined perspective than her earlier book *In Memory of Her*,[29] though I shall also draw on that work. It is Schüssler Fiorenza who has been foremost among those who have argued that we should promote a solidarity of sisterhood with the women of the earliest Christian community. She writes:

> We participate in the same struggle as our biblical foresisters against the oppression of patriarchy and for survival and freedom from it. We share the same liberating visions and commitments as our biblical foremothers. We are not called to 'empathize' or to 'identify' with *their* struggles and hopes but to continue *our* struggle in solidarity with them. Their memory and remembrance – rediscovered and kept alive in historical reconstruction and actualized in ritual celebration – encourage us in historical solidarity with them to commit ourselves to the continuing struggle against patriarchy in society and church.[30]

It should be noted that what we are said to share with them is their vision: there is one continuing struggle against patriarchy. Biblical interpretation is to be done '*for* biblical communities today. ... It ... can sustain, encourage and challenge ...'[31] A constant theme in Schüssler Fiorenza's work is that we draw strength for our struggle from our knowledge of the past. In *In Memory of Her* she once and again quotes Judy Chicago: 'Our heritage is our power.'

Schüssler Fiorenza has shown in an impressive way in *In Memory of Her* that women's contribution to the life of the church was not so marginal as has often been assumed. She enables women today to see that women have been historical agents in the past, and to envisage the past from the perspective of women. As a piece of reconstruction of history (or herstory) there can be no reason to find fault with her work. But it is clear that Schüssler Fiorenza aims to be very much more than a historian. It is also her intention to speak theologically. It is here that it seems to me that there are basic problems which are not thought through, and moreover that moves are made which are deceptive, in that they give the impression that a solution has been found where in fact the main issue has not been tackled. In what follows I shall try to elucidate what I believe the problems to be.

In the first place, such a stance tends to minimize the gap between past and present, even though Schüssler Fiorenza may say that she wishes to 'preserve the historical distance between the present and the past'.[32] (I think that *Bread Not Stone* is more hesitant here than *In Memory of Her*: she speaks of there being one vision, whereas in *In Memory of Her* she appears simply to suggest that in our suffering and our courage we are one with first-century women.) But even if one considers those women in the modern western world who are less fortunate, they still have, for example, an entirely different legal status than had a first-century woman. The difference in life-style between myself (and herself) as white, middle-class women living in the western hemisphere today and that of first-century women is such as to make all comparison meaningless. To be asked to see myself as one in solidarity with first-century women strains my credulity. It is then not immediately apparent why 'our heritage is our power': we are in a radically different situation, with different problems and different options. I may indeed want to stand by women living in less fortunate circumstances than I today. (I cannot help the dead.) It is, I think, no chance that I have chosen over the years to support women rather than men political prisoners in Chile. But it is not their wish that I put myself into their shoes, rather than living free and wishing that for them also. I find then this 'universal solidarity of sisterhood'[33] – as though women across the ages had a like situation – to be far-fetched.

But in fact the call for solidarity comes from an unacknowledged motivation. Schüssler Fiorenza wishes to look to the women of the earliest church because she is a Christian. If one is Christian, one must, in some way, make reference to Christ. For a feminist, the most obvious way in which to do this (for Christ is a male figure) is to make reference to the earliest community of disciples, particularly the community of women. It appears to be a clever move to make. It is however to evade the issue as to whether Christianity and feminism are compatible. The whole *raison d'être* of that early Christian community was that it believed certain things of Christ – at the very least, that it was he whom God had raised from the dead. Indeed one's own reason for looking to this community was presumably that, as a Christian, one needed oneself to make some reference to Christ. Like it or not then, one is forced to confront the questions which Schüssler Fiorenza, through her strategy, seeks to avoid. Is it possible for feminists to be Christians, when Christ is a male figure? (Indeed, is Christianity true: could it possibly be that one was raised from the dead?) It is of significance that one finds mention of Christ to be singularly absent from Schüssler Fiorenza's work. She at one point quotes another, James Barr, who says: 'The true believer is a believer in God and in Christ ...'.[34] But she herself neither acknowledges this, nor explores what problems a religion of which this is true holds for women. Meanwhile she has given the impression that, by looking to the earliest community of women and men, she has found a way for women to be Christian.

If it is simply that 'our heritage is our power', and women gain strength today by looking to their sisters in the past, if what interests her is the vision of an equality between women and men, Schüssler Fiorenza might well be better advised to look to other communities in the ancient Near East. There is considerable evidence that greater equality prevailed between women and men in the cult of some ancient polytheistic communities.[35] It is of interest for example that Ruether, as she has increasingly wanted to find models for women in the past, has been forced to look outside the ancient Hebrew and Christian tradition.[36] Indeed one may ask whether there is any possible community in the past which, through its vision of equality between women and men, could inspire one? It may be more fruitful to create a utopian, and as yet unrealized, vision to hold before our eyes. One might at least look to the best examples there may be today. Schüssler Fiorenza herself agrees that all early Christians shared an androcentric mind-set.[37] Why then look to them? She comments that a postbiblical (*sic*) feminist stance 'too quickly concedes that women have no authentic history within biblical religion'.[38] But why (if it were not for the fact that one is a Christian) should one be wanting to stay with the experience of women within the biblical tradition?

Schüssler Fiorenza however wants to suggest (as at times Trible does also) that we have in any case to live within – and thus also we need to try to redeem – the trajectory of biblical religion. 'Western women', she writes, 'are not able to discard completely and forget our personal, cultural or religious Christian history. We will either transform it into a new liberating future or continue to be subject to its tyranny whether we recognize its power or not.'[39] This is a very different kind of argument, a pragmatic one. But is it the case that western women, living today in the United States, let alone in secular modern Europe, live in societies so dominated by the Christian myth, so ready to point to the place of women within the biblical tradition, that the best that women can do is to try to give a better reading of that past? To suggest that a re-reading is the only option open to us is a counsel of despair. We are not so trapped. The younger

generation (at least in Britain) is profoundly ignorant of their biblical past. The society has enshrined in law a status for women far
different from that of biblical women. Surely one does not spend one's
life as a biblical scholar reinterpreting the tradition because that is
all that can be done in view of the fact that, like it or not, we live
within this trajectory? We may today distance ourselves from, indeed reject, this tradition should we wish. Carol Christ well writes in
disagreement with Schüssler Fiorenza: 'To acknowledge a kind of intellectual and conceptual debt to Western biblical traditions is not
the same as to acknowledge loyalty to those traditions.'[40]

I would want to argue that if our goal is a religious situation in
which women and men are accounted equals, we shall need to
promote not continuity but rather discontinuity with the past. Unless one is Christian, there is no particular reason to find the past
normative. It may be far more powerful to live free from the past,
weighed down as little as possible by how women have been perceived, or have perceived themselves, in that past. For myself, I wish
to say to men that as long as they associate me with an idea of
'woman' drawn from the past, or suppose that a model for gender
relations is to be found in that past, they have failed to see me for the
person who I am, or to envisage what equality might mean. Such a
stance provides a challenge. So long as one's own eyes are fixed on
the past, it is difficult to make the point that the past should not be
prescriptive for the future.

To encourage a solidarity of women across all ages is moreover
profoundly separatist. One's basic identity is found in relation to a
community of women. It is clear why, if one wishes to remain within
the Christian context, one should want to side with women (and
women-identified men) against the 'male' establishment. But (unless
one be Christian) why not hold as one's vision a community of both
women and men who, having essentially left the past behind, live in
the present?

Above all I fail to see how one could worship God or expand one's
religious sensibilities by looking to this past. Schüssler Fiorenza
believes that a people that has no history loses its sense of itself. It
may well be true that Black people are inspired by the memory of
their courage under slavery. That they are prepared to take on board
such a past, one must hold in awe. But – quite apart from the issue of
whether a woman like myself can in any meaningful way identify
herself with women in the remote past – one must ask how could this
be useful theologically? There is a theodicy question here which I

believe makes such a move as Schüssler Fiorenza wishes to make highly problematical. She writes: 'The process of inspiration must be seen as the inspiration of those people, especially of poor women, struggling for human dignity and liberation from oppressive powers, because they believe in the biblical God of creation and salvation despite all experiences to the contrary.'[41] Though I might, in working for a different future, find the struggle of women politically inspiring, I am unlikely to find a community in which women were not counted equal a medium through which I can gain a glimpse of God. Does Schüssler Fiorenza mean that one is inspired by these women, although the religion in which they were involved is sexist (in which case one is inspired to act against the biblical God)? Or that one is to continue to believe in the biblical God despite all experiences to the contrary, that is to say believe that God is bound up with a religion and a community in which women are counted inferior (in which case one is attempting to believe in an evil God)? She herself thinks, of biblical texts, that if one cannot accept the 'religious, political, and personal ethos' of a text 'one cannot accept its authority as revealed and as Holy Scripture'.[42] I would suggest that no more can one make use of the early Christian community or its religion as a medium which is transparent of God.

Like Schüssler Fiorenza, Phyllis Trible seeks to close the gap between past and present. By re-reading texts in a more favourable light, she would allow feminist women the better to be able to appropriate the scriptures. Looking to the past, she seeks to illuminate the present, believing there to be no unbridgeable gap between the two. It is not only those texts which women might be able to estimate positively which she exegetes. In her book *Texts of Terror* she considers the stories of four women of the Hebrew scriptures who are subjected to terror; rape, murder and dismemberment at the hands of men.[43] She writes: 'Ancient tales of terror speak all too frighteningly of the present.'[44] She describes the circumstances in which she chose to focus on these tales: 'hearing a black woman describe herself as a daughter of Hagar outside the covenant; ... reading news reports of the dismembered body of a woman found in a trash can'.[45] Evidently the present is in some respects not unlike the past. Of the biblical stories she remarks: 'To account for these stories as relics of a distant, primitive, and inferior past is invalid.' Her hope is that 'by enabling insight, they may inspire repentance'. She 'interprets stories of outrage on behalf of their female victims in order to recover a neglected history, to remember a past that the present embodies, and to pray that these terrors shall not come to pass again'.[46] Concluding her exegesis of the story of Jephthah's murder of his daughter in the keeping of a foolish vow, an event which was remembered ritually by women in ancient Israel, she writes:

> Like the daughters of Israel, we remember and mourn the daughter of Jephthah the Gileadite. In her death we are all diminished; by our memory she is forever hallowed. ... She becomes an unmistakable symbol for all the courageous daughters of faithless fathers. Her story ... evokes the imagination, calling forth a reader's response. ... Let us in the spirit of the daughters of Israel remember and mourn the daughter of Jephthah.[47]

Unlike Schüssler Fiorenza who seeks to move behind an androcentric text to the community which gave rise to it, Trible remains with the text itself. She employs a method called 'rhetorical criticism', a form of literary criticism, in which the text is criticized using clues given in the text itself. The principle which guides her exegesis is that one should 'use scripture in interpreting scripture'. Although conceding, in a footnote,[48] that one may use extrabiblical material to 'illuminate scripture', her basic stance is to grant to the text the status of a self-contained entity.[49] This is well captured by the opening line of her book *God and the Rhetoric of Sexuality*: 'The Bible is a pilgrim wandering through history to merge past and present.'[50] The text has a certain givenness; it may be interpreted anew in each age. Trible re-reads from a feminist perspective. She believes that the scriptures contain what she calls 'counter-cultural' motifs and themselves critique patriarchy. Thus, in an early essay, she writes: 'I affirm that the intentionality of biblical faith ... is neither to create nor to perpetuate patriarchy but rather to function as salvation for both women and men.'[51] Many feminists, she says, read the bible to reject: 'My suggestion is that we re-read to understand and to appropriate.'[52]

Trible's work could well be criticized in its own terms. It is questionable that texts can always be read as favourably as she seeks to do. I shall make mention of her reading of the story of Ruth,[53] suggesting however that that story does not escape patriarchal parameters. Her interpretation of the Genesis creation story in particular has been the cause of considerable interest. She argues that the creation of woman is the climax of the story, that the phrase 'helper' connotes equality, and that man 'discovered a partner in woman rather than a creature to dominate'.[54] Others qualified to judge have however found this re-reading too optimistic.[55] Again, the same question may be asked as that which I have asked in relation to Schüssler Fiorenza's work: given that in every age women have been mistreated at the hands of men, how much do present-day women really have in common with biblical women? The story of Ruth illuminates for me the unbridgeable difference, rather than the similarity, between her situation and mine.

It is however a rather different criticism which I wish to bring to Trible's work, one which runs in parallel to my critique of Schüssler Fiorenza's work. Why, unless one is a Christian, should one be wanting to undertake such a re-reading? Indeed, in Trible's case, unless one is a conservative Christian who believes the text to be the word of God? If one is a fundamentalist Christian who believes the text to be inspired, then one sees why the text is alone to be interpreted in terms of the text. But if one is not fundamentalist (and not simply working as a literary critic) then there are questions which need to be brought to the text. What authority could, for example, the text of the creation story possibly have post-Darwin? Trible's reading of such a text is certainly very different from that of, say, Barth. But, if only by default, through simply reading the text in terms of the text and not bringing outside considerations to bear, she, as does Barth, shores up its authority.

Trible is in fact very ambivalent as to what is her position. In her major book *God and the Rhetoric of Sexuality* she writes: 'The Bible as literature is the Bible as scripture, regardless of one's attitude toward its authority.'[56] (One may think this no more to be the case than Schüssler Fiorenza's proposition that we cannot but live within the trajectory of biblical religion.) Particularly in her more recent work however, she seems to want to give herself out simply as a literary critic. Unlike Schüssler Fiorenza, Trible never explicitly names herself a Christian feminist. But if Trible's position is that she is a literary critic, pursuing rhetorical criticism without commitment to the text, then it must be said that the impression she gives is often very different. This is true not least of her more recent work. In *Texts of Terror* she comments that 'wrestling with the silence, absence, and opposition of God' is the context of her work.[57] Indeed, she comments of the story of Jacob at Jabbok, that the 'man' with whom he wrestles is deity; and, of Jacob, on his 'refusing to let the man go unless he blesses him'. She writes: 'As a paradigm for encountering terror, this story offers sustenance for the present journey. ... We struggle mightily, only to be wounded. But yet we hold on, seeking a blessing.'[58]

But – other than if one is a Christian theologian of a rather fundamentalist variety who believes this text to be the inspired word of God – why should one be struggling with it? If I read Shakespeare's *The Merchant of Venice* and notice the anti-semitism which surrounds the character of Shylock, I may be bothered by it, even condemn Shakespeare for his anti-semitism. But I do not try to re-read the text to make it more acceptable; I dissociate myself from Shakespeare's outlook. Trible's whole approach suggests that we should be granting authority to these texts, texts which convey the most fearful misogyny. Of two women whom she mentions in her acknowledgements in *Texts of Terror* she remarks: 'They themselves rendered to God, even the God of terror.'[59] But why be wrestling with this God and seeking a blessing from him – other than if one believes that the text is of God? Why not dismiss it? Indeed, the theodicy question as to how one could ever use such texts as a medium through which to worship God may be thought to be even more insoluble than is Schüssler Fiorenza's finding inspiration in the early Christian community. Of course it would be possible for Trible to maintain that she is re-reading the text because it is an important western text and she wants to understand more accurately what its authors meant. But that this is her intent is clearly not the import of her words.

It is of interest that Schüssler Fiorenza, who looks to the continuity of the tradition, is a Roman Catholic. Trible, to whom the integrity of the text is crucial, comes from a Southern Baptist background. Of course a theologian may move far from her background and Trible may well want to claim that she has done so. What must be said however is this. If one's position is that one is a literary critic, there can be no reason to wrestle with the text that one may appropriate it. If one is a conservative Christian who grants the text authority, one sees why, as a feminist, one should need to wrestle with it. But, in wrestling with it, it should be noted that one is not addressing the more fundamental question as to whether in fact feminism is compatible with Christianity. Meanwhile the effect of taking such a stance towards the text is to bolster its authority, or at least to fail to question it. Indeed Trible's work has precisely been useful to women of conservative disposition who, accepting the text's authority, need to interpret it as best they may.

It must be said then of the attempt to re-read the history or literature of the past, that the only motivation for doing so can be that one
is a Christian. Other than if one is Christian, there can be no reason
for one, in relation to one's religious life, to want to give more positive
accounts of the past. Furthermore that while the history or literature
of the past is re-read – and the impression given that the position of
women is better than one might have expected – the more fundamental questions which need to be asked are not tackled. Can there ever
be an equal place for women in Christianity? Is Christianity true in
any case, or is what the early church believed about Jesus simply not
possible? What of the fact that our knowledge of evolution makes the
Genesis text invalid? Readings such as that of Schüssler Fiorenza
and Trible may make it easier for Christian women who are feminists to associate themselves with the Christian tradition. But the
issue as to whether feminism and Christianity are compatible is not
entered upon, let alone shown to be the case.

A POST-CHRISTIAN POSITION

One may believe of God that God is equally available to people in all
times and places. Such is my position. That is to say I deny that there
could be a particular revelation of God in any one age, which thence-
forth becomes normative for all others. It should be noted that this is
equally as is a Christian position a religious position. I am simply
denying that God (whatever we may mean by God) could be of such a
kind that God could intervene in human history, or be revealed
through particular events in history, or through a particular person,
in a way in which God is not potentially present to us in and through
all acts and persons. It will be clear that my not being a Christian has
nothing to do with any feminist stance which I may espouse. I am not
a Christian because I do not credit, as I earlier put it, that nature and
history could be other than closed causal nexuses or believe that
there can be events which are in some way qualitatively different
from other events. Again I cannot believe of Jesus Christ that he is
related to God in a way which is qualitatively different from that of
all other human beings.

To be religious in such a way is to understand theology to have the
same relation to the past as do all other human disciplines. It is
Christianity which is here the exception. In no other human discipline, not in philosophy, nor science, nor music, is it believed that

there has been a particular revelation of God in history, so that that point in history is then necessarily taken up into the discipline. Other disciplines are not historical in the sense in which I have named Christianity a 'historical' religion. Take the case of Beethoven (but equally of a scientist working today). Beethoven is unthinkable without the tradition of western music, indeed one might say without the very specific background of late eighteenth-century music in Vienna. His music, though unique to him, is clearly a creation of the late eighteenth- and early nineteenth-century tradition. In this sense it is rooted in history. But Beethoven could take what he would from the past, and invent what he would. There was no point in past music with which he had to reconcile what he wanted to say, or to which he had necessarily to make reference. Again a scientist stands at the point which has at present been reached within a long tradition of enquiry. But she is essentially faced with thinking out what she believes truth to be. She may work within a paradigm, and not be uninfluenced by how her mind was formed as she grew up within the discipline of science. But if that paradigm seems untrue, to her or to the scientific community in which she works, it can be jettisoned in favour of a new construction of reality.

Not so in the case of Christianity. Christianity, as we have seen, necessarily has an anchor in history. For it is believed that God has been revealed in a peculiar way to a certain people, and in particular made known through the person of Jesus Christ. Christianity is then a historical religion in a way in which religion need not necessarily be historical. And in a way in which other disciplines are not. This is not to say that, as a religious person who is not a Christian, one has no relation to the past. Indeed it may well be that it would be impossible to stand in no relation to the past, or to the framework in which one's mind and one's awareness as a religious person were formed. But one need not believe that God revealed God's self at a particular point in history, so that one need necessarily make reference to that point in history in one's religion. It is in such a sense that I am post-Christian. Post-*Christian* because Christianity (and not Islam) is the historical context within which my religious sensibilities were formed. But definitely *post*-Christian because I do not believe that there could be this uniqueness: that God could be related in a particular way to a particular age or to one particular person Jesus Christ.

What should the post-Christian then hold of the religion that there has been down the ages? How is she or he to make sense of the fact that the Christian tradition has reigned for two thousand years? The answer is clear. There is no reason but to think (if one is a religious person) that people were in tune with God in other ages, as indeed one believes oneself also to be. They were not deceived. What one must say however is that people interpreted their awareness of God in terms of the age in which they lived. That is to say they constructed a picture of the world, a picture which one oneself no longer believes to be viable. This picture could be expressed in the following way as a religious myth. God created the world, humans fell, in time He sent His Son Jesus Christ, who lived, died and rose again, and who will come at the end of time. Such a picture of reality, through which people have interpreted their awareness of God, has also been expressed in more abstract terms. Thus God is said to be trinity in unity, the second person of the trinity becoming incarnate in Christ. To reject the picture is not to suggest that people did not have a very real experience of God.

To believe that people have been sensible of God in other ages is not however to accept what I may call the 'vehicle' of the Christian myth which has carried their religious sensibilities. As it will have become clear, I do not believe that this vehicle is tenable. Many Christians of a liberal disposition have come to this conclusion of some aspects of the myth. Thus as we have seen Darwin pulled a plank out from under the creation stories. Again the virgin birth, in view of what we now know of human reproduction, has become highly suspect for people. In the face of the untenability of various parts of the Christian story of former ages, many Christians have made the move of saying that, however, these things are 'symbolically true'. Of course one cannot say this of the whole story; were one to say that one would no longer be a Christian. One would think (as I think) that this story has served as a vehicle through which people expressed their love of God, but not that it is true. Christians I have suggested, if they are rightly to be named Christians, must in some sense believe that God was in a unique way related to Christ, so that he becomes particular for them, and they are (as I am not) in their religion related to history.

It is here however that the feminist questions arise. Why should one want to say of a myth that it is 'symbolically true' if it is a sexist myth? What possible meaning could it have for one's life? Why symbolize one's deepest beliefs through a myth which jars with all that one believes to be moral in the realm of relations between human beings? It is such questions which one must ask of Christians, particularly Christians who would be feminist, who explain that the creation story (or any other part of the Christian story which may be said to be sexist) is to them a 'true myth'. The Genesis story, for example, does not symbolically convey a perfect creation in which human beings were equal, but one which carries (as feminists must believe) a false moral message. The further question arises as to whether the myth is not false to what we know to be the case concerning the origin of humankind. As we have already said, a creation myth which was symbolically true would have to convey that neither woman nor man was present before the other; moreover, not that they were created out of dust but that they were integrally related to the rest of the animal creation. If one believes it to be true that Christ is the Son of God one sees why one should be Christian. But if the Christian story is a myth why not, as a feminist, dispense with it?

It is sometimes said that all religion is mythological in form, and operates through concrete stories and symbols; that religion must necessarily have what I have called a vehicle and that there can be no pure awareness of God. This may very well be true: let us grant for the moment that it is. But this – it will be clear – is quite beside the point. If one realizes that one is dealing with myths and symbols, then one might as well create myths and symbols which are true to what one would symbolize. Many feminists who wish to be religious are indeed doing just that. If a symbol does not symbolize what one thinks good or true, there can be no reason to retain it. Nor do I believe that it can be said that in no way can we disentangle ourselves from the religious myth which we have inherited. Many people are precisely dispensing with Christianity because they can no longer believe in it. The 'vehicle' of Christianity which has carried people's love of God is no longer viable to them. Nor is it the case that we in fact need a vehicle, a mythological story to carry our awareness of God, of the kind which has been fabricated in the west. We may need some conceptualization, some image, some words, if we are to speak of God; but scarcely a picture of the universe and a history of humankind such as we have inherited in the Christian creeds.

I do not think then that we can 'blame' earlier generations for believing Christianity to be true. 'Blame' is not the right word. They thought in terms of a picture of the universe and of the origin of humankind (one which we now know to have been in large part mistaken), and they interpreted their awareness of God in conjunction with this picture. Again, I do not think that individuals are to be

blamed for this: whole societies were caught up in this sexist interpretation of reality. (One may however ask after the nature of men –
in so far as it has been men rather than women who have created
these pictures of the world and of the 'place' of woman within it –
such that they should have needed to construct such a misogynist
picture.) But whether people should not be called to account for continuing to hold such a picture today is another question. One would
have thought that a deep incompatibility should have become apparent to them between what they believed about the equality of human
beings and the misogynist, or at least highly patriarchal, nature of
this myth. (It is because Christian feminists see such an incongruity
that they want to adapt or reinterpret the myth.) Not least, as I have
suggested, the question arises as to how God can be good if God can
have revealed himself through such a history and if such a myth is
true.

Indeed there may be reason to think that such a dichotomy cannot
for ever persist. As long as people find the Christian story good there
is reason to believe in it, or to believe it with the exception of some of
the more minor matters such as virgin birth or the creation stories
which they have had to decide are untrue (or only symbolically true).
But once doubt comes to be cast on the goodness of this story, then
human beings will raise questions also as to its truth. It is this situation with which many women are faced. They realize, as feminists,
the extent to which this Christian story has hurt women, indeed how
far the fact that God has been seen as 'male' in the west has served to
undermine a sense of women as also made in the image of God.
Questions will then inevitably be raised as to whether the Christian
myth is true in any case. I would suggest that many women are
coming to doubt that it is. In so far as our religion is our vision of the
world, if that vision comes no longer to seem ethical, then it will be
discarded. One's religion, at the end of the day, one might suppose,
has to conform to one's ethical beliefs.

The question of the truth of the Christian picture of the world has
increasingly come to be raised during the last two hundred years. In
our age this has become an urgent question for many people and
many others have left Christianity behind them. The further question which feminism raises – to an extent to which, I would contend,
this has not been raised before – is that of whether it is moral. It is
possible to say that Christian beliefs are 'symbolically true'. But if
one does not believe them to be symbolically 'true' but false to one's
belief in human equality, there is no point in having made this

sideways move. It is precisely at the level of symbolism that, feminists are saying, the Christian story has harmed women. Thus many a feminist no longer has any use for Christianity. But this does not necessarily mean that she can no longer be a religious person. Indeed one might well argue that unless this generation is able to distinguish between what has been the religious vehicle which has carried people's love of God, and the love of God itself which needs to be interpreted in new ways, there may be scant hope for the future of religion in the west.

NOTES

1   I have sometimes heard it suggested that modern physics changes the situation here and makes Christianity somehow more possible. But this suggestion results from a confusion. If it is the case that there is randomness at the sub-atomic level, then there has always been randomness at the sub-atomic level; a fact of which we have only recently become apprised. It is not in modern physics claimed that nature has changed, so that something was possible in the first century which is now not possible. In speaking here of uniqueness, one is simply saying that each event within a category of a certain type of event has a uniqueness. One is not speaking of unique occurrences, which are not one of a category. But Christians believe in uniqueness in the sense of events which do not belong to a category: they proclaim particularity.

2   For a debate as to whether or not Christianity is necessarily sexist see Daphne Hampson and Rosemary Ruether, 'Is There a Place for Feminists in a Christian Church?', *New Blackfriars*, 68, no. 801 (January 1987) and republished as a pamphlet.

3   Speech to the General Synod of the Church of England, 8 Nov. 1978 (The Church Literature Association for the Church Union, copy in the possession of the author).

4   *Inter Insigniores: Declaration on the Question of the Admission of Women to the Ministerial Priesthood*, 15 Oct. 1976, in L. Swidler and A. Swidler (eds), *Women Priests: A Catholic Commentary on the Vatican Declaration* (New York: Paulist Press, 1977), p. 39.

5   It was reported of a Roman synod, at which the question as to whether women might be deaconesses was under discussion, that one bishop commented that, had Jesus wanted women to be deaconesses, he would have made his mother a deaconess (*Guardian*, 31 Oct. 1987).

6   See pp. 86–90.

7   See pp. 67–70.

8   *Commentary* on the *Sentences* of Peter Lombard (*Opera Omnia* XI, 'Commentum in Lib. IV Sententiarum', qu. II, art. 1). The text is not readily available in English translation. Francine Cardman, 'The Medieval

Question of Women and Orders', *The Thomist*, 42 (October 1978), pp. 586–8 however follows it closely in her discussion. (The text in the *Summa* (part III, supplement, qu. 39) was added after Thomas' death and quotes the *Commentary* word for word. Thus we do not know what he would have said in his maturity.) English translations of this question, of part I, question 92 (see note 10 below), and of other relevant parts of the *Summa* are to be found in E. Clark and H. Richardson (eds), *Women and Religion: A Feminist Sourcebook of Christian Thought* (New York and San Francisco: Harper & Row, 1977).

9   See pp. 67–8.

10 ST I, qu. 92.

11 Reply to objection 1.

12 I Cor. 11:7–9; I Tim. 2:11–14.

13 *Women Priests?* (pamphlet) (London: The Church Literature Association, 1977, first edn 1972), p. 11.

14 Synod Speech, 1978.

15 'The Theological Case for the Ordination of Women: A Letter to Members of the General Synod', 6 Oct. 1978 (distributed by the Anglican Group for the Ordination of Women).

16 I find it a matter for astonishment that proponents of the ordination of women should argue within a theological and scriptural framework without drawing attention to the fact that past views were based on ill-founded knowledge. In a recent collection of essays neither Darwin nor the falseness of previous understandings of reproduction are mentioned from start to finish. (M. Furlong (ed.), *Mirror to the Church*, London: SPCK, 1988).

17 '[Man and woman] stand in a sequence.... A precedes B, and B follows A. Order means succession. It means preceding and following.... How could she reject or envy his precedence, his task and function, as the one who stimulates, leads and inspires? To wish to replace him in this, or to do it with him, would be to wish not to be a woman.... Why should not woman be the second in sequence, but only in sequence? What other choice has she, seeing she can be nothing at all apart from this sequence and her place within it? And why should she desire anything else...?' *Church Dogmatics*, III.4, *The Doctrine of Creation* (E.T. Edinburgh: T. & T. Clark, 1961), pp. 169–71.

18 John Austin Baker, 'The Right Time' (pamphlet) (London: Movement for the Ordination of Women, 1981).

19 See p. 167.

20 Galations 3:28.

21 For such an approach see my pamphlet 'Let Us Think About Women' (The Group for the Ministry of Women in the Scottish Episcopal Church, 1979).

22 Thus I have heard of one woman's comment, of the first century, 'if only we could find one woman priest'. Such a matter should be irrelevant.

23   *Sexism and God-Talk: Toward a Feminist Theology* (Boston, MA: Beacon Press, 1983; London: SCM Press, 1983), pp. 23–4.

24   Ibid. pp. 31–3.

25   *In Memory of Her: A Feminist Theological Reconstruction of Christian Origins* (New York: Crossroad Publishing, 1983; London: SCM Press, 1983), p. 16.

26   Letter to the author, 20 Feb. 1989.

27   A term drawn from the above letter.

28   'Toward a Critical Theological Self-Understanding of Biblical Scholarship', in *Bread Not Stone: The Challenge of Feminist Biblical Interpretation* (Boston, MA: Beacon Press, 1984).

29   See note 24 above.

30   'Remembering the Past in Creating the Future', *Bread Not Stone*, p. 115.

31   'Self-Understanding', p. 143.

32   Ibid. p. 147.

33   *Memory*, p. 31.

34   'Self-Understanding', p. 147.

35   Cf. the argument of Judith Ochshorn's impressive book *The Female Experience and the Nature of the Divine* (Bloomington, IN: Indiana University Press, 1981) considered below p. 98.

36   See her book *Womanguides: Readings Toward a Feminist Theology* (Boston, MA: Beacon Press, 1985).

37   Cf. *Memory*, p. 61.

38   *Memory*, pp. xviii–xix.

39   Ibid. p. xix.

40   *Laughter of Aphrodite: Reflections on a Journey to the Goddess* (San Francisco: Harper & Row, 1987), p. xii.

41   'Self-Understanding', p. 140.

42   Ibid. p. 140.

43   *Texts of Terror: Literary and Feminist Readings of Biblical Narratives* (Philadelphia, PA: Fortress Press, 1984).

44   Ibid. p. xiii.

45   Ibid. pp. 1–2.

46   Ibid. pp. 2–3.

47   'A Meditation in Mourning: The Sacrifice of the Daughter of Jephthah', *Union Seminary Quarterly Review*, 36, Supplementary Issue, 1981, p. 67.

48   *Texts of Terror*, p. 6 n. 6.

49   Ibid. p. 2.

50   *God and the Rhetoric of Sexuality* (Philadelphia, PA: Fortress Press, 1978), p. 1.

51   'Depatriarchalizing in Biblical Interpretation', *JAAR*, 41, no. 1 (March 1973), p. 31.

52   'Eve and Adam: Genesis 2–3 Reread', in C. P. Christ and J. Plaskow

(eds), *Womanspirit Rising: A Feminist Reader in Religion* (New York and San Francisco: Harper & Row, 1979), p. 74 (1973).

53 See p. 103.

54 'Eve and Adam'; 'Women in the O.T.', in K. Crim et al., *The Interpreter's Dictionary of the Bible: Supplementary vol.* 1976, pp. 963–6; *Rhetoric of Sexuality*, pp. 12–21. (Quotation, *Dictionary*, p. 965.)

55 For (devastating) critiques see Ochshorn, *Female Experience*, pp. 210–17; David Clines, 'What Does Eve Do to Help?: And Other Irredeemably Androcentric Orientations in Genesis 1–3' (unpublished paper given at the SBL Annual Meeting, Boston, MA, 7 Dec. 1987).

56 *Rhetoric of Sexuality*, p. 8.

57 *Texts of Terror*, p. 2.

58 Ibid. p. 4

59 Ibid. p. xiv.

CHAPTER 2

Christology

THE LIMITS OF CHRISTIANITY

The nub of the question as to whether feminism is compatible with Christianity is that of whether a Christology can be found of which it may be said that at least it is not incompatible with feminism. By Christology is meant the portrayal of Jesus as the Christ. I have suggested that a meaningful way to set the limits as to what may rightly be called a Christian position, is that Christians are those who proclaim Jesus to have been unique. Such a definition does not only include those Christians who construe their belief in orthodox terms; who proclaim of Christ (following the definition of the Council of Chalcedon) that he was fully God and fully human, these two natures existing in one person. It includes also those who wish to speak of uniqueness in some other way. For example I shall later consider Bultmann, who has no classical two-nature Christology, but who says of Jesus, as of no other, that this was the man whom God raised from the dead; so that for him this man's resurrection becomes the pivot of history. I do not intend to have a restrictive but rather an expansive definition. To say of persons however who simply believe of Jesus that he had a very fine moral teaching, but who wish to say nothing of Jesus himself, that they are Christian surely does not make sense theologically – whatever they may say of themselves. Such a position should rightly be called humanist. Christians have always proclaimed not simply Jesus' teaching, but something about Jesus. There can rightly be no Christianity without a Christology.

The question of the compatibility of feminism and Christianity then is that of whether there can be a way of speaking of Christ's uniqueness which is not incompatible with feminism. (Let us take also a minimalist definition of feminism, as meaning the proclaimed equality of women and men.) The problem of course with Christology for feminists is that Jesus was a male human being and that thus as a symbol, as the Christ, or as the Second Person of the trinity, it would seem that 'God' becomes in some way 'male'. It should be noted at the outset what is the nature of the problem with which we are concerned. It is not a question of whether feminists have something against 'men'. Whether or not that is the case, the problem here is not that Jesus was a man, but that this man has been considered unique, symbolic of God, God Himself – or whatever else may be the case within Christianity. The Godhead, or at least Christology, then appears to be biased against women. Feminists have been very aware of the power of symbolism and ideology. It is no small matter then to suggest that western religious thought, which has been so fundamental to western culture, has been ideologically loaded against women.

Before we proceed to consider the question as to whether there can be a Christology which is not incompatible with feminism, I should like to point to the significance of this question for Christians. It is not simply that it is a vital matter for some small group of people (as some may think them to be) called 'Christian feminists' who would reconcile their feminism with their Christian faith. For Christianity has always proclaimed Christ to be an inclusive concept. In him, it is said, there is no East nor West, he is the new Adam, the first-born of all humanity; there is in Christ no Jew nor Greek, no more male and female. The question which feminists are raising then strikes at the very core of Christology. For it is being questioned whether a symbol which would appear to be necessarily male can be said to be inclusive of all humanity. Does it not give male human beings privilege within the religion? As far as women who would be Christian are concerned, how may they see in the Godhead an image of themselves? The contention that Christology is not inclusive represents the undoing of what, classically, has been claimed of Christ.

Why has this question now come upon the scene? What has changed in human relations between men and women, or how is it that women sense themselves differently, such that this matter has become urgent? It would be difficult to give a definitive answer, but we may have some clue. In other ages, the female seemed in some sense to be 'included' in the male, in a way in which this is no longer the case. This made Christology seem natural. Men were normally held to represent women also. Humanity could then as a whole be thought to be summed up in Christ. Mistaken biological beliefs, such that the male alone was thought to be a full human being, underlay western culture, making this seem the more plausible. Today men are not in the same way held to represent women: there are two sexes and women represent themselves.

It may then be that today situations where men alone are priests, or equally the fact that Christ is a male symbol and God is conceptualized using male metaphors, may make God appear to be 'male' in a way in which this was not earlier the case. If we see a procession of only men we ask 'where are the women?'. As we have said, in an age when men alone filled the professions, it appeared only natural that those who led the church were likewise male. When this is no longer so, the fact of a male priesthood makes God appear to be in some way peculiarly male, such that He needs a male priesthood to represent Him.[1] The belief that men alone represent humanity, whereas a woman is an individual who only represents herself, never absolute, does not wash any longer. A symbol which is a male symbol appears in our culture to represent maleness, in a way in which earlier this may not necessarily have been the case. Hence the urgency of the question as to whether Christ is an inclusive symbol, and the feeling of many women that it is not.

In this chapter I turn first to patristic Christology. I do this because it was in the period of the church fathers that what was to become orthodox Christology was worked out. But I also believe patristic Christology to be more hopeful than that of any other period in our quest to find a Christology which is inclusive of women. I shall suggest however that the philosophical framework which allowed the fathers to have a Christology which could be in some way inclusive of women has disappeared; and moreover that even patristic Christology does not solve the problem. I turn then to recent feminist Christological positions. I conclude that none of them succeed in overcoming the biased nature of Christology and moreover that such attempts cannot, through the very nature of Christology, succeed. Next I proceed to what may be called conservative Christologies, Christologies in which the maleness of Christ is said to be of the very essence of Christology. Obviously such Christologies are not acceptable to feminists. Both conservatives and feminists however, as I shall then consider, may take refuge in the suggestion that whereas Christ is a male figure, Mary (or the Holy Spirit) is an equivalent 'female' representation. I shall suggest that these attempts to find what I call compensatory factors not only fail to be counterbalances, but also represent the undoing of Christology. I shall then, having concluded that feminism and Christology are not compatible, turn to the feminist critique of Christology (on the part both of those women who would be Christian and those who are not) and discuss the crucial nature of symbolism.

I wish finally in this introduction to say something of the nature of the question which feminism is raising here for Christianity. It will be clear from what I have already said that I myself do not have a Christology and am not a Christian. I do not believe that the uniqueness which Christians attribute to Christ is possible. That is to say neither do I believe, in the terms of classical Christology, that Jesus of Nazareth could have had, as well as his human nature, a divine nature; nor do I believe that he could have been raised from the dead, so acquiring uniqueness through God's act of raising him. I put this earlier by saying that I do not believe that the causal nexus of nature or that of history could be broken. (I may believe Jesus' teaching to have been exemplary, or that he was a man singularly in tune with God; but this, as I would argue, does not make me a Christian.) The question for me then is whether Christianity is true; and I do not believe that it is. The question which feminism poses for Christianity is however other. It is that of whether Christianity is ethical. That is to say, is it not the case that a religion in which the Godhead is represented as male, or central to which is a male human being, necessarily acts as an ideology which is biased against half of humanity? Is it not the case that such a religion is by its very nature harmful to the cause of human equality? That is a serious charge against Christianity; and one which has not been raised in quite the same way by other moral issues (such as slavery) which have in the past confronted Christians.

PATRISTIC CHRISTOLOGY

Were it to be that Christian orthodoxy were that a man, Jesus of Nazareth, was God (or we may say 'a god'), then there would be no hope that Christianity and feminism could be reconciled. We should simply have a male God. The religion would consist in the deification of a human person. (We might indeed say of such a theology that it was a Jesuology, rather than a Christology; and Christianity has, at its worst, we may think, come to resemble this.) It is in the fact that this is not however orthodoxy that our hope lies.

Patristic Christology is subtle, for the fathers were trying rightly to express a complex issue. They were in the first place monotheists.

They did not therefore want to suggest of Christ that he was another God, which would create a polytheistic situation. Indeed their background as Greek intellectuals would have made it nonsensical to them to have said of a particular item in our world (a particular human being) that he was 'God'. They did not intend to equate the man Jesus of Nazareth with God. To have made such an equation would have been to create an idol: an item in the creation (not this time a golden calf but a person) would have been deified. (Obviously in this case it would follow that women are not 'like God' in the way in which men are 'like God', and Christology could not be compatible with feminism.)

The problem for the fathers was how to express that God could be said to have uniquely identified God's self with Jesus of Nazareth, without making Jesus into God. Hence the development of a two-nature Christology: that Jesus was fully God and fully human, these two natures being predicates of one 'person' or entity. The patristic scholar Richard Norris, a student in particular of the Antiochenes (that school which emphasized the distinction between the two natures) and who himself, in the sentences I quote, inclines towards an 'Antiochene' position, puts this point well. He writes:

> Classical statements about the Incarnation begin with the assumption that God is anything but a particular human being. ... To say 'the Word was made flesh', then, refers not to a simple identity of God and Jesus but to a relationship in which God lovingly identifies himself in and with a real human person, so that that person can truly be called the Word, the self-communication and self-objectification of God in human terms. ... The church fathers, with their doctrine of two distinct but unified natures in Christ, tried to say [this]. They were entirely clear in their minds that one must not 'confuse' God with a human being.[2]

The question to be asked then is, given that women are unlike Jesus of Nazareth in the form of their humanity, may it not be said that a woman baptized into Christ is not differently related than is a man to Jesus as the Christ? For this is what matters in Christology; we are speaking of Jesus as the Christ. At the outset we may note the following about the practice and theology of the early church. Christians were baptized into 'Christ', not into 'Jesus', that is to say into a relationship to Jesus as God, not into the human Jesus. And Jesus as God, as the second person of the trinity, presumably has no sex. Indeed both women and men were so baptized and entered the people of God which was the church – in differentiation from the Jewish background in which only men were circumcised and fully a part of the religious people of Israel. Secondly, it must be said that, from the very start, Christians strained ordinary human language in order to speak of the significance of Christ; the term Christ was an inclusive term, such that one could speak of persons as being 'in Christ'. They did not simply speak of the human Jesus of Nazareth and of the relation of persons to him as a human. As Christian doctrine developed, and it was said that God in Christ took on humanity, in both Greek and Latin the inclusive term for humanity was used, not that specifically for a male human being. (English is confusing here, for the same term 'man' has – until recently – been used both to encompass all humans, and specifically to speak of men.)

In an article written in support of the ordination of women to the priesthood in the Episcopal Church in the United States, Richard Norris, whose scholarship I have just mentioned, argues that the tenets of patristic Christology are such that it cannot be said that a baptized woman is differently related than is a man to Jesus as the Christ. Indeed that to say that she was, would be fundamentally to undermine patristic Christology. The most definitive statement to which attention may be drawn in this regard is the much-quoted reply of Gregory Nazianzen to Apollinarius: 'What is not assumed, is not redeemed' – or in Greek, 'not taken on, not healed'. The context was Apollinarius' denial that Jesus' was a humanity like ours. Gregory argues that if God did not take on a humanity like ours, then we are not redeemed; for it was through sharing our humanity that Christ redeemed it. Now if it could be said that God in Christ took on specifically 'male humanity', then women would be outside the scheme of salvation – and that has never been suggested. If it is to be held that both women and men find salvation in Christ, then it must be simply 'humanity' which is of significance as having been taken on. Norris in fact claims that in the patristic period nothing was made of Christ's maleness, as also not for example of his Jewishness, as being of Christological significance. Were his maleness (or Jewishness) to be brought into play, Christ would not be the saviour of all.[3] Such a Christology is in no way specifically a 'feminist Christology'. It simply does not allow that differences of sex, as also not of race, are of significance Christologically.

The implications of this for the eucharist would seem to be that a woman, equally as a man, can represent Christ. (Of course not all traditions believe that Christ is represented by the celebrant.) For it has always been said of the eucharist that precisely it is not a play about the last supper – in which case the celebrant had best be male and semitic in appearance. Rather the eucharist (as also the passover) is a re-presentation, yet anew each time, of an action which took place in the past. Indeed one might contend that, were a woman to celebrate, it would, through her very physical dissimilarity to Jesus of Nazareth, be the more apparent what was intended. (Indeed it could be that the fullness of humanity summed up in Christ would be well represented by a woman and a man concelebrating.) But in any case it follows that the necessary prerequisite for ordination is the presence of a baptized human being (not a monkey – in that God in Christ took on humanity). Furthermore, it could be said that if, in baptism into Christ, there is no more 'male and female', it is an aberration to introduce such a distinction again in ordination.[4]

At the time that I was contending for the ordination of women to the priesthood of the Anglican Church, I made use of another argument, drawing out the implications of patristic thought. I have never seen this particular argument put forward in quite this form; and I believe it to be the best argument for the ordination of women that there is. The argument arises from the fact that patristics was developed within what was philosophically a Platonist tradition. It was therefore assumed in the culture that there were 'universals' and that it was the universal, rather than particular instances of that universal, which could be said most truly to exist. To understand what is meant by a 'universal', and the implications of this way of thinking for Christology, consider the following example. Let there be shirts on a washing line. Some are blue and some pink, some have pockets and some not, but they are all examples of what it means to be a shirt: they all exemplify 'shirtness' – the universal. That is not to say that they do not have particularities, for a particular instance of a shirt has to be of a certain colour, and have pockets or not, or it would not be a shirt. Now what is in fact being said in a Christology created within such a cultural framework, is that God in Christ took on 'humanity' – the universal. Of course to be a human one has to be male or female, Jew or Gentile: a being which did not have sex and race would not be human. It is not then that this particular instance of a male, semitic human being 'is God' – one would in this case have to say 'a god'. But rather that in the incarnation God in Christ took on humanity (the universal); which is not to imply that he did not have particularities, which indeed one has to have to be human. The latter is a very different kind of statement from the former. God in Christ, through taking on a particular instance of humanity, shares with all human beings the universal, humanity, and it is that which is of significance, even though he may have different particularities from some other individuals.

What attracted me to this way of speaking is that it would seem to allow for a celebration of the diversity of human beings, this held together with an emphasis on the commonness of their humanity. Indeed one could say that, in that Jesus had particularities, such a way of thinking would allow one to celebrate the particularity of each human being. While at the same time we might say of all of us that God in Christ took on a humanity which, with him, we share. The whole tenor of such a Christology would be other than what has often been the case in western theology, whereby Christ has been conceived as male (and white!) so that women (and earlier Blacks) have seemed to be somehow less like Christ. In a world in which women are understood to be the equals of men, and in which we must promote the equality of people of different races, a Christology as that which I was proposing would seem to be fruitful. It should be noted moreover that such a Christology is not predicated upon saying that the difference between the sexes is of minimal importance, or simply to be compared with differences of race, with the implication that women can be said to be like Christ and so for example be ordained. It allows for a variety of views on how alike, or unalike, human beings are in their particularities, in particular what is the significance of the difference of sex between men and women.

What has happened however is that we have lost the philosophical framework which made the development of patristic Christology possible. Today people conceive as 'real' that which, within a dominantly Platonist framework of thought, would have been held to be a particular instance of what could be said most truly to exist. That is to say they think in terms of particular human beings (and the term human beings tends to be understood to be a collectivity of the sum total of human beings). So the question then becomes for them how this particular human being is God, rather than their thinking in terms of a humanity in which he too participated. Furthermore, many people tend to collapse the distinction between the two natures. When these things are the case then the man Jesus, with his particularities, tends simply to be equated in their mind with 'God'. Indeed we may say that there has always been such a tendency, in the patristic period likewise, to collapse the distinction between the two natures. In consequence some human beings appear to be more like Jesus (who is simply equated with God) than are others, in that they share his maleness.

The problem has been yet further exacerbated in the modern age as compared with the patristic period by what one must see as the demise of the doctrine of the trinity and its replacement by a tri-theism. A trinitarian position is that God is one (it is monotheistic), and that that one God exists in three ways, as Father, as Son and as Spirit. The divinity of the second person of the trinity is then understood with reference to the other two persons of the trinity. In so far as it is the case that, in the classical doctrine of the trinity, it is said that the three persons are alike in all save their mutual relations, when we are speaking of Christ as God, as the second person of the trinity, it cannot be said of Christ that he is 'male'. For sexuality is not a property of God. If however Christ, in and of Himself, in isolation from the other two persons of the trinity, is considered to be 'God', then there will be a greater tendency to predicate maleness of Christ as divine. That the classical doctrine of the trinity has in this manner been departed from may be thought to be of no small consequence. The extent to which there has been such a departure is well shown by the fact that, when the World Council of Churches was originally formed in 1948, the basis of that Council (to which churches which wanted to join must subscribe) read: 'The World Council of Churches is a fellowship of churches which accept our Lord Jesus Christ as God and Saviour.'[5] (It has subsequently been amended, adding a trinitarian formula.) In such a case the impression is given that Jesus is, as it were on his own, and with no reference needing to be made to the other persons of the trinity, God.[6]

The emphases of modern Christology may then be much more problematical for human equality than was the original doctrine. But it would seem to be impossible for us to return to patristic sensibilities, for the framework of thought which made that Christology possible is no longer with us. Moreover, it must be said that even the patristic position in no way solves the problem that the symbolism of Christ is somehow male. Even though it may be said that what is taken on in the incarnation is a humanity in which we all share, it is still the case that the form in which this universal nature is said to have been taken on is that of a male human being.

FEMINIST CHRISTOLOGIES

I shall now turn to the attempts by feminists of recent years to find a Christology which is at least not incompatible with their feminism. I shall suggest however that, through the very nature of Christology, there can be no Christology which is compatible with feminism.

There may be said to be three different types of Christology: 'high' Christologies, 'low' Christologies, and 'message' Christologies. A 'high' Christology is one which emphasizes Christ's divinity, a 'low' Christology his humanity, and a 'message' type Christology one which looks to his words rather than to the nature of his person. Feminists have advocated Christologies of all three types.

The problem in reconciling Christology with feminism is the very fact that, by definition, Christology speaks of Jesus as the Christ. However 'high' a Christology one may have, the divine nature of Christ is still bonded to the human nature of a human who was male. However 'low' a Christology, this human person, who is a man, is not simply human but his human nature is bonded to a divine nature. One might say that the feminist problem is that one cannot simply speak of the one nature without the other. Inescapably, if one is to have a Christology, one must bring the two natures together, and herein lies the problem. A 'message' Christology cannot simply consist in a message, a message which exists independently of the person who preached it. If it is to be a Christology, it must also concern Christ's person – whereupon all the problems which Christology entails are again present.

High Christologies

The advantage of a 'high' Christology would seem to be that there is less concentration on the maleness of Jesus, because less concentration on Jesus. If one thinks in terms of the 'cosmic Christ', or the second person of the trinity, one conceives of Christ as God rather than as a human. Moreover, in speaking, as one would tend to in a high Christology, of humanity as being summed up in Christ, or in saying that through the second person of the trinity humanity is taken into the Godhead, differences between humans may also be minimized. The problem is that this divine Christ is, in the second of his two natures, the human person Jesus, who is male. This tends to make Christ as God appear male.

A Christian feminist who has propounded what is clearly a 'high'

Christology (though it may also be a 'low' one, for she wants to speak clearly of the humanity of Jesus) is Patricia Wilson-Kastner, in her book *Faith, Feminism and the Christ*.[7] Wilson-Kastner is an Episcopal priest and patristic scholar. Her theology is in effect a cosmology: through the Logos all was created; on the cross Christ gathers up our brokenness; his resurrection is proleptic (a making present through a prefiguration of what lies in the future) of the fact that alienation will in the end be overcome. Feminism likewise, she argues, is concerned for the overcoming of dualism and alienation. Hence we should '[understand] the significance of Christ as embodying values and ideals which also are sought for and valued by feminists'.[8] Trinitarianism too fits well with a feminist ethical position. '[Just as] feminism identifies interrelatedness and mutuality – equal, respectful, and nurturing relationships - as the basis of the world as it really is and as it ought to be, we can find no better understanding and image of the divine than that of the perfect and open relationships of love.'[9] Wilson-Kastner finds her 'high' Christology and her feminism to embody the same ideals.

Wilson-Kastner's emphasis is on what persons hold in common in their humanity. 'The unity of humanity is essential if humanity is to fulfill its vocation in creation. Any feminism which does not also begin with an assumption of one human race, composed of female and male, black, white, yellow, short, tall and so forth, each equally human and not bound by preconceived roles, is not compatible with the Christian faith.'[10] With this of course one may agree. I too have suggested that Christology should embrace a multiplicity. But for her the difference of sex is essentially of no more import than are differences of race. 'The division of persons into male and female is significant, but it is one category among many.'[11] That women are of the opposite sex to Christ should then, she believes, be of no great moment. The fact that she is basically thinking in terms of the resurrected, cosmic Christ again tends to minimize any distinction which there might be between a woman and Christ in regard to sex. Thus the question which confronts Christian feminists – how should they deal with the fact that the basic symbol of their religion is that of a male Christ – does not really impress her. Nor does she have a sense for the impact which the fact that Christ has been seen as male and as part of the Godhead has had on the relations of women and men in western culture. It is as though, for her, Christ is beyond sex. The question with which we are concerned is not tackled.

Furthermore, I think there is a problem for Christians today in thinking in terms of this non-gendered cosmic Christ which forms the key to her Christology (and I am sure I would have thought this at the time that I counted myself a Christian). Wilson-Kastner apparently makes no distinction between, on the one hand, a factual account of what is the case, and, on the other, a mythological symbolism. She moves (for example) between speaking of the crucifixion of Christ (fact) to the cosmic nature of Christ – which can hardly be said to be 'true' in the sense of an empirically known fact. She will frequently tell us that the fathers of the church, or the bible, state such things to be the case, as though that were the end of the matter. I do not doubt that people in an earlier age may well have thought in terms of the kind of cosmic world picture in terms of which she herself thinks. (It is difficult to tell how far theologians in the patristic period believed themselves to be, when they spoke of the cosmic Christ or the doctrine of the trinity, stretching language to its ultimate and speaking metaphorically. One like Gregory of Nyssa, an architect of the doctrine of the trinity, was deeply conscious that God was beyond all human description.) To simply state that the fathers or biblical authors believed something does not address the question as to whether they were right, or whether our picture of the world has not so much changed as to make theirs fantastic. In an age in which we have a keen sense for the difference between fact and symbol, Wilson-Kastner makes no distinction. For example, she takes the Nicaean expression of belief as literally true, speaking not simply of the Logos but of Jesus (sic) becoming incarnate. What can that mean?

Wilson-Kastner believes that Christianity proclaims (as indeed it may well) that alienation is overcome in Christ. Again, we may ask, is this a faith statement, or a statement of what is the case? Further, she argues from the fact that one wills alienation to be overcome, that indeed it is overcome. 'There must be some reality that can heal the fragmentation of the world.'[12] Must there be? One could argue that brokenness and alienation are fundamental to the world. Though she has much to say of brokenness, my problem with her book is precisely that, through her swift movement to a triumphant conclusion, symbolized by the resurrection and the unity of humanity, she does not allow there genuinely to be brokenness.

I would then at any stage have found it difficult to believe in the cosmic Christ in whom, for her, lies the key to the solution to the world's affliction and the alienation of women. Evidently moves which for one person seem plausible are simply not moves which others can make. The debate is interesting, for it becomes evident that women who count themselves feminists may otherwise have a very different sense of reality.

Low Christologies

The advantage of a low Christology would seem to be that Jesus is considered to be just another human, one among us, our brother. Such a Christology stresses Christ's humanity rather than his divinity. The fact of Jesus' maleness then would seem to be of no more import than is his or her sexuality in the case of any other human being. It is not, in a low Christology, that we have a divine Christ who is male. The problem however is that were it simply to be said of Jesus that he was a human like any other who lived in history we should not have a Christology. A Christian position must necessarily hold of this human being Jesus that he existed (or exists) in relation to God as has no other. Either it must be said, in traditional terms, that, together with his human nature, he also had, in one person, a divine nature; or in some other way he must be held to be unique. But then we have present a male human being who, in some sense, is considered unique.

The problem with a low Christology becomes apparent through considering a liturgical situation. We have already said, that of a liturgy in which no mention was made of Christ, we might hold that it was meaningful, even theistic, but that it could not rightly be called Christian. In a Christian liturgy mention of Christ must necessarily be made, as is the case of no other human being. Indeed, through the fact that he is spoken of as though there present, something different is being said of Christ than of anyone else. No Christology can be so low that it overcomes the feminist difficulty by saying of Jesus that he was no different from every other human who has lived. A Christian position must necessarily have a *Christology*. The question is then posed as to whether one can reconcile that Christology with feminism. Indeed one might argue that talk of Jesus as our 'brother', emphasizing his humanity, makes Jesus more intrusively male than if one were casting him in the role of the cosmic Christ.

The difficulty a low Christology poses for feminists was brought home to me some years ago in attending a eucharistic liturgy, which I believe had been written by Carter Heyward, whose work I shall shortly mention. Only women were present and the service was orientated towards women. In place of a sermon there was a time of quiet in which women present spoke to the theme of 'creation', some from the perspective of giving birth. How jarring it seemed then that, at the consecration, reference had necessarily to be made to the man Jesus of Nazareth: he had to take centre stage. Not simply was he mentioned, as men may well have been in the prayers of intercession, but he was actively made present as lord of the situation. In such a liturgy it becomes apparent, in a way in which in a traditional liturgy, with a man celebrating, it does not, because there is not the same incongruity, that women are, at the very core of their religion, dependent on the male world.

Contrast the situation which pertains when a group of men celebrate the eucharist together, as has often been the case for example in a monastic setting. The central action revolves around persons of the same sex and figures of speech having the same gender reference as they themselves. Mention is made of a male Christ, God is conceived in male terms, and biblical readings doubtless largely concern the doings of men. Incidentally women may be mentioned, in prayers or as subsidiary figures in readings. How much more is the lack of symmetry between men and women apparent when one considers the fact that a congregation of nuns must invite an outsider, an outsider who, in many countries in the present Anglican and in the Roman Catholic context, has to be a man, to celebrate for them. If he does not arrive the action cannot proceed. Within the Christian context women must necessarily refer to, and exercise a dependence upon, the world of men, of a kind which men would not conceive of having in relation to the world of women.

Heyward, of whom I have just made mention, writes of Jesus as follows: 'Jesus matters only if he was fully, *and only*, human.' And further: he was 'a human person who knew and loved God'.[13] If this is all she thinks, she surely cannot be considered Christian. I too, as one who is not a Christian, might well say of him that he knew and loved God. Why then should she look in particular to Jesus? She writes: 'We cannot simply shift Jesus from center-stage and replace him with humanity or God by wishing it were so.'[14] Why she should think this, apart from consideration of her own biographical context, is unclear. She, evidently, is Christocentric, while another (as I have always been) is theocentric. But I too would want to say that (as someone has expressed it) we see God through a Christ-shaped window: I have no doubt that, as a western person, my understanding of God has, in part at least, been shaped by the person who was

Jesus of Nazareth. But again this does not make me a Christian. Heyward however shifts ground: 'I am hooked on Jesus. I could no more pretend that the Jesus-figure, *indeed the Jesus of the kerygma*, is unimportant to me than I could deny the significance of my parents and my past in the shaping of my future.'[15] The term *kerygma*, proclamation, is normally held to refer, in such a phrase as 'the Jesus of the kerygma', to the proclamation concerning Jesus; that is to say the proclamation of him as the resurrected one, as Lord and Saviour. To say this is very different from the assertion that he was simply human – and that is all. Jesus, in such a statement, is held to be unique, if only through the fact that this is the human of whom it must be said that God raised him. Heyward has a Christology (one close to the primitive Christology of the second chapter of Acts for example). If Jesus is our brother, he is a brother of a very special sort. But then the problem returns.

A 'message' Christology

The advantage of a 'message' Christology would seem to be that, with the shift of concentration from the person of Christ to his message, we circumvent the problems which present themselves when the symbol of a male person is understood to be central to Christianity. Many feminists who are Christians are surely attracted to Christianity through the compelling nature of the person who was Jesus of Nazareth and the power of his message, which resonates with their own beliefs and values.

A problem however presents itself similar to that which we have discussed when considering a 'low' Christology. To be concerned simply for Jesus' message, a message which anyone could have preached and which is now acknowledged quite independently of the person who preached it, is not to hold a Christian position. It is to hold a humanist position, to be one who, like Gandhi, finds Jesus' message striking. Compare such a position with the position that there is a kerygma to be preached about Jesus. An example of one who held this latter position is the existentialist theologian of the last generation Rudolf Bultmann. Bultmann, as I mentioned, never speaks in terms of a two-nature Christology of the type which arose in the Greek world. But Christ does for him have a uniqueness; and thus I count his position a Christian one. For Bultmann, the resurrection is not an event in our world (for resurrections he would hold, as I, do not occur in our world), but something of far greater magnitude, an eschatalogical event which represents the breaking in of another world order. It takes place in another dimension from our normal history, in God's history. Now the resurrection (an event of another order) is however the resurrection of the man who died (a normal event in our world). Thus Jesus is unique, for it is to be said of him as of none other that this is the man whom God raised, and his resurrection forms the turning-point of history. There is then, in Bultmann's theology, a necessary reference to the Christ event. (There are concomitant problems for the feminist.)

An interesting comparison here can be made with the position of Rosemary Ruether. Ruether's interest (as that also of Bultmann) is in Jesus' message, a message in her case held to concern the coming of the kingdom, the vindication of the poor and the creation of a just social order. The centre of her theology is the Christian vision. Women – who have been among the poorest of the poor – are primordially those who will be liberated. But how may this be said to be a Christology? If all she wants to speak of is a message and a vision then there is no reason to call this position Christian. Humanists too may have a vision, perhaps one which draws from Jesus Christ. Marxists have a vision, and Ruether is very much in tune with left-wing thought. There can be no incompatibility between being a feminist and taking on board the Christian vision. But to speak in terms of a vision involves no necessary reference to history, or to any particular person; one could make the vision one's own without knowing with whom it originated. If one simply wishes to speak of a social vision, one may without further ado drop any reference to the Christian 'myth', a myth which is so problematical for women. One need make no reference to a male human person who is proclaimed Lord. But to be Christian is not simply to preach Jesus' message. It is also to proclaim a message about Jesus – and therein for a feminist lie all the problems.

If one holds, of Christ, that he was, in whatever way, unique, then one is clearly a Christian. There arises the problem of reconciling a religion which has a unique Christ (who in his human nature is male) with feminism. But if Jesus of Nazareth is not thought to be unique, and the Christian story is just a myth, why, one must ask, should one who is a feminist choose to take up this particular myth when it is so male, and has central to it a male person who is held to be unique? Bultmann's is clearly a Christian position (and the problems arise for feminists). Ruether's, if she is not saying in any sense of Christ that he is unique, surely cannot be said so to be. In which case why not jettison this religion which has been so harmful to women?[16]

CONSERVATIVE CHRISTOLOGIES

I call 'conservative', for the purposes of the discussion in this chapter, Christologies which hold the maleness of Christ to be essential to his nature, and the fact that Christ was male to be central to Christianity. Conservatives do not essentially believe that the maleness of Christ in any way harms women. Women also have their place in God's creation. Indeed conservatives who are Catholics understand the feminine, as also the masculine, to be woven into a cosmic picture. The maleness of Christ may be said to form the linchpin of this picture.

Such an understanding of reality on the part of a Catholic conservative was well expressed by the Anglican bishop Graham Leonard, in his speech against the ordination of women to the General Synod of the Church of England in 1978.

> I believe that the Scriptures speak of God as Father, that Christ was incarnate as a male, that he chose men to be his apostles ... not because of social conditioning, but because in the order of creation headship and authority is symbolically and fundamentally associated with maleness. For the same reason the highest vocation of any created being was given to a woman, Mary, as representative of mankind in our response to God because symbolically and fundamentally, the response of sacrificial giving is associated with femaleness. I do not believe it is merely the result of social conditioning that in the Scriptures, in the Jewish and Christian tradition, mankind and the Church is presented as feminine to God, to whom our response must be one of obedience in contrast to those religions in which the divine is regarded as contained within creation and is to be manipulated or cajoled in order to provide what man needs. For a woman to represent the Headship of Christ and the Divine Initiative would, *unless her feminine gifts were obscured or minimized*, evoke a different approach to God from those who worship.... As the American Protestant layman Thomas Howard has said 'Jews and Christians worship the God who has gone to vast and prolonged pains to disclose himself to us as he not she, as King and not Queen, and for Christians as Father not Mother, and who sent his Son not his daughter in his final unveiling of himself for our eyes. These are terrible mysteries and we have no warrant to tinker with them.'[17]

It is thus believed by Catholic conservatives to be no chance that the incarnation took place in a male human person. The Vatican declaration that women cannot be ordained to the priesthood states:

[The incarnation] cannot be disassociated from the economy of salvation; it is, indeed, in harmony with the entirety of God's plan.... For the salvation offered by God to men and women ... took on, from the Old Testament Prophets onwards, the privileged form of a nuptial mystery: for God the Chosen People is seen as his ardently loved spouse.... Christ is the Bridegroom; the Church is his bride, whom he loves because he has gained her by his blood.[18]

Again, the Anglican V. A. Demant, arguing against the ordination of women, writes of the Christian religion: 'It is a Logos religion. And in so far as we can use gender imagery for these things the Logos is a masculine principle.... The Logos is the active, manifesting, creative-destructive, redemptive power of the godhead.' Again, Hans Urs von Balthasar, at a later date the author of a statement officially sponsored by the Vatican in support of its declaration, describes Jesus' self-giving on the cross, re-enacted in the mass, in explicitly sexual terms.

In its origin [Christianity] presents to man and woman a glorious picture of sexual integrity: the Son of God who has become man and flesh, knowing from inside his Father's work and perfecting it in the total self-giving of himself, not only of his spiritual but precisely also of his physical powers, giving not only to one individual but to all. What else is his Eucharist but, at a higher level, an endless act of fruitful out-pouring of his whole flesh, such as a man can only achieve for a moment with a limited organ of his body?[20]

For Balthasar, Mary plays the 'female' part. She is 'the favoured place where God can, and wills to, be brought into the world'.[21]

It is within such a framework of thought that it is contended that a priest must necessarily be male. (It should be noted however that not every argument for the necessity of a male priesthood necessarily entails a complete picture of God's dispensation as embodying male and female principles. It may simply be said that it is just a 'fact' that Jesus was male, and that therefore priests should be.) The Vatican declaration puts forward, as one argument among others, a Christological argument against the ordination of women. The context which it presumes is the Catholic teaching (found for example in

Thomas Aquinas) that that which becomes the sign of the sacrament must be appropriate to that which it signifies. Thus in baptism water must be used; for extreme unction there must be the presence of a sick person. The declaration states: 'The whole sacramental economy is in fact based upon natural signs, on symbols imprinted upon the human psychology: "Sacramental signs", says Thomas Aquinas, "represent what they signify by natural resemblance".' It is then contended that: 'There would not be this "natural resemblance" which must exist between Christ and his minister if the role of Christ were not taken by a man. In such a case it would be difficult to see in the minister the image of Christ. For Christ himself was and remains a man.' The priest 'acts ... *in persona Christi*, taking the role of Christ to the point of being his very image'.[22] The official commentary explains that the word 'persona' designated, in the ancient theatre, a part played using a particular mask: 'The priest takes the part of Christ, lending him his voice and gestures.' Thomas Aquinas says: '"The priest enacts the image of Christ."' The division of sex, it is said, goes much deeper than that for example of race and is fundamental to creation.[23]

Let us juxtapose this argument and that put forward by Norris, which I propounded in my discussion of patristic Christology: namely that Christ took on humanity, such that maleness is not of Christological significance. Those who hold the position expressed in the declaration may in turn respond that indeed women are, as are men, 'in Christ'; the declaration speaks of Christ as the first-born of all humanity. Yet they may also say that they believe it to be of significance that the particular instance of humanity taken on by the second person of the trinity in the incarnation was a male human being. This, they say, was not chance, for maleness is intrinsic to the symbolism of God's initiative taken towards humankind in the act of redemption. If this is to be represented symbolically, the one who acts *in persona Christi* must be male. I do not see that there is any counter argument to this. One should however perhaps comment on the fact that in this case sexual imagery has been understood to be fundamental to the act of salvation, and indeed to the action of the eucharist. It may be held to be doubtful that early Christians conceived of the eucharist in such terms. Was it not considered by them rather to be a celebratory meal, one which recalled the liberation from Egypt of the children of Israel and foreshadowed the banquet which should take place in the eschaton?

An interesting response to the Vatican's theology by one who is a

Catholic is that of Christopher Kiesling. Kiesling argues that what constitutes the priest as the image of Christ is the character of orders, that is to say that the person is a priest. (A character, in Catholic Aristotelian theology, is a similitude or image impressed by another.) He comments: 'It is not a person's maleness which constitutes that person the representative image of Christ, but a person's having the sacerdotal character, the instrumental priestly power to perform those actions signifying the giving of divine gifts, a power deriving through ordination from Christ, *the* donor of God's grace.'[24] Thomas Aquinas indeed thinks that a woman cannot receive the character of ordination. But why? Because, as he believes, the state of woman is that of subjection: *quia mulier statum subjectionis habet*. Kiesling concludes: 'It does not appear that femaleness, femininity, womanhood *as such* is the barrier to woman's receiving holy orders, but femaleness *in a state of subjection*.'[25] Likewise Kari Børresen notes that (in this respect unlike Bonaventura) 'Thomas does not say expressly that a priest ought to belong to the male sex because Christ, whom he represents, became incarnate in this sex.'[26] Thomas' belief that woman's state is one of subjection derives, as we have seen, from the false biological presuppositions which he took from Aristotle. An indication as to what his position would logically have had to be, had he not held these false presuppositions, is evident from his discussion of the validity of baptism when administered by a woman. An initial objection which he poses is, interestingly, that it is not fitting that a woman should represent a father. He answers this objection however with the reply that, whereas in human generation a woman can only be the passive principle, in spiritual generation neither man nor woman function by virtue of their own powers, but only as instruments of the power of Christ. The baptism is valid.

However, the framers of the declaration have not quite been answered; for Thomas clearly thinks that God chooses certain things and persons to become sacramental signs because they provide the more suitable signification. Kiesling writes: 'We must take seriously ... all the implications in the psychological and sociological realms of male priests to represent Christ.'[27] And Børresen concedes (of Thomas): 'His thought definitely is, that there should be conformity between the two kinds of instruments of Christ: His human nature and the priest.'[28] The Dominican Jerry Miller however has argued that the Vatican Declaration has 'misapplied [Thomas'] teaching on the issue of sign-value to support its argument from natural resemblance'. With Kiesling he argues that it is that femininity signifies inferiority to Thomas, and not femininity as such, which makes a woman unsuitable.[29]

A further line of argument which may be pursued against the declaration is that, according to Catholic theology, the power of orders lies in the soul, which is the same for both sexes, and not the body. Arguing against those who said that women could not be ordained, the Anglican theologian of the last generation Leonard Hodgson comments that to say 'that a woman is incapable of receiving the priestly or episcopal character involves saying that her sexual differentiation carries with it a deficiency in spiritual receptivity and power'.[30] Intriguingly, in his third proposition in *favour* of the argument that women can be priested, Thomas himself comments that orders lie in the soul, which is the same for both sexes, a point to which curiously (as George Tavard has pointed out) he makes no reply.[31] Thomas seems however to contradict himself in this matter, presupposing elsewhere that orders relate to the body, as when he writes: 'Since in matters pertaining to the soul woman does not differ from man as to the thing, ... it follows that she can receive the gift of prophecy and the like, but not the sacrament of Orders.'[32]

The Vatican declaration furthermore expressly rules out the objection that, in the eucharist, it is the risen Christ who is represented; and that as such he has no sex. Referring to the biblical saying that in the resurrection men and women do not marry, the declaration comments that this does not mean that the distinction between man and woman is suppressed in the glorified state. (Such a position must, one would think, constitute the strongest provocation for feminists to conclude that maleness is, in Christianity, intrinsic to the Godhead no less!)

Conservative Protestant Christians may pursue what is a rather different Christology which issues in opposition to the ordination of women. Headship and authority are, it is said, properly vested in the male: thus Christ is head of the church, and hence also women should not exercise the authority involved in being in charge of a congregation. Such a line of argument is based primarily upon scripture, and does not necessarily involve a notion of there being male and female principles in the universe. In the case of some evangelical writers (though not Barth) it may also be said that male dominance is fundamental to creation and found in all known human societies. The evangelical Gordon Wenham pursues this line.[33] An interpretation of scripture is presupposed in which all verses must comport with one another. The scriptures are then read, from Genesis to Paul, as supporting male headship.

In response to this line of thought it may well be pointed out that the subordination of woman to man is depicted in scripture as having resulted from the fall. Subordination is, in the Genesis text, the punishment meted out to woman. It is of interest that it would seem to be the case that the Galatians verse, that in Christ 'there is neither Jew nor Greek, there is neither slave nor free, there is no 'male and female', makes direct reference to Genesis. (The parallelism of the three statements is interrupted by the different form of the third, and the particular words used for male and female, which are not those which one would expect, are the same as those which the Septuagint – the Greek translation of the Hebrew scriptures with which Paul would have been familiar – uses in the Genesis verse.)[34] If this is the case, then Paul is in effect saying that the subordination, which owes to the fall, is overcome in Christ, the second Adam. It is surely the redeemed order of creation, in which there is no subordination, rather than the fallen order, which should be symbolized in the ministry of the Christian church. If however a writer believes the creation of woman from man prior to the fall to imply subordination, then there is no answer possible.

COUNTERBALANCES TO CHRISTOLOGY

Both conservative Christians and, more surprisingly, Christian feminists suggest that there are what might be called counterbalances to Christology in the form of female figures or feminine motifs present in Christian theology. I say surprisingly in the case of Christian feminists because it is so clear to me that women, or the feminine, can never hold an equivalent place to male figures or motifs within what is a deeply masculine religion. What is to be understood as happening is perhaps that, given that someone wants to be Christian, she as a feminist will look for what female representation there may be in the religion, whether or not this is fully satisfactory. Personally, when I counted myself a Christian, I had no interest in finding female figures or 'feminine' motifs within the religion. I just wanted a religion in which gender was not of significance. Once I grasped the centrality of symbolism to the religion and grasped its effect, it was time for me to leave. I have never been a Christian feminist, with typical Christian feminist concerns and sensibilities.

The compensatory factors which are suggested are various. It is said that if the Logos is to be conceived to be in some sense male, then equally the Spirit is to be held to be female. A second, though less common suggestion, is that the undivided unity of the Godhead is symbolically female, whereas the three individuated persons, the energies of the Godhead in their differentiation, are symbolically male. Thirdly, it is contended that whereas Christ is male, an equivalent figure is to be found in Mary who is female. The suggestion that though God is to be conceived as male, humanity is to be understood as female in relation to God, I shall leave until the next chapter.[35] But it too is a compensatory move which is sometimes made. I believe it to be true of all such moves that they are dubiously orthodox. Moreover I do not think that it can be said that they succeed in righting the imbalance in the symbolism of Christianity.

The suggestion that the second person of the trinity, the Logos, is 'male', but the Spirit should be seen as 'female' would appear to be common among more conservative Christians, Catholic, Anglican and Orthodox, and has been taken up by Christian feminists. In the course of arguing against the ordination of women, the Orthodox theologian Thomas Hopko writes: 'As the Son and the Holy Spirit are not the same and are not interchangeable in their unique forms of their common divinity, so the male and female are not the same and not interchangeable in the unique forms of their common humanity.'[36] One may think such a suggestion to be far from orthodox. Patristic doctrine (which it might be expected that one who is Orthodox should revere), when expounded for example by the Cappadocians (the authors in large part of the doctrine of the trinity) is that the persons of the trinity are alike in all respects save in their mutual relations.[37] Thus it would be difficult to say that the second person of the trinity is somehow male and the third female. Further, Hopko finds there to be 'a direct analogical, symbolic ... relationship'[38] between, on the one hand, Adam and Christ, and, on the other, Eve and the Spirit. Of Genesis 2 he writes: 'Women are created and called to be men's "helpers" in their service of self-emptying love. (Gn 2:18). They are to be "submissive" to men's love and service, and as such to enable and empower it – as the Holy Spirit, "incarnate by grace" in saved humanity, enables and empowers Christ himself to "fulfil" his divine ministry among his creatures.'[39] Responding to such an equation of the spirit with femaleness, Norris points out that Gregory of Nyssa (one of the Cappadocians) does indeed speak of Christ as casting out demons by the power of the Spirit, but that there is nothing in his language to imply a subordination of the Spirit to Christ!

The suggestion that the Godhead in its undivided unity be 'feminine', while the three persons 'masculine', is explained by Demant. He writes: 'If we are pressed to see in the doctrine of the Trinity some clue to the sense that gender ... must have something corresponding to it in the God-head, one would find in the unconditioned Unity of God something like the feminine in creation, while the differentiated Persons, on the other hand, have each a masculine denomination.' But, he adds: 'This attribution of femininity to the undivided unity, and of masculinity to the threefold divine energy, is not found explicit in the Church's teaching traditions.'[40] It is an interesting reflection of how gender, both masculinity and femininity, has been construed in the west. One should comment however that God in God's unity, if we are speaking of monotheism, has in fact been conceived as male and not female!

I turn finally to the suggestion that the compensatory figure to Christ who is male, is Mary who is female. Many a feminist seems to have become fixated upon Mary in recent years. That this should be the case is perhaps a good indication of the need that Christian women feel to find themselves represented symbolically in their religion. I find myself incredulous. There is nothing whatever upon which Mariology could be built! It is a castle in the sky, a male construction of an earlier age, for which there exists no possible basis. We know today (as the ancient world did not) that a new human being comes from chromosomes from both the male and the female. If moreover there were to be a case of parthenogenesis, the resulting foetus would be female, for there would be no 'Y' chromosome present! Nor is there textual evidence which carries any conviction. The passage in Matthew (in which talk of Mary's virginity occurs) is late, unreliable, and contains some of the most fanciful and non-historical writing in the new testament. Paul evidently knew nothing of so remarkable an event, for he never mentions it. How the myth came to be seems clear enough. The Greek version of Isaiah 7 uses a word which refers specifically to a virgin, whereas the underlying Hebrew simply denotes a young girl. It is this Greek version of the Hebrew scriptures with which the author of Matthew – who intends to say that the prophecy has been fulfilled – would have been familiar. One must add that there is nothing particularly remarkable about the fact that such a myth should have grown up; it would almost be surprising if it had not. It was frequently said of great men in the ancient world, for example of Plato, that they had had a god for a father and a human mother. Indeed Origen, the early Christian apologist, replies to attacks on the notion of the virgin birth by referring to other stories of virgin births circulating in his world.[41]

Quite apart from the impossibility of virgin births, it must be said that symbolically the figure of Mary is surely of little avail. The Christian religion has always resisted the idea that Mary is part of the Godhead; she is in no way equivalent to the male Christ. Biblical religion is not about Mary, who is wholly peripheral, but about Christ. Furthermore, Mary is scarcely a woman whom women today might be expected to find to be a symbol who represents them. She fulfils a typically female role: she is the one who receives from a God conceived as male. That is to say she conforms to the masculinist construction of femininity. The chief, indeed only, reason for her appearance on the scene is that she gave birth to a (male) child! Indeed her title of the patristic period, *theotokos*, the God-bearer, conceives of her simply in relation to him to whom she gave birth.

What an extraordinary position has been reached in some Christian theology, such that it is thought, at least at a subconscious level, that somehow Christ and Mary are a pair, Christ male and representative of men, and Mary female and representative of women, was brought home to me by the following incident. Some years ago when I was on the edge of Christianity, I spoke to a large gathering about the problematic nature of the Godhead for women. The Latin American liberation theologian Jon Sobrino responded that there was no problem: men should emulate Christ he said, and women Mary. It had never occurred to me. However widespread such an attitude may have been in popular piety (and perhaps it has been widespread), and though it may be thinkable to a Latin American theologian today, it is hardly orthodox. The early Christians clearly did not think that Mary provided a role model for women and Christ for men! Christians modelled themselves on Christ. One has the sense that, in such a theology, there are two glorified persons in heaven retaining their sexuality, Christ and Mary. (The two-nature Christology of Chalcedon has disappeared: Christ is a male deity.) Nor is Mary equivalent to Christ. The suggestion is in fact a good symbolization of the inferior position of women.

Quite apart from the fact that they would appear to be unorthodox and a distortion at its best of Christian theology, I believe it must be said of all these suggestions that, if what is intended is that they should give an equal place to women or to the 'feminine' within the Christian religion, they fail. What is said of the Spirit by Hopko is that the Spirit exists in the service of the male Christ. Again it may not be thought to be particularly helpful that God in God's undifferentiated nature (or indeed the Spirit in its rather vague nature) are to be understood as 'female', while 'divine energies' (*sic*), that which is clearly differentiated and self-determining, is to be seen as 'male'. Mary is in no way the equivalent of Christ in the Christian religion. The religion is centred on him. Indeed she only has a place in the religion in relation to him. For men to have a male deity, and women a lesser female 'deity', would create a polytheistic religion.

Finally, of all schemes which assign gender to different persons of the Godhead, which suggest that God in God's undifferentiated unity is female and as differentiated is male, or which see God as 'male' and humanity as 'female' in relation to God, it must be said that they necessarily fuel gender differentiation. Certain attributes are said to be 'masculine' or 'feminine', 'complementing' (it is often said) the other. When symbol systems to which a certain ultimacy is attributed, as is the case of symbols for the nature of God, or the relation of God to humanity, are conceived in terms of male and female, certain understandings of gender are legitimized and reinforced. This is ultimately unhelpful to women.

CHRIST AND FEMINISM

We have concluded therefore that the maleness of Christ is not to be evaded. Even if we take patristic Christology, in which it is said that God in Christ took on humanity in which we all participate, it is still the case that that human nature was the human nature of a male human being. In any symbolization of Christ the symbol will be male not female (or neuter). This necessary maleness is equally the case if one moves from the Greek to the original Jewish framework. The Messiah had to be a male figure. The repercussions of this maleness of the concept of Christ may be thought to be incalculable. The onus, one would have thought, lies on those who would show that it is not the case that the fact that God, whether in the form of the Father or of Christ, has been seen as 'male', is an underlying factor in western culture, distorting human relations. All the evidence would seem to point to the fact that this is the case.

It is conservatives and feminist radicals who grasp the importance of symbolism. Both see that the fact that God, and Christ, have been seen as 'male' is crucial to the religion. It establishes a particular place both for men and for women, for the 'male' and for the 'female', within the religion. But feminists who are alerted to the importance of symbolism believe Christianity accordingly to be judged. One may think that as the ethical equality of human beings comes to be recognized in our society, the masculine nature of their religion will become an ever more pressing question for Christians. Christian feminists often fail to recognize the crucial nature of symbolism. In so far as they do, they are troubled: they try to find a way for women to be represented in a religion where the Godhead is conceived in male terms, and a way indeed to be able to associate themselves with a male God or Christ. Conservatives (and Christian feminists also to some extent) seek alternative ways in which the female can be symbolized in the religion, ways which it must be thought are less than satisfactory, and which become increasingly unsatisfactory as that for which women stand in our society changes.

It should be pointed out once again that those feminists who say that, on account of the male symbolism, Christianity is impossible for them, are not thereby necessarily 'anti-men'. It is a retort which is sometimes given, but quite beside the point. For we are not here, in speaking Christologically, conceiving of Jesus as simply one human being among others who have lived in the past. Christology gives a male human being a status which is given to no woman. A Christian service revolves around Christ. Indeed it may be (as in my case) because one deeply cares that there should be good and equal relations between men and women that one is adamant that no one human being can be given the kind of status which Christians give to Christ. Such a religion as Christianity is a symbolic distortion of the relationships which I would have. Above all in religion, one would think, when religion is so potent for how human beings conceive the world, it is important that there be no such bias. I am therefore not Christian not least for the sake of the kind of human relationships which I want to see flourish.

It will be useful in conclusion to look at some incidents which illuminate the way in which symbolism operates in the religion. It is sometimes said that the difference of sex is of no more significance than the difference of race. Thus it is thought that the fact that some human beings are of the opposite sex to Christ is not of importance. I would argue that this is not the case. Symbolically at least (and in Christology we are dealing partially with the realm of symbolism) the difference of sex is a divide. This indeed is the origin of the word: the 'se' root of 'sex' means to cut or divide – as also in section, secateurs, segment – and sex is the great cutting of humanity. It may be that biologically we are on a continuum, and on rare occasions a child is born whose sex is uncertain. But symbolically (and in large part biologically) there are two sexes. Again, that this is the case is not contradicted by the fact that, in many spheres, I may have much more in common with first world men than with third world women.

Consider then the following. A book, edited by Hans-Ruedi Weber (until recently of the World Council of Churches), *On a Friday Noon*,[42] shows illustrations of Christ crucified, drawn from all cultures and times in history. The variety is fascinating. There are yellow Christs and brown Christs, Christs who are serene and Christs in agony, Christs who are stylized and Christ in the image of the people who depicted him. But one thing these pictures – which reflect a spectrum of human art and imagination – have in common: they are all images of a man. If there were to be an image of a woman in that book, that one picture would stand out as the exception. However Christ is understood, as people take him up into their culture, or make of him what they will, they know him to be male. A woman is the 'opposite' to Christ in a way in which someone of another race is not.

Consider then again the following, an example which shows well how far feminists who are Christians feel the lack of a male figure with which to associate. In the Anglican cathedral of St John the Divine in New York there was placed a female figure on a cross. It was designated 'The Christa'. (It is significant that it could not be called 'Christ' but had to be given another name; moreover that it had to be explained what this was, whereas a man on the cross would have required no explanation.) The fact that such a statue could be produced, and was apparently meaningful to women, shows something of women's yearning in their religion in a culture which is now deeply conscious of feminist issues. There followed an uproar. As could have been the case of no male figure, the Christa for many people represented a distortion of Christianity. This incident highlights the tension. Yet what can be done? For it is indeed a distortion of the historical religion, in a way in which no figure of a man can be (consider the book showing images of Christ), to depict a female Christ.

Consider again the following. Many years ago, at a race relations meeting held in the church hall of a Black church in the American South, I saw a striking picture of the head and shoulders of a Black man on the cross, simply called 'Black Christ'. I realized, in a way in which it had never struck me before, what a need there was for Black people (naturally) to see themselves as in the image of their God, and their God as in their image. This the more particularly when the surrounding society has discriminated against them. When I became in a conscious way feminist I pondered long what it meant that a woman could not in such a way depict Christ as being in her image. Yet the need is there, as evidenced by the Christa.

It will be appropriate to end this discussion by recognizing the fact that it is fundamentally on account of Christ's maleness that still today, throughout the greater part of Christendom (and in countries where women now play a leading part in public life), women may still not be ordained. In my own case it was not that I was considered pastorally unsuitable, or academically unable, which led to my being refused ordination. I could not even be considered. Let us compare this with situations in which the issue of race has been involved. There was last century a question as to whether Blacks could be ordained, but they have been. Today, were a Black to be refused ordination on account of his race, there would be an outcry. One may imagine that bishops would rush to ordain him to make the point. Again, when Jews were refused ordination in the national protestant church in Germany during the Third Reich, the church split, for there were those who said that on principle (whatever might be the case in the state) this could not be in the church. But men have not, on the whole, one may note, considered it necessary to break ranks in order to ordain women. They have agreed that there was something to be discussed. So apparently have the majority of women. That this is so shows how deep is the division of sex to human beings. But one may also say, from the fact that this has needed to be discussed – and from the fact that, as I say, throughout the greater part of Christendom women have not been ordained – it would be difficult to argue that the fact that this religion has had at its centre a male figure has been of little significance.

NOTES

1 I owe this point to John Riches. ('The Case for the Ordination of Women to the Priesthood', unpublished paper given to the meeting of the Anglican Orthodox Joint Doctrinal Discussions, Athens, 1978 (London: Anglican Consultative Council AO/JDD 185), p. 34.)

2 'Interpreting the Doctrine of the Incarnation', in D. R. McDonald (ed.), *The Myth/Truth of God Incarnate* (Wilton, CT: Morehouse-Barlow, 1979), p. 80–1.

3 'The Ordination of Women and the "Maleness" of Christ', *Anglican*

Theological Review, Supplementary Series, 6 (June 1976), pp. 69–80.

4 Unless it be said that maleness belongs to the essential character of priesthood, an argument which will be considered below (pp. 67–70).

5 The Constitution of the World Council of Churches, adopted at Amsterdam, 30 August 1948. (W. A. Visser 't Hooft (ed.), *The First Assembly of the World Council of Churches*, vol. V, London: SCM Press, 1949, p. 197.)

6 How different from for example Gregory of Nyssa, who writes that the three persons are as links in a chain, so that in the presence of one the others are immediately present; or from the patristic analogy of the trinity as being like the moving pattern on a wall caused by the reflection of the sun's rays on water, so intimately are the three ways in which God is God one.

7 *Faith, Feminism and the Christ* (Philadelphia, PA: Fortress Press, 1983).

8 Ibid. p. 92.

9 Ibid. p. 126.

10 Ibid. p. 60.

11 Ibid. p. 57.

12 Ibid. p. 52.

13 *The Redemption of God: A Theology of Mutual Relation* (Washington, DC: University Press of America, 1982), pp. 31–2, emphasis mine.

14 Ibid. pp. 31–2.

15 Ibid. p. 196, emphasis mine.

16 For further discussion of Ruether's position in relation to Bultmann's see Daphne Hampson and Rosemary Ruether, 'Is There a Place for Feminists in a Christian Church?', *New Blackfriars*, 68, no. 801 (January 1987).

17 Speech to the General Synod of the Church of England, 8 Nov. 1978 (The Church Literature Association for the Church Union, copy in the possession of the author).

18 *Inter Insigniores: Declaration on the Question of the Admission of Women to the Ministerial Priesthood*, 15 Oct. 1976, in L. Swidler and A. Swidler (eds), *Women Priests: A Catholic Commentary on the Vatican Declaration* (New York: Paulist Press, 1977), p. 44.

19 'Why the Christian Priesthood is Male', *Women and Holy Orders: Report of the Archbishops' Commission*, appendix C (London: Church Information Office, 1966), p. 101.

20 'The Christian and Chastity', *Elucidations*, tr. J. Riches (London: SPCK, 1975), p. 150 (1971).

21 'Welches Gewicht hat die ununterbrochene Tradition der Kirche bezüglich der Zuordnung des Priestertums an den Mann?', hg. von der deutschsprachigen Redaktion des 'Osservatore Romano', *Die Sendung der Frau in der Kirche: Die Erklärung 'Inter insigniores' der Kongregation für die Glaubenslehre mit Kommentar und theologischen Studien* (Verlag Butzon & Bercker Kevelaer), p. 57, my translation.

22 'Vatican Declaration', Swidler, pp. 43, 44, 43.
23 'The Ordination of Women: Official Commentary from the Sacred Congregation for the Doctrine of the Faith on its declaration *Inter Insigniores*: "Women and the Priesthood" of 15th October 1976' (pamphlet) (London: Catholic Truth Society, undated).
24 'Aquinas on Persons' Representation in Sacraments', in Swidler and Swidler (eds), *Women Priests*, p. 254. It should be pointed out that we do not know what Thomas' opinion would have been in his maturity. The text in the *Summa*, added after his death, is taken word for word from the early *Commentary on the Sentences of Peter Lombard*.
25 'Persons' Representation', p. 255.
26 *Subordination and Equivalence: The Nature and Role of Women in Augustine and Thomas Aquinas*, tr. C. H. Talbot (Washington, DC: University Press of America, 1981), p. 242.
27 'Persons' Representation', p. 257.
28 *Subordination and Equivalence*, p. 242.
29 'A Note on Aquinas and Ordination of Women', *New Blackfriars*, 61, no. 719 (April 1980), p. 190.
30 'Theological Objections to the Admission of Women to Holy Orders' (pamphlet) (The Anglican Group for the Ordination of Women, 1974), p. 8 (1967).
31 'The Scholastic Doctrine', in Swidler and Swidler (eds), *Women Priests*. ST, part III, supplement, qu. 39, art. 1, ad 1 obj.
32 ST, part III, supplement, qu. 39, art. 1, ad 1 obj.
33 'The Ordination of Women: why is it so divisive?', *Churchman*, 92, no. 4 (1978), pp. 310–19.
34 Cf. Krister Stendahl, 'The Bible and the Role of Women' (pamphlet) (Philadelphia, PA: Fortress Press, Facet Books, Biblical Series 15, 1966), p. 32.
35 See pp. 97–101.
36 'On the Male Character of Christian Priesthood', in T. Hopko (ed.), *Women and the Priesthood* (Crestwood, NY: St Vladimir's Seminary Press, 1983), p. 107.
37 Cf. Gregory Nazianzen, *Oratio* XXXIX.16 (MPG XXXV1, 93C–96B), quoted by Norris, 'Ordination and Maleness', n. 16.
38 'Male Character of Christian Priesthood', p. 106.
39 Ibid. p. 111.
40 'Why the Christian Priesthood is Male', p. 101.
41 Cf. Frances Young, 'Two Roots or a Tangled Mass?', in J. Hick (ed.), *The Myth of God Incarnate* (London: SCM Press, 1977), p. 89.
42 *On a Friday Noon* (London: SPCK, 1979; Geneva: WCC, 1979).

CHAPTER 3

Concretion

THE CONCRETION OF RELIGION

Religion lives through its concretion. By concretion I mean the parables, the stories and the history, the images, symbols and metaphors by which it is carried. Of course it would be possible to have a religion which was largely abstract, which consisted of philosophical formulations and moral maxims. But Christianity is not like that. It lives through a wealth of images. For a start Christianity, and Judaism before it, arose amid the history and literature of a people. Within Christianity, people have sought out symbols through which they could formulate their faith, such as the doctrine of the trinity. It is through this concretion that the religion is conveyed from one generation to another. Biblical figures have become paradigmatic. The parables of Jesus have entered the culture. It is the particular way in which its doctrines have been expressed through concrete imagery which has shaped those doctrines. Above all the understanding of God is an imaginative construct, for we have no access to what God may be in God's self.

Clearly the shaping of Christianity has been largely masculine. God is conveyed using male metaphors. Christ is central to the religion. As we shall see, his parables largely concern male characters. Prophets and priests, disciples and church leaders are male. Of course women too are present. But the way in which they are present may be less than helpful. If they are placed in secondary roles, or it is assumed that women's identity is to be found in mothering, then the fact of their presence reinforces a certain understanding of the feminine. The concretion conveys a subtle message to us at a subconscious level. The parable of the prodigal son conveys at a conscious level a message about the need for forgiveness and acceptance. But at another level we come to learn that God is to be compared to a good father (not a mother) who divides his property between two sons (not daughters). The concretion is potent. It forms the religious imagination. One may respond (in relation to the parable of the prodigal son) that one knows that today women may pass property to their daughters. But it is still the case that through the reading of it in church a certain image of what it means to be male or female is conveyed. Again it may be said that though prophets and priests in the bible are male, there is no reason why women should not be ordained or exercise leadership today. But the past situation makes women appear an aberration.

Of recent years, not least through the coming into their own of women this century, the question has arisen for Christians as to how far the concretion is itself inspired. Is the imagery God-given, or is it the product of the human imagination and so subject to alteration in another age? When in effect, through changing the symbols or language used, should we have another religion? C. S. Lewis speaks for the conservatives here:

> Suppose the reformer stops saying that a good woman may be like God and begins saying that God is like a good woman. Suppose he says that we might just as well pray to 'Our Mother which art in Heaven'. ... Suppose he suggests that the Incarnation might just as well have taken a female as a male form, and the Second Person of the Trinity be as well called the Daughter as the Son. ...
>
> But Christians think that God Himself has taught us how to speak of Him. To say that it does not matter is to say either that all the masculine imagery is not inspired, is merely human in origin, or else that, though inspired, it is quite arbitrary and unessential. And this is surely intolerable. ... A child who had been taught to pray to a Mother in Heaven would have a religious life radically different from that of a Christian child.[1]

For Lewis the concretion is given. And concretion is not incidental to what is conveyed. This would also be the position of conservatives such as Leonard (whom we have considered)[2] who believe masculinity and femininity to be built into God's ordering of reality.

Likewise Austin Farrer believes that a translation process cannot be undertaken without the substance of the matter being lost. He pokes fun at the modern person who says:

> 'As for the terms in which St Paul expressed it – well, there you are – he used any sort of figure that came to hand: he picked up a rhetorical

metaphor from a cynic preaching in the market. ... He would have
been amazed to learn that subsequent generations would make such
stuff the foundation of dogmas. We should strip off the fashions of
speech; but keep the substance, of course.' ... But what is the substance? It has an uncanny trick of evaporating once its accidents of
expression are all removed. ...

Now the thought of Christ Himself was expressed in certain dominant images. ... These tremendous images ... are not the whole of
Christ's teaching, but they set forth the supernatural mystery which is
the heart of the teaching. ... It is because the spiritual instruction is
related to the great images, that it becomes revealed truth. ... We have
to listen to the Spirit speaking divine things: and the way to appreciate
his speech is to quicken our own minds with the life of the inspired
images. ... Theology is the analysis and criticism of the revealed
images. ... Theology tests and determines the sense of the images, it
does not create it. The images, of themselves, signify and reveal.[3]

For Farrer too the images are given.

What may a liberal say to this? How may the message be disen-
tangled from the original imagery through which it was conveyed, or
is this to distort and change its meaning? Farrer has been criticized
by Ian Barbour who writes: 'By his appeal to authority, Farrer makes
"authorized images" immune to criticism. ... By detaching religious
images from the human experience in which they occur, he mini-
mizes the influence of psychological forces and cultural images (from
literature, mythology, art, etc.). ... I submit that the images themselves are not directly God-given but arise from man's analogical
imagination.'[4] Of course one may (as a liberal) agree with this.
Human beings chose the imagery through which they would capture
their understanding of God. Jesus looked to material close to hand
for the subject matter of his parables. Yet this does not really speak
to the conservatives' point. For that which is conveyed is clearly
shaped by the concretion. A feminist will agree with Lewis that a
child who prayed to a mother in heaven would have a fundamentally
different conception of God! She might well say that she would have
a different sense of herself as well had she grown up counting herself
as made in God's image.

Criticism of those who see concretion to be fundamental to religion
may be quite beside the point. The Lutheran scholar Robert Jenson
chastises Christian feminists for being so foolish as to think that the
term 'Father' is being used univocally (having the same connotations) when used of human fathers and of God; as though to imply

that there is sexuality in God.[5] But feminists may be well aware that, in calling God Father, it is not intended to say that God literally has sexuality, while yet wanting to maintain that this is problematic. When Jenson continues that the reason why the biblical God is called 'Father' is that the attempt is being made to get away from sexuality, with which women are more naturally to be associated, we may think that he has given the game away! For it is precisely the fact that men have tended to be associated with that which is above, spiritual and 'like God', whereas women have been associated with that with is below, of the earth, sexual, and 'unlike God' which lies at the heart of the problem! To continue to use exclusively male language for God (or female language for humanity in relation to God) reinforces these perceptions. The biblical material is not innocent.

The problem is that Christianity cannot shed its concretion. For Christianity is a historical religion. It is rooted in a particular past, a past that was patriarchal. It would be difficult to think of God as anything other than 'Father' and 'Son' when the biblical metaphors for God are male, and Jesus was a male human being. Of course supplementary imagery may be found, but the core imagery remains male. The Hebrew scriptures are bound up with the history of a particular society, and that society was patriarchal. The church arose in a social setting in which women were not equals. Jesus' teaching is conveyed through the particular examples which he used. In Christian worship, or through the reading of the bible, this language and imagery is transported from the past into the present. Moreover this language and imagery is brought from the past into the present not just as any language and imagery, but as having a certain givenness. The bible is considered to be inspired literature which is in some way normative for the religion. Change to the concretion may be thought to be extraordinarily difficult, for the imagery is built into the literature and thought structure which form the basis of the religion. In some cases it is, if one is to retain the historical character of the religion, impossible: for example the fact cannot be altered of Jesus having been a male human being. One thinks of the feminist cartoon of the three wise men arriving at Bethlehem, one saying to the others, with down-turned mouth: 'Its a girl!' That would disrupt the whole story.

The impact which the bible and the imagery of the Christian religion has had on our society is not to be overestimated. It has been fundamental to western consciousness. This is still the case today, although its hold may be lessening and our societies becoming radically secular. Children who read western literature absorb the impact which religion has had on that literature. In Britain children still hear biblical stories in schools; much of American society is steeped in the bible. For many people in our society the bible is a book like no other book. People who never normally go to church find themselves called upon to express their emotions through religious symbols and imagery at moments of transition and crisis in their lives: at baptisms, weddings and funerals. The church is full of concrete symbolism: the priest may have to be male, the words of the prayer book or liturgy are used, the hymns of former generations sung. At Christmas, the most celebrated festival of the year, a particular story is depicted on Christmas cards or in nativity plays. It has one woman character, and she is there *qua* mother. Men are shown in different roles, as innkeepers, shepherds, wise men and fathers. The story celebrates the birth of a boy, who is to be the redeemer of humankind.

Christian feminists too are of course deeply conscious of these things. The concretion of the Christian religion drives them to its edge; indeed makes them wonder whether there is a place for them within it. They attempt a process of translation. But the biblical material may simply not be amenable to what they would say. They may look to parts of the tradition which are less inimical to them, for example stories that tell of the lives of women. But the women whom they find may well not match their feminist consciousness. It struck me as incongruous when I heard of a parish church, in a commuter town south of London, which was to enact a nativity play. What had those educated women in that church, many of them with responsible jobs in London, in common with that story? As we have said, in concluding the last chapter, women need to find images with which, and persons with whom, they can in their religion form some association, or perceive a reflection of themselves. Men generally fail to realize that there are women in the pews in pain – and others have left. Women are disrupted in their worship by the masculinity of the religion to the point that it ceases to be for them a vehicle through which they can love God. The question thus with which we are confronted is that of whether this religion can contain the new consciousness of women.

I shall in this chapter first look at the biblical material. The bible forms the basis of the Christian religion and is the source of its concretion. That the bible is deeply patriarchal may be taken as read. What I shall endeavour to show is the extent and depth of this bias towards the male. I shall then, secondly, move to the language of

Christian theology, the imaging of God. I shall consider the success of attempts of recent years to mitigate its masculine nature. Thirdly, I shall look at the understanding of the 'feminine' which has been built into the tradition. I shall then fourthly look at the various ways in which Christian feminists try to relate to and to appropriate the biblical material. Finally, I shall consider the conclusion to which some women have come, that feminism is incompatible with a religion of which the core symbolism of which is male. I shall look at the endeavour of women both within and outside Christianity to create a different concretion.

BIBLICAL RELIGION

That the bible reflects a patriarchal world is clear. The majority of biblical figures, whether partriarchs, prophets, priests, disciples or church leaders, are male. The scriptures largely concern the interaction of men with one another and with their God. The central figure of the tradition for Christians, Jesus Christ, is of course male. A handful of women who play a part on the stage form the exception. Likewise parables and ethical sayings are largely directed to the world of men. But it is not simply that women are notable by their absence. When they are present they are present for the most part performing female roles as defined by that society. The problems are thus multi-faceted.

In general terms these things are evident: one need not demonstrate them. What I wish rather to do is to show the extent to which it is the case that the bible is patriarchal in its presuppositions. I shall therefore do two things. Firstly, I shall consider Jesus Christ. For it is often supposed that his attitude towards women stands in stark contrast to that of the surrounding society. Here at least, it is thought, feminist women may find some solace. Jesus' attitudes and teaching are moreover central to the biblical witness: they tend to be the reference point to which Christians turn. Moreover, his parables and ethical sayings are among the most well-known passages in the bible. Secondly, I shall discuss textual analysis of the bible which has been carried out by feminists in recent years. Such readings of the text lead one to the conclusion that patriarchal presuppositions are woven into the writing in such a way that they cannot be extricated. The fact that a negative view of women is conveyed at a level which must be largely subconscious makes these texts all the more dangerous. Biblical stories, and the narration of history in the bible, may be profoundly damaging to human relations.

To turn first to the words and attitudes of Jesus. We should of course be aware that we do not know what Jesus himself said: we do not have his words verbatim. Nor do we know precisely what he did. 'Jesus' as we have him may have been filtered through the patriarchal world which remembered him and wrote about him (if the biblical authors were male). Nevertheless, this is not of importance in relation to our present consideration. For it is Jesus as he was remembered and his words as we have them which have played the part which they have in western culture. What I wish to discuss then is the contention of some in recent years that 'Jesus was a feminist'. This has been suggested by male authors who wish to support the cause of women,[6] and by many a Christian feminist. For such a contention there would seem to be not a shred of evidence. Even if one takes a minimalist definition of feminism, the equality of women and men, is this the case. Indeed, one might well say how could such equality have occurred to Jesus, given the society in which he lived. Still less can it be said that Jesus had a feminist interpretation of social realities. That Jesus reached out to women as individuals in their need (as he did also to men) is certainly so. But there is no evidence that he mounted a critique of the position in which women were placed in his society.

It must in the first place be said that there was probably nothing particularly exceptional about Jesus' behaviour and attitudes towards women. True he was not, so far as we know, misogynist: there is evidence to the contrary. But it must not be thought that he was in this alone in his society: there were others also who were not. Judaism (as Jewish scholars have pointed out) was much more diverse than Christians, keen to suggest that Jesus stood out from his surroundings, have sometimes allowed.[7] It is important moreover that one not give overtones to stories surrounding Jesus which they may in no way have carried. Thus for example it is sometimes held to be of significance that the first appearance of the resurrected Christ is said to have been to a woman.[8] Judith Ochshorn, a specialist in Near Eastern culture, points out that there is a long history of women as mourners and attendants on the dead: thus 'in its cultural context, the presence of women at the cross or at the tomb of Jesus was not exceptional'.[9] Again the context of Jesus' statement against divorce may not, as has sometimes been suggested, be that of a prohibition of a double standard for men and women. He was simply advocating one of the two strands of thought already present in the legal thought and practice of Judaism.[10]

Inasmuch as the parables provide us with some indication of how Jesus saw the world, it must be said that women would appear to have been marginal to his perception. Nicola Slee provides some interesting statistics.[11] Taking alone the synoptic gospels, for they are likely to be closer to the words of Jesus, the facts are as follows. There are in the parables in Mark's gospel 18 main characters, all of whom are men; in Matthew's 85, 12 of whom are women, but this includes 10 bridesmaids; in Luke's 108, of whom 9 are women. Moreover, and perhaps even more significantly, among the men there is a rich spectrum of life represented: they are farmers, builders, merchants, kings, judges, stewards, doctors, bridegrooms, servants, sons, fathers, priests, publicans, rich men, poor men, thieves, fools, scoundrels. By contrast the roles in which women are portrayed are wholly conventional. The women can be listed exhaustively as ten bridesmaids, a woman searching for a lost coin, a widow seeking justice, and a handful of unspecified wives, mothers and daughters mentioned in general terms. The facts speak for themselves.

There is no positive evidence that Jesus saw anything wrong with the sexism of his day. He did not, so far as we know, see the necessity for structural change to remedy the oppression that women were under. One may make a comparison here with his attitude towards the poor; for one could evidently make out a case that, in relation to the poor, he preached the need for revolution. He suggests that a woman may be allowed to sit at his feet, rather than preoccupy herself with cooking. But there is no suggestion that the service of others, in which discipleship was to consist, should involve taking some of the burden of housework from women. His parables never challenge male privilege. The father in the parable of the prodigal son divides his property between sons. The 'owner of the house', the person who builds a house, and the one who has authority over servants, are all presumed male. In John 3 Jesus is reputed to have said that 'the bride exists only for the bridegroom'. Mention is made, in Matthew 18:25, of a man selling his wife and children into slavery to pay off his debt. What more need one say?

It has been pointed out by Ochshorn that Jesus' message is evidently addressed basically to men. The life which Jesus advocated must have necessarily had an appeal to men rather than to women, for it would in many cases have put women in an impossible position. Ochshorn comments:

> It seems likely that in ways we can never measure, the preachings about the superiority of the life of the spirit may have been profoundly discouraging and alienating to mothers of very young children, who knew about the realities of their own lives and realized that these preachings were profoundly insensitive to those realities. ... It is not that Jesus viewed women with ambivalence, but his emphasis on the superior value of the spiritual may have placed women more than men in an ambivalent relationship to the divine.[12]

Jesus urges that land and possessions should be abandoned. But only men had these. He forbids divorce, but implicitly accepts that it is a man who initiates divorce, 'the man who divorces his wife...'. When a man says he will follow him 'but let me first say farewell to those at my home', Jesus reprimands him, and when a woman cries out 'Blessed is the womb that bore you, and the breasts that you sucked', he replies 'Blessed rather are those who hear the word of God'. In both these cases he rejects the ties of family.[13]

Nor, significantly, in the realm of religion does Jesus appear to have done anything to counter the inferior position in which women were placed. We have records of frequent clashes with the Pharisees over the sabbath and other traditional observances. Not once is Jesus recorded as challenging the oppression of women. He heals a woman with a flow of blood, but haemorrhaging is a disease and is referred to as such: 'Be healed of your disease.' He nowhere confronts the whole issue of menstruation and childbirth, which marked woman as either ritually unclean or sinful.[14] He never for example suggests that women should be allowed into the inner courts of the temple, or take upon themselves the obligations of prayer laid on men. And we must certainly say that he never saw the issues of language and imagery which feminists today believe to be crucial: he evidently refers without second thought to God as 'Father'.

In saying these things one is, of course, not 'blaming' Jesus – any more than one is blaming, as individuals, any of his contemporaries for not comprehending the ethical necessity of human equality. We may think that 'blame' would be a mistaken judgement on the peculiar blindness in that society to the situation of women. But when one realizes what that situation was,[15] the blindness becomes horrific. That Jesus was personally kind to women there is no reason to doubt. That he freed people to be themselves and to be present for others is the undeniable witness of the texts. But that he had a feminist analysis of society is something for which there is no evidence. To contend under these circumstances that Jesus was a feminist, or that he spoke out for women, must imply a very low estimate of what being a feminist (or speaking out for women) might mean. It becomes important to say these things in view of the fact that Christian people tend to look to Jesus' teaching and actions as exemplary of what human relationships should be. He was in no way concerned with those issues which must concern us. Ochshorn writes: 'Jesus was neither a feminist nor a misogynist. His central message simply lay elsewhere.'[16]

I turn then, secondly, to the readings which feminist scholars are giving of biblical texts. The techniques used are those learnt in literary analysis, particularly literary analysis as influenced by French (post-modern) thought. I take here as my example Nelly Furman's intriguing essay 'His Story versus Her Story: Male Genealogy and Female Strategy in the Jacob Cycle'. Other effective examples of such work are Esther Fuch's two essays in the same volume, *Feminist Perspectives on Biblical Scholarship*, in which Furman's essay appears.[17] Fuchs, in an analysis of women as mothers in the Hebrew scriptures, shows how women are considered entirely in relation to the male world. In her other essay she considers the theme of female deceptiveness in those scriptures, arguing that it is the text itself which is deceptive through its failing to name the real problem: namely that the power relations which pertained between men and women forced women to seek to obtain their ends through underhand means, while at the same time the deviousness of women is used to justify their inferior position.

I turn however to Furman's essay. A text, says Furman, quoting the French semiotician Roland Barthes, is a reading of a text: a reader, like a musician faced with a score, appropriates it in a way that is meaningful. She proposes a feminist reading. She will gain entrance to the text through a consideration of how articles of clothing function for women and for men. For men, as she shows, articles of clothing signify a specific bond between them. Thus when Joseph escapes the embrace of Potiphar's wife (Gen. 39:9–10), who would seduce him, leaving his coat in her hands, the coat stands for his loyalty to another man. Likewise Jacob, his father, had given him a long robe with sleeves, for he 'loved Joseph more than any other of his children' (Gen. 37:3). 'In both cases, a piece of attire represents an emotional link, a trust between men.'[18] Again when Pharaoh makes Joseph vizier of Egypt he gives him special clothes, as does Joseph his brothers to mark his reconciliation with them. Garments, for men, express feelings. When overcome with grief, men rend their clothes. (Gen. 37:29, 34; 44:13). Clothing sets up a hierarchical order founded on a father's liking for a child. Items of clothing are thus 'textual signifiers'; 'they implement the new hierarchical order of elective dominance'.[19]

When however we turn to women, items of clothing have a very different signification, a signification corresponding to women's lack of power in the society. Thus Tamar, the widow of Judah's son, substitutes for her widow's dress a prostitute's veil. Whereupon Judah asks for her favours, for which she takes his signet, cord and staff as a pledge for payment – so that, when pregnant, she is able to prove that he is the father of the child and so legitimize her twins and perpetuate the line of her husband. Potiphar's wife, likewise, had made an article of clothing serve her own purpose, in that case to convince her husband that Joseph had tried to seduce her. Again, Rebekah secures Isaac's blessing for Jacob by dressing him in Esau's clothing. Furman comments:

> When Rebekah, Potiphar's wife, or Tamar uses a piece of attire for their own personal ends, they do not create a gratuitous disturbance in the order of things. Although in a world under divine guidance their actions can be said to actualize the Lord's will, these actions can also be seen as the expression of women's resentment and rebellion. When Rebekah suggests that Jacob take his brother's place, or when Potiphar's wife tries to seduce Joseph, or Tamar calls attention to Judah's progeny, their interference breaks up the exclusive father–son dialogue and forces recognition of their presence. ...
>
> Women use pieces of attire ... to reinscribe themselves in the patriarchal system. ... As used by men, garments form a communicative channel from which women are excluded; but when used by women, garments function as communicative devices between the sexes. For the men, garments are symbolic markers of filial love and recognition, whereas for the women they serve as a means of self-inscription in a system that neglects them. ... Whereas for the men garments have a determined, precise meaning, that is to say, a truth value, for the women clothes are nothing but signifiers open to a variety of meanings; they are items whose function and referential meaning can easily be changed. ... [Garments] are the place of juncture for a multiplicity of meanings, the locus for the expression of divergent desires.[20]

One may furthermore point out that the anonymous biblical narrator sides with Potiphar and Joseph. 'In siding with Joseph, the
narrator embraces the ideological structure which Joseph serves,
namely, the male desire for an exclusive bond between men. ... The
position of the biblical narrator is no more "neutral" than that of the
feminist reader.'[21]

Such textual analysis, undertaken with a feminist pair of eyes, is
uncovering the depth at which sexism must be seen to be present in
the text. It shows to be wholly naive claims that the problem of the
patriarchal nature of the biblical literature could be solved by for
example substituting certain female words for male words, or con-
centrating on those stories which concern women. The text is the
product of a sexist, indeed misogynist, culture: the presuppositions
of a patriarchal world are written into it. Moreover, such texts are
the more dangerous in that they affect us at a subconscious level. The
fact that the narrator evaluates the story from a patriarchal perspective only compounds the issue. There is, one must conclude, little
that can be done. Yet these texts are read as sacred texts.

THE IMAGING OF GOD

Central to the concretion of the Christian religion has been the way
in which God has been conceived. I shall here consider the imagery
and the symbols which have been used for God. In particular I shall
look at the attempts of recent years to unearth other, female (or
feminine) imagery, present in the scriptures and in the Christian
tradition. I shall argue that the suggestions which have been made
carry with them grave problems. Moreover that they do not do the
work which it is intended that they shall do.

The source of Christian shaping of the concept of God is the biblical
language and metaphors. In the Hebrew scriptures, God is of course
overwhelmingly conceived using male figures of speech. It may be
noted that, in this, the Israelites were unlike surrounding cultures
which, polytheistic rather than monotheistic, conceptualized the divine through the use of both female and male imagery. This prevalent masculinity does not change in the Christian scriptures. The
naming of God as Father is added to the previous designations of
King, Lord and Judge: all of them, it should be noted, denoting in
that society high-ranking males. God is called 'Father' 170 times by
Jesus in the gospels, and in his prayers never invoked by any other

name.[22] By contrast God is never once throughout the bible addressed as 'Mother'.[23]

With the development of Christian theology, God comes to be symbolized as trinity. It may well be that this development makes matters worse. It could well be argued that inasmuch as there is a relationship between the second person of the trinity and the male human being Jesus, God becomes relatively more anthropomorphized, so appearing more masculine. Don Cupitt indeed suggests that the fact that Jesus, a human being, came to be seen as God, made for a situation whereby God the 'Father' also was conceived more anthropomorphically than was the case within the Jewish background. In Christian art it becomes acceptable to portray God 'the Father' as a male figure, whereas within Judaism this would have been unthinkable.[24] In Christian theology, God comes to be conceived as 'Father' and 'Son'. The fact that Jesus referred to God as 'Father' made this move seem axiomatic. In this context it is of interest that the Jewish scholar Rita Gross argues that there is no intrinsic reason why, within Judaism, God should not be named 'She'. She writes: 'The familiar ... "the Holy One, blessed be He" is also ... "the Holy One, blessed be She" and *always has been*. Only the poverty of our religious imagination and the repressiveness of our social forms prevented that realization.'[25] This may be more difficult within Christian theology.

I turn then to the interest in Christian circles of late in trying to mitigate the exclusively male, or masculine, way in which God is understood in the bible and in Christian symbolism. It is suggested that the God of the bible, called by masculine names, has however characteristics which are more 'feminine' as feminine has traditionally been conceived, and that there is imagery to be found which is female. Trible points to the use of the metaphor of a womb to convey God's compassion.[26] In Isaiah God is compared to a woman in travail.[27] Jesus says that he would comfort Jerusalem as a mother hen takes chicks under its wings. The German Protestant theologian Jürgen Moltmann speaks of God as a 'motherly father'. He suggests that trinitarianism implies 'a radical transformation of the Father image'. For 'a father who both begets and bears his son is not merely a father in the male sense. He is a motherly father too.' The Council of Toledo (675), he tells us, spoke of the Son as being born out of the Father's womb.[28]

There is interest also in showing Christ in the past to have been conceived to have more feminine, indeed female, characteristics. In particular there has been appreciation of the medieval tradition in this respect. Thus Anselm of Canterbury, referring to Galatians 7:19, speaks of St Paul as his 'sweet nurse, sweet mother'; and continues, with reference to Luke 13:34: 'And you Jesus, are you not also a mother? Are you not the mother who, like a hen, gathers her children under her wings?... Then both of you are mothers. Even if you are fathers, you are also mothers.... Fathers by your authority, mothers by your kindness. Fathers by your teaching, mothers by your mercy.'[29] In passages which have become well known, the medieval woman mystic Julian of Norwich speaks of God as both Father and Mother and of the trinity as exemplifying fatherhood and motherhood. Of Christ she writes: 'By the skill and wisdom of the Second Person we are sustained, restored, and saved with regard to our sensual nature, for he is our Mother, Brother, and Saviour.' Again she says:

> For the merciful ample flood of his precious blood and water suffices to make us sweet and clean; the Saviour's blessed wounds are open, and rejoice to heal us; the dear, gracious hands of our Mother are ever about us, and eager to help. In all this work he functions as a kindly nurse who has no other business than to care for the well-being of her charge.[30]

An interesting gloss on the medieval understanding of Christ as a nurturing mother is provided by Caroline Bynum, who tells us that in the medical theory of the time breast milk was believed to be processed blood.[31] Eleanor McLaughlin has argued effectively that, in comparison in particular with modern Protestantism, the medieval tradition allowed for a more androgynous understanding of God and, since the human was seen as 'female' before God, also of the human being.[32]

This suggestion that the masculine God should be understood in a more female or feminine way is however not without problems. The effect of such imagery is to enrich or enlarge our concept of the male, or of what may truly be said to be 'masculine'. God (who is basically seen as male) is portrayed as nurturing and caring, Christ as feeding and protecting. It may well be said that the patriarchal understanding of what it means to be male is abandoned. But such a move does nothing for women, or for the concept of the feminine *per se*: it expands our understanding of what is to be considered authentically male. In order to change the understanding of women, or enlarge the conception as to what is to be considered authentically female, we should have to apply what have been thought to be characteristically male attributes to a female symbol. For example the female should be seen to embrace headship or authority. Indeed one might well say that, through this augmentation of what is to be considered male, the male now absorbs all in himself. While remaining male, the male symbol has taken over female tasks and properties as well. What place then is left for the female? As one of my students remarked: 'If men now have wombs, women are superfluous.'

Furthermore one may remark on the fact that that which is considered 'feminine', which the male also now takes on, corresponds simply to what have traditionally been women's tasks (nurturing and caring). Through suggesting that God should be seen in these ways, for example that those biblical verses which give feminine attributes to God should be drawn upon, one does nothing to change the conception of what are authentic roles for women. The idea that femininity is in the first place to be associated with motherhood is simply writ large. Thus for example in the quotation which I gave from Anselm, it is to be noted that God is to be seen as a Father in authority and teaching, as a Mother in kindness and mercy. This is hardly a feminist revolution. The whole approach then, though it may in helpful ways mitigate an authoritarian image of the male, does not change our understanding of women.

I have already commented on the suggestion, made by both conservative Christians and Christian feminists, that the Spirit should be seen as specifically female.[33] Certainly the word for spirit is female in Hebrew, and there is a long tradition of the divine wisdom being conceived to be feminine. It may be that Christianity has lost something here which was present in the tradition. If we are speaking however within a Christian context of the Holy Spirit, such a suggestion may be far from helpful. The Spirit becomes in effect a weak counterpart to the male Logos: I say weak because clearly the Spirit is not differentiated in the sense in which the Logos is associated with a male human being. What is to be understood as female is something vague; indeed the Spirit is often designated as neuter. The two 'male' persons of the trinity by contrast are anthropomorphically conceived entities, 'persons' to whom people direct their prayers. Moreover the Spirit has ever played second fiddle to the male Christ within trinitarian theology. Talk of the Spirit as female may moreover once again tend to fuel a certain understanding of what is to be considered feminine. The process theologian John Cobb can write as follows of the Spirit: 'It is the receptive, empathetic, suffering, redemptive, preservative aspect of God, whereas Logos is order, novelty, call, demand, agent, transformer and principle of restlessness.'[34] This may be thought scarcely auspicious.

That the God of Judaism and of Christianity is in conception profoundly male is clear. It may be more honest to face this for what it is. The various attempts to find more female aspects to the tradition can retrieve very little. Moreover, as we have seen, the attempt to elicit more feminine aspects to a God (or Christ) otherwise conceived of as masculine is really beside the point as far as women are concerned. The Spirit fails to be a counterpart to the two 'male' persons of the trinity, and is scarcely female. The extent to which God in all three persons of the trinity has simply been seen as male is well captured by the liturgy of *The Alternative Service Book* used in Anglican services of confirmation in Britain. The candidate replies 'I believe and trust in him' three times to the successive questions 'Do you believe and trust in God the Father/his Son/his Holy Spirit ...?'. When one speaks of the biblical God, one automatically says 'He': that God is profoundly male. It strikes a very foreign note to call the God of this tradition by anything other than male names. Of course it may help feminists when, in a Christian invocation to worship, God is referred to as for example 'Creator, Redeemer and Sanctifier'. But when, in the next moment, the bible is read, we shall again hear talk of 'Father' and 'Son'. As long as one remains within a biblical and Christian tradition, the problem may be thought to be without solution.

THE 'FEMININE' AS CONSTRUCT

It is not simply that women have been singularly absent from western religious texts and symbols; they have also been present. But the way in which women have been perceived, and the understanding which there has been of the 'feminine' has been largely determined by men. Women then have a double task. Not only do they want women to be present in the religion and the female to be represented in its symbolism, but they need a false understanding of 'woman' and the 'feminine' to be overcome. This false understanding has meant that particular roles have been given to women, limiting them in what they might be. In this section I shall therefore consider the notion of gender in western religion. By gender I mean the construction of the 'masculine' and the 'feminine' which has been imposed on the biological difference of male and female. Of course the conceptualization of the feminine and the understanding of what women should be has not simply been determined by men and imposed upon women. Women, in a process of socialization, have internalized the role models set for them. As Simone de Beauvoir commented in what have become famous words: 'One is not born a woman, one becomes one.'[35]

We should be clear that it is men who have been the creators of that cultural reality which is western theology. It has been they who have shaped its basic framework. A patriarchal society has given rise to the concept that God is to be conceived as peculiarly male. God is seen as transcendent above humankind in what is an ordered hierarchy. Since men also see themselves as above women, 'humanity' has been designated as 'feminine' in relation to God. We arrive then at a whole social construct, whereby men are seen as good and strong and more spiritual, in relation to women who tend to be seen as sinful, weak and closer to things of the earth (particularly as they have to do with reproduction); just as God takes on the characteristics of being good and strong and spiritual in relation to humankind, which is by contrast designated sinful and weak and more material in relation to God. What female and the feminine stands for thus becomes locked into a whole interpretation of reality. And it should be noted that it is a hierarchical interpretation, in which woman and the feminine are conceived as inferior and often as sinful.

How far this sense of things has been internalized within western culture has been shown by the American psychotherapist Anne Wilson Schaef in an experiment which she has carried out with groups of people. The group is given two sheets of paper on which they are asked to write respectively the characteristics which they would ascribe to God and the characteristics they would ascribe to humanity. The exercise is then repeated with another two sheets of paper on which they are asked to write the characteristics which respectively they would ascribe to men and to women. She then takes the four sheets and puts up side by side the sheets showing the characteristics which have been ascribed to God and to men; and in another place those which have been ascribed to humanity (in relationship to God) and to women. There are direct parallels between how on the one hand God and men are seen, and on the other hand humanity and women. God and men are generally conceived as good, intelligent and powerful, whereas humanity and women (whose characteristics it should be remembered have, in the exercise, been described in comparison with God and men) are seen by contrast as emotional, weak and sinful.[36]

The extent to which the feminine is a social construct, seen in polarity to what is understood by the masculine, and understood as inferior, is clearly present in the tradition from the beginning. It is markedly present in the Hebrew scriptures, which form the basis of western religion. In her fascinating book *The Female Experience and the Nature of the Divine* Judith Ochshorn compares ancient Israel in this regard with the surrounding polytheistic societies. She analyses the relationship between the type of religion espoused (monotheism on the one hand and polytheism on the other) and the social structure of Israel as compared with the social structures of other societies. In particular she looks at the relationship between men and women and at the way in which gender is conceived, firstly in the religion and secondly in the society. She comes to some interesting conclusions. In the societies in which divinity is imaged as consisting in relationships between a number of gods and goddesses, there is, in the religion, less construction of gender. For example gods and goddesses may move from one sex to the other, being a god in one society and a goddess in another; goddesses go to war, while gods are connected with fertility. In parallel, in the societies with polytheistic religions not only do women fulfil roles (such as priestess) in the religion, but there is in the society less construction of gender. For example there are few taboos surrounding female sexuality. In Israel, by contrast, not only do women seem to be worse off within the society and have no proper place within the religion, but there is a marked concept of the feminine, which is held to be inferior.

The Jewish scholar Drorah Setel considers how imagery functions in the writings of the books of some of the prophets in the Hebrew bible. She looks in particular at Hosea.[37] Using insights which have been gained through feminist analysis of pornographic writing, Setel shows the same mechanisms to be operating in the biblical text. That which is good, God (or Hosea) is conceived as male. That which is wilful and in the wrong, Israel or Gomer, Hosea's unfaithful wife (the word used is that for a prostitute), is symbolized as female. It is Gomer/Israel who is portrayed as going astray and committing adulterous and idolatrous acts. Moreover, the patriarchal nature of the society is reflected in presuppositions built into the text. Husbands, it is implied, should have possession and control over their wives, as does Yahweh over Israel. Hosea takes the initiative in marrying

Gomer. Yahweh is seen as the true provider of sustenance, and the female (as Israel) is understood to be dependent on the male. The female is made into an object, thought to be lower and associated with sexuality, and then denigrated. Gomer, interestingly, is associated with the land – as indeed in pornographic literature the female is often associated with nature: that is to say with that which it is for man to dominate and conquer. Yahweh (and thus men) are understood to control fertility, while women are depicted as having no control over reproduction. The theme of public degradation and humiliation of females is present. Though an obvious example, the book of Hosea is not, in these respects, an exception. An objectification of the female, and a perception of female sexuality as evil, is present in Isaiah, Jeremiah, Ezekiel and the twelve 'shorter' prophets.

It is in Catholicism in particular, within Christian history, that there has been a construct of the 'feminine'. This is not necessarily to say that women are worse off within Catholicism than within Protestantism, but they are faced with a different situation. In Catholicism the feminine is at least present, either through the position given to the virgin Mary, or through a certain place being reserved for 'the feminine' as symbolized by the church and humanity. The problem is that this understanding of the 'feminine' is very different from how feminist women (and perhaps most women) see themselves. Protestantism, by contrast, one may think to be peculiarly masculine. In one sense this may be an advantage. Women do not face a false understanding of themselves with which they must do battle. But the question arises as to whether that religious consciousness has a place for anything which is genuinely other than a masculine God in His relation to His sons.

In Catholicism the 'feminine' has almost an ontological quality. It is as though the masculine and the feminine are written into creation. (We have already considered this.)[38] Such a construction of the masculine and the feminine is markedly present in the understanding of God in relation to humanity, Christ in relation to the church, and the priest in relation to the people. It becomes necessary therefore, in order that she may fit this whole philosophy, to advocate that woman should be a certain kind of being. She is to represent that which is bodily rather than spiritual; she must be receptive, obedient, humble and serve others. For her to attempt to be anything else would be for her not to be herself. This is not necessarily to say that men look down on women. There is an ambivalence. On the one hand woman or the feminine is placed on a pedestal, as representing all that is pure and that which humanity should attain to in relation to God. Men, by contrast, are seen as marred through being caught up in the rough and tumble world and prone to pride. On the other hand, woman tends to be connected with the body and with sexuality, that is to say with that which represents temptation and is sinful. What woman is not allowed to be is simply herself, another human person. The fact that Catholic theologians and priests have been celibate and had little day-to-day contact with women has certainly been a factor in making for this unrealistic idea of the feminine. Indeed one may be permitted to think that in some cases a certain romance with the 'feminine' (exemplified by the virgin Mary or the church) has been a substitute for real relations with human persons of the opposite sex.

The pivot of this understanding of the feminine within western history, the symbol on to which it has been plastered, is the virgin Mary. Was ever anything more of a construct! – a construct, we may say, which came out of human need. The purely masculine religion which had come to the west from ancient Israel, lacking any female or mother figure, was inadequate to the religious needs of Christendom. What was missing was taken from other religions of the ancient Mediterranean world and woven into Christianity. There is a direct link between the goddess Isis and the iconography of the virgin Mary: they both sit, in like posture, their child-God on their lap.[39] Mary (and woman) are designated primarily as mother, in Mary's case mother of the male God. What Mary has been taken to symbolize in Christian thought is then a far cry from the representation of her in the Christian scriptures. In the scriptures there is put into her mouth a powerful magnificat, which speaks of the overturning of an unjust order and the creation of social justice. The picture of Mary in Christian history has, by contrast, been of one who is submissive, docile and gentle. Barth too, a Protestant, speaks of Mary as 'this non-willing, non-achieving, non-creative, non-sovereign, merely ready, merely receptive, virgin human being'.[40]

It is these things which humanity is supposed to be in relation to God, and Mary thus who represents humanity. Her fiat, her 'be it unto me according to thy word' in response to God, is seen as the perfect human response to God; which is to be modelled on the female response to male initiative. It will be said by men who want to convince women that they, equally, have a place within the Christian scheme of things, that of course we are all 'feminine' in relation to God. (Indeed it is frequently said that, if it is the case that only men can be priests, only women can be mothers.) But this is scarcely of help to women. In the first place it tends simply to fuel a certain understanding of gender, so that the feminine has a particular place and women are supposed to be a certain way. But secondly it is no equivalent. It is yet another example of that for which the masculine stands (through the male being seen as 'female' in relation to God) being augmented by qualities of passivity and gentleness. But it does nothing to augment the understanding of the female. For that to happen, women would have to be leaders and exercise headship. The equivalent to the male taking on the 'feminine' role of humanity in relation to God, would be that women should take the 'masculine' role of representing God to humanity as priests.

Conservatives want preciously to preserve a world which has passed. The pressure put on women to conform results from the fact that the conservative understanding of the feminine, and what woman should represent, forms part of a complete world-picture. It is in relation to this picture that conservatives gain their self-under-standing as to who they are as men and priests. One may wonder if the real world of women has ever been what these men represent it as being. Women have always had more gumption. But what is certainly doubtful is that women any longer occupy a place which makes this imaginative world possible. Marina Warner describes the demise of the role of the virgin Mary in western culture. 'The reality her myth describes is over; the moral code she affirms has been exhausted. The Catholic church might succeed, with its natural resilience and craft, in accommodating her to the new circumstances of sexual equality, but it is more likely that, like Ishtar, the Virgin will recede into legend.'[41] She quotes Roland Barthes: 'It is human history which converts reality into speech, and it alone rules the life and death of mythical language.'[42] If this is the case, then the conser-vative and Catholic world order is collapsing. No wonder feminism poses such a threat.

It is then questionable that this construct of the feminine can in any way persist within western civilization, or whether it has not simply been outgrown. Fundamental to the ordering of reality which we have been considering is a belief that there is a 'complementarity' between male and female. When C. S. Lewis heard of the proposition that women should be ordained priest, he wrote (in an essay which may be said to concern gender polarity) of the thoughts which came to him. They had to do with dancing. 'This parallel between the

Church and the ball is not so fanciful as some would think. ... The ball exists to stylize something which is natural and which concerns human beings in their entirety – namely, courtship. We cannot shuffle or tamper so much.'[43] The understanding of the feminine as complementary to the masculine which Lewis describes in this essay has, I would suggest, in large part ceased to exist. (Within ten years of his writing, that is to say in the sixties, men and women dressed much alike to dance, and jived with one another, the women dancing together if the men were more interested in drinking beer.) The younger generation, though they be men and women, do not, for the most part, one might think, understand their relationships in terms of a polarity.

It is not however unique to Catholicism that the female is seen as complementary to, and secondary to, the male – for that which 'complements' is always in some sense inferior to that which it complements. In conservative Protestantism this complementarity takes the form of subordination. We have already seen how Barth designates Mary. For him too woman is complementary to man. He writes: 'She is his glory as he himself is the glory of God (I Cor. 11.7).... It is the peculiar glory of her creation, i.e., that she was "taken out of man", that she completes the creation of man from man himself.'[44] The respective roles of man and woman are not to be confused: 'It is always in relationship to their opposite that man and woman are what they are in themselves.' One must, he says, have a 'firm adherence to this polarity'.[45] The lengths to which a patronizing of women can go in some evangelical writing may be illustrated by a quotation from John Stott.

> The husband's headship of his wife ... is a headship more of care than of control, more of responsibility than of authority. As her 'head', he gives himself up for her in love. ... And he looks after her, as we do our own bodies. His concern is not to crush her, but to liberate her. ... The husband gives himself for his bride, in order to create the conditions within which she may grow into the fullness of her femininity. But what is 'femininity' that it needs conditions to be created for its flowering? ... 'weakness' ... Under the rubric of 'weakness' we should probably include those characteristically feminine traits of gentleness, tenderness, sensitivity, patience and devotion. These are delicate plants, which are easily trodden under foot, and which wither and die if the climate is unfriendly.[46]

The independence of women must challenge this world.

APPROPRIATING THE PAST

Feminists who would be Christians endeavour to find ways to appropriate the world of the scriptures. The most obvious line of approach is to concentrate on those passages which have to do with women. The relatively few stories in which women are prominent and in which there appears to be a positive estimation of them have been the subject of innumerable women's bible studies and feminist sermons of recent years. Looking at the positive estimates of women is not however the only approach to have been suggested. As we have seen, Phyllis Trible advocates that women should study so called 'texts of terror'.[47] Nicola Slee also believes this to be fruitful. Slee moreover (who has pointed out what a poor showing statistically women have in the parables)[48] makes the interesting suggestion that the imagery present in the parables (not necessarily those having to do with women) may make them peculiarly relevant to the world of women.

The attempt by Christian feminists to find examples of a positive portrayal of women in the scriptures is, I believe, fraught with difficulty. Those stories which might be thought to be good candidates turn out, upon closer inspection, to be far from adequate. One does indeed find examples of women who were ingenious or brave; even of women who may be read as having been sceptical of the values of a male world. But if what one wishes to find is women who may serve as models, who exemplify the values for which feminists stand, I would suggest the outlook to be bleak. This is perhaps not surprising when one considers that biblical literature arose in a patriarchal society. But the point is that Christian women look to these texts as scripture, and therefore they must find ways in which this literature can speak to them. What however even the possible candidates as stories which feminists might pick up seem rather to show is, the depth of the sexist presuppositions of the biblical world.

Let us consider as examples three such stories: stories which might typically be used by a woman wishing to preach a feminist sermon or participate in a bible study with other women. I take one from the Hebrew scriptures and two from the Christian gospel. The story of Ruth would seem to be a good candidate, and indeed Trible gives a fascinating re-reading of this story.[49] It is true that Ruth puts loyalty to another woman high on her agenda, that she is resourceful and courageous. Let us be clear nevertheless that the context in which Ruth acts is that it is considered to be her duty, in a patriarchal world, to raise children to her dead husband and so perpetuate his name. Indeed, that she and her mother-in-law may eat is dependent on the goodwill of a man. She is not present at the meeting at the town gate at which her fate is decided. It lies wholly within the power of men what will become of her. Ruth is rewarded for the faithfulness of her behaviour within this patriarchal context. But the story in no way questions that context or the rights of men.

Then take again the story of Jesus' visit to Martha and Mary. It would seem that the notion that women should only fulfil a domestic role is questioned. Mary is allowed to sit, as at the feet of a rabbi, at Jesus' feet. But – as I have already mentioned – there is no suggestion that the men should on this occasion do the work of preparing the food. Moreover, what is the picture that we are given? As Ochshorn rightly remarks: 'Mary was hardly being intellectual in any creative way, or initiating any original ideas of her own, by sitting at [Jesus'] feet and listening.'[50] If the story were to be useful to feminists one would have thought that it would have to show role reversal. It would need to concern on this occasion a man sitting at a woman's feet and learning from her. But that is unthinkable in the context. The story does not even portray a dialogue between two equals. The image we are given simply serves to confirm the picture of teacher and listener given to men and women respectively within a patriarchal order.

Consider again the story of Jesus' conversation with the Samaritan woman at the well. It is indeed a story which breaks the bounds of convention: Jesus converses with a person who is firstly a woman (and a sinner at that) and secondly a Samaritan. Yet consider the dialogue. Jesus asks her to draw water for him: a task apparently allotted to women, as is carrying water in many parts of the third world today, despite the fact that men have stronger shoulder muscles. Throughout the dialogue she calls him, in deference, 'sir'. He pontificates to her, without discussion, on her marital relations. She elicits from him something of his importance – and the story ends by her proclaiming him to be the Messiah! Of course this may not be what exactly took place: the story has been arranged by the evangelist to show a Samaritan woman coming to believe in Jesus' Messiahship. But it cannot be said that the story, as we have it, portrays relationships of equality between women and men. It simply shows something of what a predicament women were in under patriarchy.

But some women, as Phyllis Trible, suggest that those passages in which women are slandered may be appropriated by women today.

Writing with reference to Trible's work, Nicola Slee comments as follows:

> I believe that it is possible for feminists to reclaim much of the biblical material in ways that enable us to celebrate and affirm and make sense of our own experience, without for a moment supposing that the biblical writers themselves (or even Jesus himself) would have intended the material to be understood in this way. I would say that it is possible, more, vitally necessary, to reclaim in meaningful ways even those 'texts of terror' where women are abused, mutilated, raped, etc., – precisely because they are there in the scriptures, because this is what has happened to women and this is what does happen to women. And as long as this has happened to women and continues to happen to women, we need women who will read these texts and will bring their feminist understanding to bear upon the terrible pain and anger and wounding of women which is witnessed to there. Perhaps it is precisely by exposing the sexism of the tradition for what it is and calling it to repentance that these texts can be reclaimed for contemporary women readers. I see this as perhaps the only viable way of rereading the texts.[51]

This is a thought provoking statement. Two things must however be said. Firstly, that a reading of these texts as texts which need to be interpreted fails to challenge the notion that they are scripture and not just ancient literature. At worst it tends to substantiate a belief that, in the case of the bible, all we can do is interpret, we cannot dismiss. If what we are looking for is some record of the constancy of male bestiality towards women we might as well look at other examples; for example at the treatment by Pakistani soldiers of Bangladeshi women during the war which led to the splitting of Pakistan.[52] Using the texts which have been designated scripture in the west for this purpose confuses the issue, making it difficult to challenge the notion that these texts are to be considered scripture. One supposes that in actuality the reason why women reinterpret these texts is because they are Christians. They cannot as Christians escape the biblical text. Secondly, it must be said that, though the study of these texts may tell us something about patriarchy, such a reading as that which Trible or Slee propose does not enable us to use this literature as a vehicle for our religious longings (that is to say to appropriate these texts as scripture). It can hardly be said that the text becomes for us diaphanous of God.

In her article 'Parables and Women's Experience' Slee advocates another approach which should allow women to appropriate the scriptures. I find it suggestive. She has of course admitted to what she calls the 'surface invisibility' of women in the parables: they are scarcely represented.[53] But, Slee continues: 'I suggest that it is possible to find beneath the surface invisibility of women a host of images and situations in the parables which are uniquely evocative of women's lives and experiences, and speak deeply to them.' Many parables are set in the domestic sphere. They tell of something erupting into the familiar scene, the wine that bursts the skins, the yeast which transforms the dough. May one not then discover the presence of God within the confines of the mundane and domestic? Other parables are parables of growth, yet contain a note of crisis and judgement. They perhaps 'afford a context for wrestling with the perpetual crises, whether they be domestic, emotional or spiritual, which disrupt and disturb [women's] sense of rhythm and pace'. Parables of feasting and celebration may speak to women 'whose lives are very much bound up with the rituals of feeding and feasting, which take on special significance at the celebration of births, marriages, anniversaries and achievements, and at the more sombre times of death and departure, but can also have a treasured place in the rhythm of daily life'. While parables of relationship speak to women 'whose lives are rooted in the relational sphere'. Such parables speak of service and denial of self, yet also there is 'a strong affirmation of other more forceful and self-assertive human qualities'. Finally, of parables which embody grotesque violence she writes: 'Can they not speak to us of our own experience of violence, conflict, anger, self-disgust and loathing?... Perhaps these harsh and violent parables are part of the Gospel tradition which can be reclaimed as words to give voice to our experience of pain, to release the anger and reshape our lives.'

What should we say to this? Clearly women (as men also) can find their lives to be reflected and refracted through Jesus' parables. That is not in question. One might well think that many a person, Christian or not, would find the parables to illuminate her or his life. Slee may be said to be working with what I earlier called a 'golden thread' approach to biblical interpretation.[54] The interest which she brings to scripture, that which she asks after when reading the text, is women's experience. 'My primary concern' she writes 'is with ... the ways in which [the parables] may function in dialogue with women's present experience.'[55] The problem with this is twofold, the two being interconnected. There is in the first place (as she realizes) a generalization about 'present women's experience'. Much of what she says relates to the lives of women in the domestic sphere and reflects the experience of women subject to discrimination. Such a life is of course the lot of many women. Yet one wonders how far such a reading can enable women to move into a new world, a world in which they are the actors. Much of what she says is indicative of a world of wounded women. She says little of women's self-confidence. Secondly, I have a sense, in part at least, of an interpretation of women's lives which is deeply separatist, and which, again, fails to advocate positively the equality of women in a mixed world.

The efforts of Christian feminists to enable the scriptures to be accessible have been ingenious. Yet they never quite succeed. The central issue as to whether feminist insights can ever be squared with the biblical literature is for the most part dodged. In reading a collection of essays like that edited by Letty Russell, *Feminist Interpretation of the Bible*,[56] one has a sense of frustration as the authors beat all around the bush, suggesting a re-reading here, a way in which women may find connection with the text there. One has the impression that women have taken a prior decision to be Christian, and, given that they are Christian, they do the best that can be done with the text. Among biblical exegetes of whose work I am aware, Mary Ann Tolbert confronts the most honestly the question as to whether Christian feminists can ever succeed in their task. Tolbert writes:

> To destroy the oppressive structure of society using the tools that structure itself supplies is a process of erosion. ... The kind of vast structural alteration that feminism demands must occur gradually over a long period ... by small, often unnoticed acts of subversion. Numerous such incremental changes, like erosion, will eventually bring down the fortress. ... Like the small seed planted in the ground which over time grows into the largest bush, or the small amount of leaven which infiltrates the whole loaf, or the seeds that almost unnoticed grow into the harvest, so vast revolutions slowly change the landscape.[57]

Might one – to be wicked – not respond by calling attention to the parable of the man who, wishing to build a tower, should first sit down and consider whether he can complete it? If one is actually talking about feminism, the equality of women and men, is Christianity ever going to be able to deliver the goods? For all the chipping away here, the re-reading there, the underlying problem remains. Christianity is a historical religion which must needs have deep roots in a patriarchal past.

BREAKING FREE

The person who first gave voice, in a way that received wide attention, to the conclusion that feminism and Christianity were never
going to be reconcilable, was Mary Daly in her book, published in
1973, *Beyond God the Father*.[58] The central theme of that book is well
captured by the line which owes to Marshall McLuhan (and which
she takes up in the 'postchristian' introduction which she wrote for
her earlier book *The Church and the Second Sex*): 'The medium is the
message.'[59] Daly analyses Christian imagery. Christianity is a religion of the 'Father' and the 'Son'. One cannot, she says, change the
overwhelmingly patriarchal character of biblical religion. Moreover,
there has been a peculiar place for women, represented by the virgin
Mary and by Eve. Women have been made the scapegoats for sin.
Daly, who grew up within pre-Vatican II Catholicism, is well qualified
to understand the construction of the world through Catholic eyes.
Ideologies, she contends, serve to legitimize patriarchal power structures. She writes of 'the power that religion has over the human
psyche, linking the unsteady reality of social constructs ... to ultimate reality through myth'.[60] As she contends, in a line often quoted
from her work, 'If God is male, then the male is God.'[61] It is however
dawning on women that they have been conned. 'The idea of the God-
Man (God-Male, on the imaginative level) – ... is beginning to be
perceived by some women as a kind of cosmic joke.'[62] The change
which is taking place in women is threatening the credibility of the
religious symbols of our culture.

Daly's basic point is never satisfactorily answered by Christian
feminists. Many appear never to have faced it (or if they have, they
find no answer). Carol Christ writes: 'A serious Christian response to
Daly's criticism of the core symbolism of Christianity either will have
to show that the core symbolism of Father and Son do not have the
effect of reinforcing and legitimating male power and female submission, or it will have to transform Christian imagery at its very core.'[63]
But how, one may ask, could one transform Christian imagery to its
very core while Christianity remains rooted in the biblical texts?
Thus Schüssler Fiorenza for example does not consider symbolism:
she analyses the role of women in the early church. Ruether, in her
earlier work as a liberation theologian, did not either. It is significant
that as she has come to pay more attention to issues of imagery and
symbolism she has increasingly moved outside the Christian tradition, finding it to be inadequate. In her more recent work she

proposes that women should supplement the Judaeo-Christian tradition with texts and images drawn from other sources.[64] The problem is that there is no solution: the core symbolism of Christianity is masculine.

It is interesting here to reflect upon the question as to which women have remained within the Christian fold, for we all (in my generation) grew up within the Christian (or Jewish) tradition, and who has moved outside. I am thinking here specifically of women who trained as theologians, or who teach in religious studies. The women who have remained within Christianity, or who at least have not positively and publicly separated themselves from that tradition, seem to be those who are historians and exegetes. Their work does not in the same sense demand (as does the work of one who, like myself, is a systematic theologian) that they come off the fence and state where they stand. They reinterpret texts or rewrite history. But also perhaps by temperament they have not wanted to stand back from the tradition and ask fundamental questions of it. Those on the other hand who have left, tend to be women trained in philosophy or theology. Through their work and by inclination they find that they ask after questions of truth. I would cite as examples Mary Daly, Carol Christ, Naomi Goldenberg – author of a relatively early book about the implications of women's changing consciousness, *Changing of the Gods*,[65] who might well be called 'post-Jewish' – and this applies also to myself. For all of these women alike, the issue of symbolism has been crucial.

Some women then have needed to make a marked break with the Christian (or Jewish) tradition. The past is too restrictive. Women are gaining the confidence to define their own lives, and this must needs mean also their religious position. Daly writes: 'When ... a woman first consciously says of her Self, "I am a radical feminist", there is a Shift in the shape of her soul.' And, of a woman who recognized in a moment of illumination that she had to be feminist: 'It is significant that the first act [she] performed after this epiphany was to "let God have it." She killed off the male "God", naturally, for the primal and essential move of Shape-shifting that accompanies a truly conscious Realization that "I am a radical feminist" is a rejection of patriarchal religious myth.'[66] Women will no longer wish to think within a patriarchal thought structure which they find to be profoundly harmful to them as women. To come into one's own is to reject the male God.

What is interesting is that in this revolutionary situation many women have chosen to retain, or recreate, a spirituality. This is true both of those who have remained within traditional religions, but have moved to the edge of them, and of those who have made a clean break. For many this has meant the creation of new myths, new symbols and new ceremonies. Many believe the concretion of religion to be central to its nature. Thus a change of perception has necessitated this kind of creativity; as indeed the creativity has been a way to articulate, and so to affirm, the change in perception. Women recognize that they have been hurt by patriarchal religion. To create symbols which express the wholeness of women is to heal. Again women have often been excluded from the action in patriarchal religion. Women's religious ceremonies embody, by contrast, a consciousness of the need to include everyone.

Some of the energy has been put into reworking patriarchal myths. To retell a story and do so differently is to relativize that which one inherited. This may be effective for women immersed in Judaism and Christianity. An early example would be the creation of a counter-story to the Genesis myth, 'The Coming of Lilith', undertaken by Judith Plaskow and others at a conference in 1973. Lilith, a figure of Jewish midrash, was created by God as Adam's first wife, and then dismissed when she tried to be equal to Adam, God creating the more subservient Eve in her place. In the feminist retelling, Lilith returns to the garden to tempt Eve over the wall: it was the early seventies, the days when women were skiving off to women's caucuses, the heady days of sisterhood. Adam is puzzled. The male God comments 'I am who I am, but I must become who I will become'. 'And God and Adam were expectant and afraid the day Eve and Lilith returned to the garden, bursting with possibilities, ready to rebuild it together.'[67] By blowing sky high the male myth women deny it power over them.

Not surprisingly a theme common to women's rituals, as I indicated, has been the celebration of women's physicality as something which is good. That this is the case speaks worlds as to what has been done to women through the strictures of male religion. After all it is not long since there were ceremonies for the 'churching' of women after the birth of a child, and there have long been taboos, social and religious, against menstruating women. Still in our generation, it is on account of her physicality that many a woman has been denied ordination. It must take an effort of imagination on the part of white males, who have never known discrimination stemming from the way in which they are, to imagine what it does to one's relation to oneself. I remember thinking it significant as I listened, as it came in, to news of the debate on the ordination of women at the 1978 Lambeth conference (of Anglican bishops from the world-wide communion) that the one man whose words spoke to those women with whom I had gathered was a Black. Comparing discrimination on grounds of sex with that on grounds of race, Desmond Tutu commented: 'A child of God subjected to that kind of treatment, actually gets to doubt that he is, or she is, a child of God.' Given such a background, women's spiritual writing and drama has often represented a recovery by women of their sense of their goodness. One may quote the well-known lines from Ntozake Shange's choreopoem and Broadway show *for colored girls who have considered suicide / when the rainbow is enuf.*[68] At the conclusion a Black woman, dressed strikingly in red, and standing centre stage, declares:

> i found god in myself
> & i loved her/i loved her fiercely

What a comment on what western culture has done to those who are both female and Black!

Some women have in this situation turned to matriarchy or to Goddess religion. It may be powerful to uncover the fact that, prior to western religion as we have known it, there were other societies in which the female was honoured. But matriarchy, and Goddess religion, are not primarily about digging up the past: to comment of the research that it is 'unhistorical' is quite beside the point. Rather do women want to use the past as a resource for constructing a different present; what is important is to feed women's imagination. Women need to regain a sense of their power. Thus most matriarchy or Goddess religion is thoroughly syncretistic, women weaving together ancient symbols and newly created myths. Some women have named themselves 'witches' and joined together in groups or 'covens'; some of which groups also admit men. Ceremonies will often be connected to the seasons of the earth, or the waxing and waning of the moon. The movement seems to have been particularly strong in California, but there has been considerable interest in it throughout the United States, and there are groups for example in Britain and in West Germany. It would seem that many women have in some degree been influenced by it who have not been directly involved.

Though it may be the case that radical Christian women who celebrate together and matriarchalists who do so, use different symbols and tell different stories, nevertheless what is held in common, and the extent to which ideas have moved across boundaries, strikes me as significant. A stress on the relationship between humans and the rest of nature (or creation) has been common to both. So too has been the explicit recognition and value accorded to each person. Women have been present to one another, through their words and actions healing one another. Symbols of light and life and also of connectedness (one thinks of the balls of wool used to form 'webs') are prevalent. Not myself being a person given to ritual or symbolic actions, I found myself, not long after I had left the church, at a gathering of mostly Christian women. We sat on the floor in the dark in concentric circles, it falling by chance to me to light the candles in the centre. Knowing that I was unlikely ever again to attend a Christian eucharist, yet among Christian women, I found myself strangely healed. There are no clear lines of demarcation. I have known Quakers celebrate the winter equinox – perhaps not in a sufficiently dedicated way! It was from Quaker women that I first learnt a song which, in speaking of self-affirmation and of the connectedness of women to the divine, sums up what women's spirituality has meant to many.

> Woman am I
> Spirit am I
> I am the Infinite within myself
> I can find no beginning
> I can see no end
> All this I am.

Women are conjuring up a new sense of themselves.

NOTES

1 'Priestesses in the Church?', in W. Hooper (ed.), *God in the Dock: Essays on Theology and Ethics* (Grand Rapids, MI: William Eerdmans, 1970), pp. 90–1 and in W. Hooper (ed.), *Undeceptions: Essays on Theology and Ethics* (London: Geoffrey Bles, 1971), pp. 193–4 (1948).
2 See p. 66.
3 *The Glass of Vision* (London: Dacre Press, 1948), pp. 37–8, 42–3, 44.
4 *Myths, Models and Paradigms: The Nature of Scientific and Religious Language* (London: SCM Press, 1984), p. 18.
5 *The Triune Identity: God According to the Gospel* (Philadelphia, PA: Fortress Press, 1982), pp. 13–16, 20 n. 33, 107.

6   The phrase that 'Jesus was a feminist' is often connected with a well-known article by Leonard Swidler with that title.

7   Cf. Judith Plaskow, 'Christian Feminism and Anti-Judaism', *Cross Currents*, Fall 1978, pp. 306–9; reprinted in E. T. Beck (ed.), *Nice Jewish Girls: A Lesbian Anthology* (Watertown, MA: Persephone Press, 1982).

8   See for example Francis Moloney, *Woman: First Among the Faithful* (London: Darton, Longman & Todd,1985).

9   *The Female Experience and the Nature of the Divine* (Bloomington, IN: Indiana University Press, 1981), p. 170.

10 Cf. Bernadette Brooten, 'Early Christian Women and Their Cultural Context: Issues of Method in Historical Reconstruction', in A. Yarbro Collins (ed.), *Feminist Perspectives on Biblical Scholarship* (Society of Biblical Literature, Centennial Publications; Chico, CA: Scholars Press, 1985), pp. 73–4.

11 'Parables and Women's Experience', *The Modern Churchman*, 26, no. 2 (1984), pp. 25–31.

12 *Female Experience*, p. 173.

13 On Jesus' social conformity in his understanding of the respective roles of women and men, see the excellent discussion of Fr John Wijngaards' *Did Christ Rule Out Women Priests?* (Great Wakering, Essex: Mayhew-McCrimmon, 1977, revised edn 1986), ch. 4. Wijngaards argues that it can in no way be said (as it is by the Vatican declaration, see p. 13 above) that Jesus 'deliberately and courageously' broke with custom in his treatment of women, and that the Vatican argument against ordaining women based on this assertion is invalid.

14 Cf. Ochshorn, *Female Experience*, p. 170.

15 For a striking description see Joachim Jeremias, *Jerusalem in the Time of Jesus: An Investigation into Economic and Social Conditions during the New Testament Period* (London: SCM Press, 1969; Philadelphia, PA: Fortress Press, 1975), ch. xviii, 'The Social Position of Women'.

16 *Female Experience*, p. 173.

17 A. Yarbro Collins (ed.) (Chico, CA: Scholars Press, 1985).

18 'His Story versus Her Story', p. 109.

19 Ibid. p. 110.

20 Ibid. pp. 113–15.

21 Ibid. p. 116.

22 Robert Hamerton-Kelly, 'God the Father in the Bible and in the Experience of Jesus: The State of the Question', in J.-B. Metz and E. Schillebeeckx (eds), *God as Father?* (*Concilium* no. 143, 1981), p. 98.

23 A. Lewis (ed.), *The Motherhood of God: A Report by a Study Group appointed by the Woman's Guild and the Panel on Doctrine on the invitation of the General Assembly of the Church of Scotland* (Edinburgh: The Saint Andrew Press, 1984).

24 'The Christ of Christendom', in J. Hick (ed.), *The Myth of God Incarnate* (London: SCM Press, 1977).

25 'Female God Language in a Jewish Context', in C. P. Christ and J. Plaskow (eds), *Womanspirit Rising: A Feminist Reader in Religion* (New York and San Francisco: Harper & Row, 1979), p. 173.

26 *God and the Rhetoric of Sexuality* (Philadelphia, PA: Fortress Press, 1978), ch. 2, esp. p. 45.

27 Cf. Isaiah 42:14; 46:3–4; 49:15; 66:13.

28 *The Trinity and the Kingdom of God* (London: SCM Press, 1981; New York: Harper & Row, 1981), pp. 164–5. See also 'The Motherly Father: Is Trinitarian Patripassionism Replacing Theological Patriarchalism?', in *God as Father?* (*Concilium*, no. 143, 1981).

29 *The Prayers and Meditations of St. Anselm*, tr. B. Ward (Harmondsworth: Penguin Classics, 1973), pp. 152–4.

30 *Revelations of Divine Love*, tr. C. Wolters (Harmondsworth: Penguin Classics, 1966). See chs 58–61. Quotations pp. 165, 173.

31 *Jesus as Mother: Studies in the Spirituality of the High Middle Ages* (Berkeley, CA: University of California Press, 1982), p. 132.

32 '"Christ My Mother": Feminine Naming and Metaphor in Medieval Spirituality', *Nashotah Review*, 15, no. 3 (Fall 1975), pp. 366–86.

33 See p. 72.

34 *Christ in a Pluralistic Age* (Philadelphia, PA: Westminster Press, 1975), pp. 263–4.

35 *The Second Sex*, tr. H. M. Parshley (Harmondsworth: Penguin Books, 1983), p. 295: 'One is not born, but rather becomes, a woman' (1949).

36 *Women's Reality: An Emerging Female System in the White Male Society* (Minneapolis, MN: Winston Press, 1981), pp. 162–4.

37 'Prophets and Pornography: Female Sexual Imagery in Hosea', in L. Russell (ed.), *Feminist Interpretation of the Bible* (Philadelphia, PA: Westminster Press, 1985; Oxford: Basil Blackwell, 1985).

38 See pp. 66–7.

39 Cf. Rosemary Ruether, *Mary – The Feminine Face of the Church* (Philadelphia, PA: Westminster Press, 1977; London: SCM Press, 1979).

40 *Church Dogmatics*, I.2 (E. T. Edinburgh: T. & T. Clark, 1956), pp. 191–2.

41 *Alone of All Her Sex: The Myth and the Cult of the Virgin Mary* (New York: Alfred A. Knopf, 1976; London: Weidenfeld & Nicolson, 1976), pp. 338–9.

42 Ibid. p. 339.

43 'Priestesses in the Church?', p. 93.

44 *Church Dogmatics*, III.1 (E. T. Edinburgh: T. & T. Clark, 1958), p. 303.

45 Ibid. III.4, p. 163.

46 *Issues Facing Christians Today* (Basingstoke: Marshall Morgan & Scott, 1984), pp. 247–8.

47 See pp. 37–40.

48 See p. 88.
49 *Rhetoric of Sexuality*, ch. 6.
50 *Female Experience*, p. 169.
51 Letter to the author, 15 Jan. 1989.
52 Cf. Joyce Goldman, 'The Women of Bangladesh', Ms., 1 (August 1972), p. 84, quoted by Mary Daly, *Beyond God the Father: Toward a Philosophy of Women's Liberation* (Boston, MA: Beacon Press, 1973; London: The Women's Press, 1986), p. 115.
53 See p. 88.
54 See pp. 25–6.
55 'Parables and Women's Experience', p. 21.
56 L. Russell (ed.), *Feminist Interpretation of the Bible* (Philadelphia, PA: Westminster Press, 1985; Oxford: Basil Blackwell, 1985).
57 'Defining the Problem: The Bible and Feminist Hermeneutics', *Semeia*, 28 (Chico, CA: Scholars Press, 1983), p. 121.
58 See note 52 above.
59 'Feminist Postchristian Introduction', *The Church and the Second Sex* (New York and San Francisco: Harper & Row, 1975; Boston, MA: Beacon Press, 1985), p. 21 (1968).
60 *Beyond God the Father*, p. 138.
61 Ibid. p. 19.
62 Ibid. p. 72.
63 'The New Feminist Theology: A Review of the Literature', *Religious Studies Review*, 3, no. 4 (October 1977), p. 205.
64 See p. 159.
65 *Changing of the Gods: Feminism and the End of Traditional Religions* (Boston, MA: Beacon Press, 1979).
66 *Pure Lust: Elemental Feminist Philosophy* (Boston, MA: Beacon Press, 1984; London: The Women's Press, 1984), p. 396.
67 Reprinted in R. Ruether (ed.), *Religion and Sexism: Images of Woman in the Jewish and Christian Traditions*, Epilogue (New York: Simon & Schuster, 1974).
68 *for colored girls who have considered suicide / when the rainbow is enuf* (San Lorenzo, CA: Shameless Hussy Press, 1975; London: Methuen, 1978), p. 63.

CHAPTER 4

Anthropology

FEMINIST ANTHROPOLOGY

I use the term 'anthropology' as the title to this chapter in the sense in which it has become used in recent years in the phrase 'theological anthropology'. Earlier such a discipline used to be called, perhaps with slightly different connotations, 'the doctrine of man'. I shall use it in the widest sense of the term. I wish to consider how our understanding of the human being affects the theology which we hold. If women are thinking differently about the human being and about human relations, then this will result in a different theology. We begin to see how profound the ramifications of the feminist revolution may be for theology. It is not simply a case of needing to make changes of language (though that in itself is not superficial). The very structures of theology as we have known it may reflect a male world.

It is difficult in a word to describe what might be called feminist anthropology. All I can do here is to indicate some of the discussion which there has been and to mention some of the books which have influenced feminist women. Feminist thinking about the self and about human relationships has been closely interwoven with praxis. It is in the sphere of praxis, in self-consciously women's groups, women's movements, or individual therapy conducted with a feminist awareness, that women have become changed. What one might today call a feminist anthropology may well be built upon ways in which women have ever tended to interact among themselves. What is new is that, within the feminist movement, women have come to articulate and to value different perceptions. Moreover, they have moved from conducting relations differently within small groups of women to the belief that large-scale public groups, such as a conference or a peace demonstration, may embody feminist ideals. Many women have, for example, learnt to work with consensus decision making, rather than a hierarchy of leaders and others, and to value the participation of all.

Whether the apparent differences between women and men (which underlie the consideration in this chapter) are in part biologically based, or are due wholly to social conditioning, has been a matter for fierce debate within the women's movement. I am not here attempting to adjudicate in this debate. Its implications may however be thought to be considerable. If there is a biological difference between men and women which significantly affects behaviour, then there is the temptation for feminist women to think that, in their striving to bring into being a very different world, they should be looking to themselves and what seems 'natural' to them. Conversely, if there is a degree of biological determination behind male behaviour, men would seem to be irreparably damned; or we may say that male sin lies deeper than we had grasped and men will need to struggle harder to overcome their faults! If however the explanation for the difference which women at present perceive between women's and men's attitudes lies wholly in social conditioning, it would appear to follow that change may be brought about by social engineering. It should be possible for men to unlearn what they have learnt and for different social arrangements to produce a a different male outlook in future generations. But the corollary of the conclusion that unsocial behaviour is the result of social conditioning is that women, as increasingly they enter into positions of power, may, if they are not careful, come to behave just as badly as they at present judge many men to behave.

For the fact that at present women do perceive themselves, and relate to others, very differently than do men, there is considerable evidence. It is that this is the case which concerns us here. Women have come to value this difference. There may also be a variety of social norms which obtain between women according to their class, ethnicity and national background. That I cannot here consider. One may think, however, that the differences between women and men in large part extend cross-culturally. The concern of the theologian is that of what may be the implications of these differences for theology. We may have reason to think that the perception of self and of the relationship between oneself and others is fundamental to our ordering of the world and the way in which we conceive reality. Differences between women and men here will then result in different emphases in theology. Feminism constitutes a major shift in perception. This must needs affect the theology which feminist women write.

I will mention here some of the work which has been most widely influential which is pertinent to our theme. In a much discussed book *In a Different Voice*,[1] Carol Gilligan reports on work she has done, mostly with young women, though in some tests in comparison with men and boys. Gilligan is trained in developmental theory, and earlier had worked (as was common) on samples of humans which consisted only of men! As she started listening to the different voice of women, she came to see that their ideas as to what is ethical behaviour simply did not fit the categories which had been proposed (largely by Kohlberg) for 'normal' human development. The result of this was that she came to evolve a different understanding of what constitutes mature development for women (and one would often wish for men as well). She concluded that women find themselves at home in 'web-like' participatory structures. They are made anxious as men try to separate themselves from the web of humanity – and then from an isolated position proceed to dominate others. In one experiment, in which people are given cards showing pictures about which they are asked to write stories, women perceived as potentially dangerous a picture of a man on his own in the window of a high-rise office block: the only picture which showed someone alone. Some of the evidence of men's fear of relationality is astonishing. In response to a perfectly peaceful scene which showed two people sitting on a bench by a river next to a low bridge (that is to say a picture which showed normal human intimacy), a significant proportion of men (and no women) wrote stories which ended in rape or murder. Gilligan concludes that men fear being 'trapped'. Women, by contrast, fear to go too far out from the centre of the web: they fear isolation – and thus putting themselves forward. What men then need to learn is to be a self in *relation*; while women, to be a *self* in relation.

In a remarkable book which was another best-seller *Toward a New Psychology of Women*,[2] Jean Baker Miller seemed to touch a chord which resonated with many women. She describes the way in which problems which women experience are the result of the social context in which their lives are set. Therapy for women then (and Miller is herself a practising psychotherapist) needs to be very different from that to which women have often been subjected. In coming to have a feminist analysis of her context, above all in achieving a new-found trust in herself and in her basic abilities, many a woman can find a greater degree of self-acceptance and self-realization. But what is attempted in feminist therapy, we may think, is not radically different from the task that women have often performed for one another in recent years in innumerable consciousness-raising or other women's groups and in one to one relationships. As women find that they are not alone in the response which they have to the circumstances of their lives, their guilt begins to lift. They start to view the world with a different pair of eyes and to have a different expectation as to what they might be. As Nelle Morton has well put it: 'Women are literally hearing one another to speech.'[3]

A theory as to wherein the cause may lie of the perceived differences between men and women which has met with wide recognition, is that put forward by Nancy Chodorow in an early book *The Reproduction of Mothering*.[4] Building on British object relations theory, whereby children are understood to become themselves in relation to significant others, Chodorow proposes that the differences arise from the fact that parenting is largely performed by women. A little girl growing up amid the world of women, of which she will one day be an adult member, feels no need to separate herself from her social context. Mothering, the ability to care for others in close social relationships, is reproduced in her. By contrast the boy knows from a young age that he is of the opposite sex, and so learns to sharply differentiate himself from his mother. This would well explain why women tend to think in terms of 'self–other relations', and men 'self–other oppositions' (Caroline Whitbeck).[5] Chodorow's proposed solution is that of equal parenting. Girls might then learn the differentiation of self from other (which Gilligan suggests women need better to establish), while boys would learn relationality in relation to a parent of the same sex as themselves to whom they were close.

This chapter will ask after this different sense of self and different sense of relationality as between women and men as it manifests itself in theology. Women are beginning to say of male theology that it is the product of dynamics which are those of the male world and of a conception of the self which is not theirs. This will become particularly apparent in the discussion of sin. Women themselves have other needs. They may also have a different sense of social relations and hence a different analysis of society. These things will affect their understanding of what it is in which salvation consists. Feminists have wanted to see humans as part of the world of nature, rather than as somehow having disembodied spirits. The domination by humanity of the rest of creation has led us to the brink. It may also be that women, in thinking more relationally about the self, are less anxious about the continuation of an individuated self after death. Indeed, through being to a greater extent tied into a web of social relationships, women may experience less *Angst*. Feminism, in common with other revolutionary movements, has produced utopian visions. Such vision is tells us something of the ideals of the more radical part of the movement.

The extent of the theological work which has been done in the field of what I have called theological anthropology is very various. Indeed the kind of material on which I shall draw ranges from the clearly theological to what is much more tentatively theological, though in some sense spiritual. We should not limit theology to what have been the bounds of male theology. If feminist women are considering the nature of the human person, the relationships between human beings, their vision for humanity, questions of ethics, politics and spirituality, then they are not far from what have traditionally been the concerns of theological anthropology. Feminism has in many ways been a deeply spiritual matrix. Feminists have been concerned with the concept of our care for one another, for the earth on which we live, for the resolution of conflict and the nature of peace. Indeed something which is striking about some of the more radical material which I shall consider is the new synthesis of ethics, politics and a certain spirituality in the women's movement. Women will to articulate their vision and their hope. Spiritual values are clearly woven into this.

The importance of such a consideration is that male theology is in the process relativized. When one is aware of the fact that theology reflects the social context in which it is formulated, it appears to be not quite so God-given. It becomes apparent that what was thought to reflect the situation of all humanity is in fact quite specific: it is the product of the world of men, often privileged men, living within patriarchy. Women are saying that they find themselves not to have been included; they only partially recognize themselves and their world. But to state this is only part of the task, and perhaps the easier part. Women have also of recent years aspired to articulate what it is that they would themselves say. Feminist theology, theology which comes out of a feminist matrix, is only in its infancy. For this reason much of this chapter must be tentative. But one may at least describe something of the matrix out of which theology will arise. It is only as we begin to approach these larger issues of politics and ethics, the nature of the self and relationships, that we begin to see what the feminist revolution may mean for theology.

SIN

I shall in this section consider how an analysis which has come out of a male world has been written into the conception of sin as we have known it. I shall indicate that this conceptualization may not be appropriate, indeed harmful, in the very different situation in which typically women have found themselves. In the next section I shall turn to the possibility that this different situation of women may lead to a different understanding of what might appropriately be termed salvation (that is to say the overcoming of sin) in the case of women.

The doctrine of sin has always been fundamental to theological anthropology. That this is the case may in itself be significant. Human beings have been seen as in apposition to God. God is considered good; humans, by contrast with God, sinful. Feminists (as I shall suggest in the next chapter)[6] may want to get away from such a dipolar construal of reality. It has also affected, as I suggested in the last chapter, the way in which women have been conceived in relation to men. Sin is connected with what is 'below' and with our bodily nature; and woman comes to be associated with sexuality. However the primary understanding of sin in the tradition (which has been a male tradition, for theology has been male) has been that sin is in the first instance not sensuality but rather pride. Here again we may think the conceptualization to have fitted a male dynamic; for men have been the ones who have been in a position to be proud.

In my consideration of sin, I shall look at feminist responses to the conceptualization of sin articulated by Reinhold Niebuhr. I turn to the feminist critique of Niebuhr for two reasons. In the first place there has been a concentration of feminist work here. And secondly, Niebuhr's analysis of sin, particularly as developed in his Gifford lectures *The Nature and Destiny of Man*,[7] is arguably the most profound that there has been. The women who have taken issue with Niebuhr (and this includes myself) have trained in theology in the United States where his thought has been influential. The argument is not that Niebuhr's analysis is false, but that it is inapplicable to the situation of all of humanity, while failing to recognize that this is the case.

The setting for Niebuhr's Gifford lectures was Scotland at the outbreak of the Second World War. Europe was faced, in National Socialist Germany, with the most overweening pride (or hubris) of a people in their desire for expansion and their submission of others, which the western world has experienced. Niebuhr's is a multi-faceted analysis, brilliantly interweaving theology with histori-cal, social and psychological insights. Sin he sees in its basic form to be pride, showing convincingly that this has been the major under-standing in the western tradition. Sin comes to be, not necessarily but inevitably, in a situation of *Angst*; that anxiety which, having no definite object, consists in a basic dis-ease. In their anxiety human beings are faced with two possibilities. Either they can trust in God; which is what the creator intended – for indeed the anxiety has only arisen through a lack of such trust. Or they fall into sin. Sin can be of two kinds: pride, in which human beings attempt to set themselves up in the place of God, to be gods themselves, subjecting others to their will; or sensuality, in which (rather than having an egotistical sense of self) human beings try to get rid of any sense of themselves and bury themselves in others or the things of this world – for example through the misuse of sexuality.

That Niebuhr's analysis contains deep insights is not in dispute. Indeed feminists might well say that Niebuhr has put his finger on what they find to be so worrying about the male world. He describes a situation in which a man, or a nation, would try to be free of the web of humanity (perhaps through insecurity) and then comes to domi-nate others. (Again the discussion of the misuse of sexuality as an attempt to escape from self rings true.) But the problem is that of the isolated male who would be free of others. He attempts self-sufficiency at the expense of other life. Women's criticism has thus been twofold. In the first place it is said that this is not a good analysis of the situation in which women find themselves; moreover that women's failings are typically other. Secondly, it is pointed out that Niebuhr (for all that he is concerned with social analysis) has an extraordi-narily individuated concept of the human being, who finds himself essentially caught up in competitive relationships.

That Niebuhr (and Tillich also) do not describe what is typically woman's predicament was first elucidated by Valerie Saiving in an article published in 1960, the article which is often taken to mark the beginning of the current wave of feminist theological writing. Saiv-ing writes:

> It is clear that many of the characteristic emphases of contemporary theology; – ... its identification of sin with pride, will-to-power, exploi-tation, self-assertiveness, and the treatment of others as objects rather than persons ... – it is clear that such an analysis of man's dilemma was profoundly responsive and relevant to the concrete facts of modern man's existence. ... As a matter of fact, however, this theology is not

adequate to the universal human situation. ... For the temptations of woman *as woman* are not the same as the temptations of man *as man*, and the specifically feminine forms of sin – 'feminine' not because they are confined to women or because women are incapable of sinning in other ways but because they are outgrowths of the basic feminine character structure – have a quality which can never be encompassed by such terms as 'pride' and 'will-to-power'. They are better suggested by such items as triviality, distractability, and diffuseness; lack of an organizing center or focus; dependence on others for one's own self-definition; ... in short, underdevelopment or negation of the self.[8]

One may remark on the fact that Niebuhr, who follows closely the Danish nineteenth century thinker Søren Kierkegaard in his under-standing of the relationship of insecurity, pride and sensuality, does not however take up Kierkegaard's dual articulation of the typically 'manly' and 'womanly' ways of sinning. Man, says Kierkegaard, would try to be Caesar, whereas woman would be rid of herself.[9] That Kierkegaard's (and Saiving's) analysis is an analysis of women as women are living under patriarchy is of course the case.

Consequently some women have wanted to say that woman's 'sin' is – to quote an effective phrase of Judith Plaskow's – 'the failure to take responsibility for self-actualization'.[10] To name such behaviour 'sin' is (as I have discovered when working with groups of women) very effective. For women to hear that it is their right and duty to take themselves seriously, that it matters who they are and what they think, is to turn Christian theology as they have imbibed it upside-down. For it is women largely who have been expected by society to take on board the Christian admonition to be self-effacing. This suggests that the fact that women have had preached to them that self-sacrifice is the message of the gospel has been wholly inappropriate in the situation in which they found themselves. Whether 'the failure to take responsibility for self-actualization' should however be called 'sin' is another question – as Helen Percy in particular has pointed out to me. If we think of women's typical 'fail-ings', as Saiving names them, they can hardly be said (in the way in which this is true of male pride) to be actively destructive of others. Rather have women been destructive of themselves and their own potentialities.

But the feminist criticism is not simply that Niebuhr has described what have been behaviour patterns of men rather than of women. It has seemed to feminist theologians, that in his sense of the individ-ual as highly individuated and 'atomic' rather than in relationship to others, Niebuhr has described what is peculiarly a male propensity. When (as I have discovered) it is said by feminists that Niebuhr fails to have a social conception of the human, this may well be misunderstood. For – the response comes back – no theologian more than he has considered the human in society. Of course this is the case. What is being referred to here however is a different level of the word social. Niebuhr sees the human being as monadic rather than as having an essential relationality. In this he is very different from much feminist thought. Very fine work here has been accomplished by Judith Vaughan. Vaughan, in work originally undertaken with Rosemary Ruether, compares Niebuhr's ethics with Ruether's ethics.[11] She shows that their different ethical and political stance relates to a different understanding of the human being. Vaughan, and Ruether, hold what I earlier designated a Marxist-Hegelian perspective.[12] They see persons as caught up in social relationships and believe that the external relations of the self form the understanding which a person has of him or herself.

It is from such a position that Vaughan mounts a critique of Niebuhr. Niebuhr, she shows, is working with an essentially isolated model of the human self. It is in a relationship between the self and God (or the lack of such a relationship) that the self comes to itself (or fails to do so). Social relations are subsequent. 'It is the relatively autonomous *pre-constituted* person who enters into social relations.'[13] In an ethic which derives ultimately from Kant, Niebuhr understands the individual to be essentially free and autonomous. Moral behaviour for Niebuhr (as may be thought to be the case in so much of the male tradition) consists in not encroaching on another's territory. Niebuhr writes that 'the other' is 'that other form of life, or that other unique community, [which form] … the limit beyond which our ambitions must not run and the boundary beyond which our life must not expand'.[14] By contrast Vaughan would say (and she shows this to be true also of Ruether's ethical outlook) that we are only persons through our relations with others. The self has what she calls, borrowing a phrase from David Rasmussen, an essential 'sociality'.

Niebuhr is moreover faulted by feminists for taking it simply for granted that individuals (and societies) hold a basically competitive stance towards one another. There is a lack of a vision that anything else might be possible. Sheila Collins writes of Niebuhr here:

Niebuhr's realism failed to penetrate to the edges of the reality system in which it was immersed. Christian realism is still very much a product of the patriarchal mentality. It continues to define sin as pride – renamed 'egoism' or 'self-interest' by Niebuhr; it is essentially pessimistic about the ability of human beings to shape creatively a more humane destiny; and its solution to the human dilemma is to accept and work within the limits of the status quo, that is, to accept the presence of competing political power blocs and the definition of collective self-interest as evil but necessary. Thus, realism positing a kind of ontological determinism offers no new vision by which to understand reality and therefore no new hope for the oppressed.[15]

It is of interest in this regard that it is a woman, Karen Horney, whom Niebuhr criticizes, in his discussion in *The Nature and Destiny of Man*, for her suggestion that the will-to-power arises from the general insecurities of a competitive civilization, holding out hope for its elimination in a co-operative society.[16]

Left-wing feminists, or perhaps one should say 'social feminists' (and many feminists are deeply socially concerned), may have a very different analysis as to what it is in which 'sin' primarily consists. Whereas, classically, sin has been understood as a disruption in the relationship between an individual and God (resulting from individual behaviour), 'sin' for such feminists consists rather in the structural sin obtaining in society. Thus sin is the sin of the domination of one class by another, and indeed (and perhaps primarily) the sin of sexism – which has gone unrecognized in male theology. With their social view of the human being as formed within the society, they believe that there must first be a social revolution, so that the conditions which lead to alienation are overcome, before individuals can come into their own. It is not simply that human pride and domination of others must needs be eliminated. There must be an empowering of those who at present are disempowered.

From this perspective Niebuhr's analysis is seen to be inadequate. He speaks of the need for sacrificial love on the part of the powerful. But he fails to speak of the need for those who are powerless to stake a claim for power. Ruether by contrast, as Vaughan shows, enables those who are involved in revolutionary movements which are engaged in claiming power to understand their activity to be moral. She is affirmative, as Niebuhr fails to be, of those striving to create a just society. Collins too criticizes Niebuhr on this score, writing:

> The most serious failure of Christian ethics has been its inability to provide a theoretical foundation for the establishment of wide-ranging social justice. It has failed in this endeavor because it has refused to look at the underlying reality paradigm upon which it has been built.

The hierarchical world view which determined that evil was to be equated with pride and self-transcendence while salvation was found in submission to the divine will is a world view which leaves intact the political status quo; in fact, to upset that status quo, to overstep the divinely sanctioned boundaries, is to commit sin. Such a set of values ... suggests that corporate evil is overcome only through a multitude of individual conversions, and it leaves the Christian bewildered in the face of political power. It provides no way of understanding or of influencing social change.[17]

Feminist politics is by contrast revolutionary and social, and feminist theology will reflect this.

Niebuhr moreover has a different ethic operating for the private sphere of the family than for the public world. In the family love should rule, but in the public sphere no more than justice is possible. The private sphere is of course understood to be the sphere of women, who should aspire to freedom and equality only in so far as this does not interfere with their function of motherhood. Niebuhr (writing in 1965) speaks of 'sacrificial love' as 'a moral norm relevant to interpersonal (particularly family) relations, and significant for parents (particularly mothers, heroes and saints), but scarcely applicable to the power relations of modern industry'.[18] Such an attitude – one which is deeply rooted in Christian ethics and in no way peculiar to Niebuhr – is one with which feminists have trouble. While handing women the sop of suggesting that they should attain to what the male world of politics is incapable of emulating, it must, in its suggestion that self-sacrifice is alone commendable, undercut women's justifiable attempts to assert their equality. Not simply love but justice too, feminists would maintain, must reign in the private sphere. Furthermore, for Ruether, as Vaughan points out, there can in the public sphere be no essential distinction between justice and love, for love entails the creation of a just order of society. Feminists, then, would wish to name as 'sin' unjust relations which prevent community, whether found in the personal or the political sphere.

SALVATION

The conception which is held as to what constitutes salvation presumably relates to the conception which is held of sin, if salvation is to be conceived as an overcoming of sin. This is certainly true of the Protestant theological tradition stemming from Luther of which Niebuhr (though not himself Lutheran) is so notable an exponent.

Salvation in that tradition is understood as the breaking of a self-enclosed self, a self which tries to become itself by itself, and a placing of trust in God. For Luther the hallmark of a Christian is that he or she lives outside him or herself; the Christian, he says, lives *extra se*. By trust the Christian lives in God; in love the Christian is present for the neighbour. For Niebuhr likewise conversion consists in the breaking of an egotistical self. Quoting Paul he writes: 'the sinful self, the self which is centred in itself must be "crucified": ... shattered at the very centre of its being.' The Christian experiences a 'new self' which is 'more truly a real self because the vicious circle of self-centredness has been broken'.[19]

The question is whether such an analysis is appropriate to women's situation. If women have not on the whole suffered from an egotistical self, if they have not been in a position to dominate others, then such a prescription is beside the point. Rather than breaking the self, women, it may be suggested, need to come to themselves. If women see themselves as only able to be themselves in relationship to others, then the whole dichotomy between being on the one hand self-enclosed, or on the other present in service to others, may not strike them as relevant. Thus Attracta Ingram suggests that the dichotomy so notably present in male ethical theory between egoism and altruism is inappropriate to women's situation.[20] It may well be that women, their lives bound up with those of others as they are, know very well that they will only find themselves fulfilled as the whole web of relationships in which they are engaged is in a state of repair. What many a woman has to learn is, rather, to take herself seriously as one who also has needs and rights. This need not necessarily involve the destruction of others.

If it is not particularly useful to women to see salvation as a breaking of the self, how then should they envisage it? Perhaps as a healing of the self; as a person coming to be all that she may be in a network of relationships. Healing is indeed the Latin root of the word 'salvation'. In the early church there were those (in particular Irenaeus in the second century) who understood salvation primarily as healing. I have found this suggestion to resonate with women. If women's ills have been the result of an undervaluation of the self, then their healing must consist in self-actualization. It is notable how many of the problems which one typically associates with women may be said to relate to an undervaluation of the self. One may name phobias, such as claustrophobia and agoraphobia, anorexia, the tendency to resort to sleeping pills, and a proneness to cry out for help (rather than actually to kill oneself) through attempted suicide. Salvation in these circumstances is to come to have self-worth. Healing – it has well been said – is the venture of discovery of one's true self.

The structure of society has often dictated against women coming into their own. That has been the root of the problem for women. The structural sin of sexism has meant that women had lower-paid jobs and little money to spend on themselves, inordinate amounts of housework and inadequate time to pursue their interests, and a lack of educational opportunities which would enable them to realize their talents. The whole context in which women's lives have been set has meant that they themselves often came last. This is why consciousness-raising groups, feminist therapy as practised in recent years, and the friendships which women have formed through the women's movement have had such a dramatic effect on so many women's lives. For women have learnt to say 'I': to find out who they are and what it is for which they hope for themselves. Thus Jean Baker Miller, whose work I mentioned, sees the dynamic of therapy as consisting in enabling women to interpret their lives with reference to the (frequently sexist) context in which they are set. Cure comes through a woman being the better able to trust in the soundness of her judgement and in her basic ability. Indeed one could say it consists in coming to value herself.

How unlike is this to the explanation of her situation which has normally been fed back to a woman within patriarchal society. Lacking the understanding with which a feminist analysis might provide them, women have simply felt inadequate. If a woman was frustrated in the often soul-destroying task of bringing up small children – frequently in a situation of considerable isolation alone all day at home – then this reflected on her. For women, it was held, were meant to mother, and her failure meant she was not a good enough mother. Her 'problems' (and doubtless they were problems) were the result of her (or women's) propensity not to be able to cope. 'Cure' consisted – from Freud forwards – in enabling her to manage in the disadvantaged situation in which she was placed. Certainly there was present no social analysis which saw the cure to be self-realization. In like manner a woman's 'problems' in an all-male working environment have often been seen as her failure to be able to fit into the (male) workplace and function within it. That that public environment might need to change has not been considered. Feminism has then provided a tool which has allowed women to radically re-evaluate their situation. In this feminism has been a spiritual movement. It has lifted a burden of guilt from women, enabling them to overcome self-blame through bringing to light the sexist presuppositions operating in the context in which their life is set.

I have questioned whether for women salvation had best be understood as a breaking of the self. The distinction, popularized by William James, between 'once-born' and 'twice-born' persons may be an interesting distinction to consider in relation to a possible difference between women and men. Could it be that women, more typically, are 'once-born'? They may wish to work with themselves, transforming an already given sense of self, rather than jettisoning the past in a dramatic break. Women have been interested in biography and in the continuity of families from one generation to another. They see their lives, and the lives of others, as bound up in an unfolding social matrix. It has been women's task to care and to tend, to encourage and to enable. Women have been present at that process of growth and maturation which is childhood and youth. They have been teachers and social workers. They have nursed the sick, and helped the dying to bring their lives to a conclusion. Typically, it may be thought, women want to understand their life history. They analyse the past and try to make sense of it. Many more women than men (and I count this positively) undertake therapy. It may then be that an understanding of salvation which propounds that one should break the self, that one should leave the past behind, fits singularly ill with where many women find themselves. Rather will it be meaningful to conceive salvation as a process of transformation of that which is already given. Salvation as healing speaks to the quest for growth and increasing integration.

On a social level too it may well be that an understanding of salvation as a redemption of that which is present, rather than as violent revolution, better fits the feminist agenda. A theology which speaks in terms of the intervention of a powerful (masculine) God, who will judge and damn the wicked, sounds more like a continuation of the same power dynamics. It does not constitute real change in the nature of relationships. We may note Mary Daly's response to the Black theology of James Cone. Daly writes:

Sometimes black theology ... resounds with a cry for vengeance and is fiercely biblical and patriarchal. It ... tends to settle for being religion as a gun. Tailored to fit only the situation of racial oppression, it ... leaves unexplored other dimensions of liberation. It does not get beyond the sexist models internalized by the self ... – models that are at the root of racism. ... The Black God and Black Messiah apparently are merely the same patriarchs after a pigmentation operation – their behavior unaltered.[21]

If revolution consists simply in another group now being on top, then the same divided society remains. What is needed is a theology which speaks to the need for fundamental change. Redemption as the healing of relationships, and the creation of non-dominative patterns of behaviour, must surely commend itself to many women. This may in turn involve a different understanding of God.

The overcoming of sexism may then well be the cure for other ills in society. Radical feminists see sexism as fundamental: it is not just one ill among others, but the school in which discrimination and hierarchy are imbibed. If a child learns to see the opposite sex as 'other', moreover to see one sex as dominant and the other as subordinate, the child learns to equate difference with opposition and hierarchy. A mentality in which one sees the world as 'us' and 'not us' and fears the other, comes to seem axiomatic. It is this that feminists would overcome. Difference need not imply the construction of the world in terms of self-other dichotomies: it may be enriching. Relationships in which difference is present may also be relationships of equality. Thus in an intriguing feminist analysis Marilyn Massey yearns for 'the creation of a society in which there is no need for a scapegoat, for a rejected object'. Women, she believes, have the opportunity to create something new. 'If women ... refuse to project all evil onto men or any other group', then their position will be that 'of a new and finally mature human'. There can be 'difference without domination'.[22]

Feminism thus may be held to be a basically optimistic creed. On the one hand a feminist analysis would suggest that sexism lies deeper in human beings than has often been conceived, for it is fundamental to a distortion of the psyche which comes about in childhood. On the other hand, if sexism basically owes to social conditioning, then it does not need to be. Conditions could be created in which difference, learnt in the first place in relation to gender difference, need not result in competition and domination. In the first place the problem must be named. Virginia Woolf commences effectively on such a task. She points to medals, uniforms and competitive sport, not as the inconsequential things which they have often been taken to be but as symptomatic of the male world. They are not to be separated from the attitudes which give rise to war. Men's treatment of women is part of a larger world of thought and behaviour.[23] But if these things are socially learnt, they are patient of cure.

Feminist women have concluded that women have a different experience of relationality. They have begun to articulate this – and to challenge the male world. Feminists may differ as to how far an individual can come to herself while she is set in a sexist environment. Some feminists emphasize the social context to the extent that they believe that no real healing can take place until there is a fundamental shift in society. Others sense that a feminist analysis of her circumstances may at least enable a woman to see herself and her world differently. Women's experience of recent years in the feminist movement has been that a very real transformation is possible. Feminists are at least involved in a sub-culture in which other values can reign. One thing is certain. For many women there is no way back; only the creation of a different future.

CREATION

A feminist critique of a male outlook often extends not simply to the way that men have viewed women but to the way that they have viewed nature. Just as men seem to have maintained themselves in isolation and not to have conceived of themselves as being part of a web of humanity, just as they have designated woman as an 'other' and then proceeded to dominate her, so too in western culture (and that culture has been a male construct) has the world of nature been conceived as something separate from humankind. This objectification has led to exploitation, as the rest of the creation has been seen in terms of its usefulness to humankind.

Western religion seems to have served humanity singularly ill in this regard. We may look momentarily at what some of the influences have been which have made it so problematic here. Both the Hebrew and the Greek strands of that religion may, in their different ways, be thought to have been far from helpful. The Hebrew religion of a transcendent monotheism, as it has flowed into western thought, conceives God as wholly separate from nature. Indeed Jewish monotheism was in large part formed in opposition to the more immanentist religions of surrounding cultures. The verse at the beginning of Genesis to the effect that humankind should have 'dominion' over the rest of creation has been read as meaning that the rest of creation exists for humankind's benefit and may therefore be exploited. We may note that the secular form of western religion, Marxism, likewise conceives humankind progressively to exercise mastery over the forces of nature. Greek thought, though different, is no more promising. That which is highest, mind or spirit, is seen to be essentially dissociated from the changing world subject to decay. The quest for the good then comes to be equated with freedom from all that would tie humans to their animal nature. It is of significance that within western thought the charge of 'pantheism', when flung at a theology, is the worst possible form of abuse. Whatever the Christian God is, that God is to be dissociated from pantheism which is a 'lower' form of religion.

We have reason to think that women's spirituality will be fundamentally different: the evidence is clearly that this is the case. Feminist women tend to be politically and ecologically conscious. A woman who plants wheat on Ministry of Defence land is making both a political and a spiritual statement. Through movements like the Goddess movement, or in connection with the peace movement, some women have explicitly taken a stand for celebrating nature. Many women have in recent years wanted to draw attention to the interconnectedness between humanity and the rest of the creation and to insist that a spirituality must take into account the fact that we are part of the earth and the cycles of nature, rather than conceiving of humans as somehow spiritual beings who are understood to be above nature.

It has at times however been difficult for women to know whether to stress this connectedness, or whether this computes the damage which the age-old association of woman with nature has done. There is a danger that if women celebrate the fact that they are related to other creatures and the fertility of the earth, they may tend to reinforce male perceptions that somehow women are closer to 'mother nature', more material (and less important than men). There is a need for a spirituality which speaks both to the fact that human beings are a part of nature, and yet does not deny their peculiar transcendence.

Most of the writing to which I shall turn, not by chance has moved way beyond Christianity (or Judaism). But it should not be thought that a sense of our connectedness with the rest of nature has been without its influence on women in the church. This is an area in which women have with one voice wanted to stress something very different from the ethereal stance of much male religion. I shall look here at some of those who have found ways of speaking of this connectedness and who have drawn on a certain spirituality in the way that they have done so. In the short space available, I can do no more than make mention of some of the writers who may be thought to be significant here. I shall also say something about two movements in which such thinking has been found: the Goddess movement and the peace movement, at least as it has been experienced within Britain.

Mary Daly has made a significant contribution here. Her book *Pure Lust* is a philosophy of woman. But it is also a political philosophy. It associates male treatment of women with male political behaviour and treatment of the earth. The only hope for our salvation is seen to lie in women bringing into being a new relationship between ourselves and the world of nature. It is I believe an important book. Difficult, it has perhaps failed to achieve the recognition it deserves. Its analyses are far-reaching and provocative. Published in 1984, at the height of the cold war when catastrophe seemed immanent, it is no less relevant in an age in which we are now understanding the impact which humans are making on the environment. Daly writes, in the opening passage:

> This book is being published in the 1980s – a period of extreme danger for women and for our sister earth and her other creatures, all of whom are targeted by the maniacal fathers, sons, and holy ghosts for extinction by nuclear holocaust, or, failing that, by chemical contamination, by escalated ordinary violence, by man-made hunger and disease that proliferate in a climate of deception and mind-rot. Within the general context of this decade's horrors, women face in our daily lives forces whose intent is to mangle, strangle, tame, and turn us against our own purposes.
>
> Yet at this very time, somehow living/longing through, above, before, and beyond it, thousands of women struggle to re-member our-Selves and our history, to sustain and intensify a biophilic consciousness. Having once known the intense joy of woman-identified bonding and creation, we refuse to turn back. For those who survive in the only real sense, that is, with metapatriarchal consciousness alive and growing, our struggle and quest concern Elemental participation in Be-ing. Our passion is for that which is most intimate and most ultimate, for depth and transcendence, for recalling original wholeness.[24]

It was Susan Griffin's book *Woman and Nature*, published in 1978, which first brought the connectedness of women with nature to the fore in a way which made a wide impact. Griffin, part of a whole movement in California, became for a while a guru to women who wanted to create a new 'nature spirituality'. *Woman and Nature* is a quite extraordinary book, defying description. But it is through its structure that it conveys its message. Griffin wants to shift our consciousness: she well describes her book as 'a description of a different way of seeing'.[25] The book is poetic and literary, rather than consisting in an analytic argument. It works by juxtaposing different texts and images; indeed her flair is for making connections which enable the reader to gain new perceptions. The book is divided into four sections or passages, through which we move from the first in which man couples woman with nature and denigrates her, to the last in which woman has come into her own in a celebration of her oneness with nature. Each passage consists of a series of vignettes. Thus for example, in the first passage, we have 'The Show Horse: And the Domesticated Learn to Please'. In this chapter passages from a riding manual for show horses are juxtaposed with passages from a book of etiquette for women – showing what dilettante persons women have been supposed to be to please men. The chapter is interspersed with quotations from Rousseau and Freud. By the last passage woman has reclaimed her body, her vision and the wildness within her. Griffin's central message is the connectedness of all of reality, which we ignore at our peril. In a later book, *Pornography and Silence*, she writes: 'We are inseparable from all other beings in the universe. Intimations of this have reached us.'[26]

One who has had an impact on theological circles is Carol P. Christ. Christ's journey from a concern with Jewish and Christian literature to her present interest in the symbol of the Goddess is significant. She has always loved literature, particularly the literature and culture of the ancient world, and has had a marked concern for the issue of suffering and theodicy. In the first place she studied the Hebrew scriptures, and wrote her doctoral thesis on the novels of Elie Wiesel. But in time she moved to the world of ancient Greece and the symbol of the Goddess. For some years dividing her time between her native California and Greece, she now lives in Greece. She is able to bring together her political concerns (particularly her work in the peace movement) with her knowledge of the roots of western culture in what is often powerful writing.

Christ points to the fact that the God of the Hebrew scriptures is a warrior. Jahweh's giving to his people 'a land flowing with milk and honey' entailed the disappropriation of others. The western conception of God is not incidental, she contends, to an outlook which has made nuclear war thinkable. Of the United States administration she writes: 'It is easy to dismiss these men as mad.... But they are not aberrations within Western civilization. They are its products.'[27] She believes our hope to lie in the development of a spirituality in which the disconnectedness between mind and matter is overcome. This for her is what is symbolized by the Goddess. Writing at Lesbos in Greece under the radioactive cloud caused by Chernobyl, Christ concludes (quoting Susan Griffin): 'I know "this earth is my sister" more deeply than I feel and know anything. My spirituality stems from my sense of connection to this earth.'[28]

The theme of the relationship between nature, women and a certain spirituality has (not surprisingly) been explored in women's fiction of recent years. Perhaps most remarkable is the Canadian writer Margaret Atwood's *Surfacing*. *Surfacing* is about a pilgrimage; a pilgrimage which takes place on different levels. On one level the protagonist returns from the industrial city in the United States in which she now lives, to the Canadian northern wilderness of her childhood. She goes in search of her lost father; and finally finds his body, drowned. But meanwhile another 'pilgrimage' is under way, a journey from the false values of civilization to an intense communion with nature. Sending on before her her three companions – who have, in their various ways, no feeling for the world of nature and lack any ability to survive in the wilderness – she becomes like an animal, donning a fur and searching out food. It is an extraordinary, dream-like book, which provides no clear answers. As is the case in much of Atwood's work, a telling critique of Christianity runs like a streak through the whole.

It is difficult in short compass to do justice to the Goddess spirituality movement. Having had little contact with it myself, I find some of the writing which has issued from the movement of greater interest than I had realized that I should. It is clear that for most women who are involved the Goddess is not conceived to be an objective reality, equivalent to the male God; rather is she a symbol which allows women to focus on their wholeness. Women's relation to their bodies has after all been badly damaged through the misogynism of masculinist religion. The Goddess moreover symbolizes the relatedness of humanity to nature. For Starhawk, a well-known witch, 'Goddess' is equivalent to 'immanence'. Immanence she defines as: 'The awareness of the world and everything in it as alive, dynamic, interdependent, interacting, and infused with moving energies: a living being, a weaving dance.'[29] The term Goddess speaks to her of 'the powers of connectedness, sustenance, healing, creating'.[30] She writes: 'Let us be clear that when I say *Goddess* I am not talking about a being somewhere outside of this world, nor am I proposing a new belief system. I am talking about choosing an attitude: choosing to take this living world, the people and creatures on it, as the ultimate meaning and purpose of life, to see the world, the earth, and our lives as sacred.'[31] From this perspective the belief in a God transcendent to the world is a root cause of the malaise which has led to human domination of nature. Charlene Spretnak quotes Gary Snyder: 'Our troubles began with the invention of male deities located off the planet.'[32] Starhawk writes: 'Let us imagine that these children, at least, have never known a God who stands outside the world, that nothing in their minds is receptive to the principle of power over.... The vision is not hard to construct.'[33] Revolutionary politics requires a different spiritual basis.

It would be difficult to exaggerate the impact which the 'Greenham' phenomenon has had on the lives of countless British women. 'Greenham' constituted much more than a peace camp. It was an attempt to articulate different values. For a start the whole form of organization was remarkable. Women assembled by their thousands in peaceful protest. They found that they could do this without named leaders and exercising consensus decision making. Women discovered that they, as women, had a different view of the world from what the dominant culture represented – and they gained a sense of their strength and of their resolution. The permanent camp at Greenham represented an experiment in a different way of living (as also the camps at other missile bases) and a school of radical feminist politics. As one woman, a frequent visitor to Greenham whose life was changed by it, remarked to me: 'Greenham is where you go to sit at the feet of wise women.' Greenham has been the place in British society where many facets of the feminist movement have come together: a radical politics, a concern for new forms of organization, and not least an experimentation with a different spirituality and a renewed relationship of humankind to the world of nature.

The world of Greenham can in no way better be represented than through citations from the many songs which grew up around it – and which have spread throughout the women's movement in Britain.

> They fear the dove, they clip her wings
> Shall there be womanly times, or shall we die?
> But still she flies, and still we sing

There will be womanly times we will not die.

The missiles wait in concrete tombs ...
Born of the head and not the womb ...

The sun has ruled this age of men ...
Now moon take up your place again ...[34]

And again:

We are gentle angry women
And we are singing, singing for our lives

We are the witches of Diana ...

We are the dreamers of the future ...[35]

And again, from 'Carry Greenham Home':

Woman tiger, woman dove
Help to save the world you love
Velvet fist in iron glove
Bring the message home.[36]

What shall we say of this? It is clearly a long way from the world of traditional male academic theology. Is it theology? In no straightforward sense is it theology. But one should be careful not to dismiss such writing or think that it has been without impact on the lives of many who work in the churches or read theology. There is present a spiritual vision. The kinds of movements and texts which I have discussed in this section are at the least bound to make many women look askance henceforth at a theology which is 'dry', 'academic', and which does not seem to have at heart a concern for a connectedness between human beings and the integrity of creation. It is a different kind of spirituality from the often intensely privatized spirituality that much western culture has known. In the creation of such a political spirituality women may be said to be leading the way.

'ANGST', DEATH AND ETERNAL LIFE

I shall in this section suggest that the male sense of self (typically) means that men are more liable to be prone to *Angst*, that they think differently than do women about sacrifice and death, and that it matters more to them that there should be a continuation in eternal life. Though such conclusions must be tentative, there is some evidence that these things are the case. Certainly the differences which I am suggesting here would fit well with what Carol Gilligan reports as to the way in which men and women see themselves: men tending to be more isolated, more egotistical and seeing the world in relation to themselves; women tending to be more caught up in a human network with a less atomistic sense of self. Theology as we have known it has written into it, in some traditions, a preoccupation with *Angst*, male religion has been much occupied with sacrifice, and Christian theology has had as a major theme the idea of eternal life. If there is a difference between men and women here, theology, as women come to write it, will reflect very different concerns.

Angst is a word which, in theology and philosophy, has particular connotations. It is anxiety without an object: thus it might be described as a basic dis-ease. The concept has been prominent in German Protestant theology and in existentialist philosophy, following upon the exposition of *Angst* by the Danish thinker Søren Kierkegaard in the nineteenth century. But it might well be said that Luther, although he may not have used this word, having these particular connotations, has a theology which is predicated upon the human condition of *Angst*. For him, as also for later thinkers, the human is not at home in the world: we cannot stand *coram Deo*, before the face of God. The concept of *Angst* is fundamental to Reinhold Niebuhr, whose discussion of sin we considered earlier in this chapter. For Niebuhr it is out of anxiety that we sin. In our insecurity we should put our faith in God, but instead we try to find that security through pride or sensuality. *Angst* is seen to arise (at least from Kierkegaard forwards) from the fact that we are double: both spirit, and yet bodily like the animals – so that we rise above our bodily limitations in our imagination and have limitless ambition, yet know that we shall die. In the writing of Rudolf Bultmann, the major existentialist theologian of the century (and again Lutheran), the human, in sin, grasps at the finite, misusing those around him in order to try to gain what proves to be a false sense of security. The secular existentialist philosopher Martin Heidegger, with whom Bultmann worked closely, believes that it is only as we face death that we may begin to live with authenticity. For the theologian Paul Tillich, the human is faced in a major way with the threat of non-being. The tradition is well summed up by David Rasmussen, writing: 'There is a profound truth in the existentialist vision of the man who must achieve freedom in a life conditioned by time and eventual death, a vision in which philosophy ... becomes the tender art of learning to die with courage.'[37]

Of course it is not the case that all theology has been obsessed with *Angst*, or even with the wider theme of facing death. Catholic theology does not speak to *Angst* in the way that Lutheran theology does; it sees the human as much more bound up in a web with others – which is interesting, as I wish to suggest that this is also true of women. Nor is the theme of *Angst* fundamental to Anglo-Saxon theology with its sometimes facile optimism. Yet it is the case that that the human has *Angst* has been basic to what has arguably been the most important and creative stream of modern Protestant theology.

What should women think of this tradition? May it not strike women as peculiarly male? Is the fact that we are both physical and yet more than physical a situation which women find to be intolerable? It occurs to many women – I do not think I am wrong in this – that men appear to be curiously unintegrated. (There is indeed evidence that the left and right sides of the brain are less integrated in men than in women.) Men's sexuality often seems to be somehow separate from themselves. And certainly many women find the men they know to be extraordinarily isolated – not least from other men. The presuppositions which allow such a philosophical school of thought to get under way may simply not seem to women to be axiomatic. Could it be that *Angst* is the hazard to which in particular the isolated, and privileged, male is prone? His minor needs having been taken care of (by wife, secretary and cleaner) he is left alone in his study, his mind able to contemplate vast reaches of thought. He seems to transcend time, yet despite his creativity, he knows he must die. He feels himself limitless, yet cruelly limited. He will attempt to secure himself through feats, whether in the writing of books, or – in the case of another – through conquering nations.

It may be that women (typically) live within a different social matrix, so that *Angst* is not a major theme. Anxiety they may indeed have: but that is different, anxiety pertains to this or that. Do they lack the time for *Angst*? Their lives are taken up with particular problems in the never-ending round of tasks. Perhaps it is her very involvement with the everyday world (which is supposed to represent inauthenticity!) which saves many a woman from *Angst*. Women's lives are more bound up with those of others, with other women and children. They are not so isolated on a personal level. Nor are they so egotistical. They are not in the powerful position which should allow them to see others in relation to themselves, nor has society trained them to see themselves in this way. Of course a woman may bend the lives of others in relation to herself. But is this not more commonly through having a 'martyr complex' – which arises rather from a low self-esteem and an identity which consists in needing to be the servant of others? Depression women do know: depression which may be thought often to arise from the circumscribed circumstances of their lives. But *Angst*? *Angst* in the sense of terror that one will die without making one's mark on the world? *Angst* that arises from a terrible isolation alone before the face of God? I doubt it.

Feminist writers have often thought men to be orientated towards death in a way that women are not. Thought about death occupies a major place in male religion. Moreover, it is often death connected with sacrifice. Indeed there is a theme of death through sacrifice and rebirth. This paradigm is obviously built into Christianity. May it be that women are more interested in giving birth to life? Nor does the life necessarily need to come out of death. Further there appears to be a preoccupation in male religion with the continuation of an individual life after death. May it be that the kind of religion which comes naturally to men here is very different from what would be the emphases of many women? The early American feminist thinker Charlotte Perkins Gilman certainly thought so, writing:

> To the death-based religion, the main question is, 'What is going to happen to me after I am dead?' – a posthumous egotism. To the birth-based religion, the main question is, 'What must be done for the child who is born?' an immediate altruism. ... The death-based religions have led to a limitless individualism, a demand for the eternal extension of personality. Such good conduct as they required was to placate the deity or to benefit one's self. ... The birth-based religion is necessarily and essentially altruistic, a forgetting of oneself for the good of the child, and tends to develop naturally into love and labor for the widening range of family, state and world.[38]

It is hardly surprising that men should be more concerned with death through sacrifice. For generations it has been for men to kill and to risk being killed, either earlier in the hunt, or in all ages through war. Of course women have also risked their lives. Until recently every time a woman became pregnant she did so. But to lose one's life in childbirth is to lose one's life in a situation of supreme connectedness to another – to give one's life in giving life. Whereas to kill, or risk being killed, must imply a certain disconnectedness and an impersonalization of the other. There must be many men also who find the centrality of sacrifice to religion to be perverse. But one should note that it is written into much male religion. Women may feel very differently here. The Anglican priest Carter Heyward writes: 'I cannot image Jesus's death as a "sacrifice" at all.'[39] Again it may be that the idea of death and rebirth fits well with the male's life-cycle, which as we have said, in conjunction with the discussion of Nancy Chodorow's work, consists in separating himself from the original matrix in which the boy found himself, and being reborn into the world of men.[40] I have suggested that women may tend to be more once-born in the type of religion which they espouse, men more twice-born. The question then is that of whether it may not be the case that the religion which we have known in the west has reflected male sensibilities rather than female.

The greater social isolation of men which may lead to a greater sense of *Angst* may also account for their being more concerned for the continuation of an individual life after death. If it is true that men tend to be more egotistical, more self-enclosed and socialized to think that they must make an impact on the world, then it is not surprising to find that this should be the case. Anne Wilson Schaef comments on the difference between men and women here which she has experienced in her psychotherapeutic practice. (Her terms 'white male system' and 'female system' designate two orientations not dissimilar from Gilligan's differentiation between the ways in which women and men typically speak about themselves.) Schaef writes:

Since White Male System persons so firmly believe that it is possible for one to become God, they are understandably concerned with the issue of immortality. Female System persons, on the other hand, realize that immortality is not a genuine possibility and spend little or no time worrying about it. Nearly every man I have ever seen in therapy spends several sessions dealing with immortality-related anxieties. ... At some level of their consciousness ... a surprising number of men really *do* believe that it's possible for them to become immortal. They only have to find the way! ... One must either have children, especially male heirs to carry on the family name and bloodliness; or one must amass material goods; or one must produce lasting things like 'great books'. ... I have yet to meet a woman who concerns herself with the issue of immortality. She may want her children to validate her own choices, but she seldom believes that they will guarantee her eternal life on this earth. She is usually too busy struggling with more mundane issues such as the need to survive and establish a sense of self-worth.[41]

The male concern seems to come out of a control instinct – such that one would, if one could, also control what happens to one's individual self the other side of death.

If women see their lives as bound up in a web of connection with the lives of others, then the theme of individual death may not seem to be quite so traumatic to them. There is no reason why one should go on for ever. What is important is that the world may continue, and others live. Carol Christ expresses eloquently an alternative perspective with which many women may resonate. She writes:

> The knowledge that we could destroy this earth weighs heavily on me. … I can imagine my own death and do not really fear it. … We must learn to love this life that ends in death. This is not absolutely to rule out the possibility of individual or communal survival after death, but to say that we ought not [to] live our lives in the light of such a possibility. Our task is here. … From the perspective of our religious heritage it might seem that such a spirituality [which acknowledges finitude and death] is a contradiction in terms. What is spirituality, it might be said, if not an answer to questions we have about finitude and death?… The spirituality we need for our survival, I would argue, is precisely a spirituality encouraging us to recognize limitation and mortality, a spirituality calling us to celebrate all that is finite.[42]

What is so terrible about death is not so much the loss of an individuated self, but rather that it marks the end of communication between those who love each other. It is in the striving not for their own individual lives, but that the whole might continue, that women have of recent years woven pictures of their children into perimeter fences.

THE ESCHATON

That feminism has given rise to a utopian literature I count to be of the greatest significance. It gives some measure of the radicalness of the movement. Sallie McFague writes: 'One of the most powerful ways to question a tradition is to imagine new worlds that challenge it.'[43] Traditionally the eschaton has come last in dogmatics, imagined as a future state. Perhaps however it should come first. One learns much about a movement from its sense of what would constitute utopia.

It is interesting that radical social and political movements in the west have so often produced a vision of the eschaton, or in secular terms a utopia. It is true of Christianity, and true of Marxism. It is also notably true of non-conformist political and religious movements in the Anglo-Saxon world. The vision is presumably an extrapolation from the best that is known in this world. Yet on the other hand it is a projection which, in turn, judges the present state of affairs when that is held up against the ideal. These things are also true of the feminist vision. Further, radical political, social and religious groups have often taken themselves apart from the world and formed separatist communes, that in a small way, in their own world, they might succeed in realizing something of the vision. This separatism too has been a mark of the radical feminist movement. One may ask after the relevance of separatism: it is an apt question. Perhaps the relevance lies in the fact that some women are prepared to go to these lengths, often sacrificing comfort and incurring social ridicule, in order to keep a light burning.

One place to look for the feminist utopia is feminist science fiction. Gwynneth Jones writes, reviewing this literature, that '(at its best) science fiction is transforming, subversive, revolutionary – defiantly refusing to validate present realities.'[44] Science fiction allows of the creation of a world in which the aspects of this world which one would like to see accentuated, and brought to readers' attention, can be magnified. Moreover, through the juxtaposition of the imagined world with our own world, one may cast light on this world. Thus in Sally Gearhart's novel *The Wanderground*,[45] a description of a separatist commune, the women are able to communicate through a sixth sense, thus accentuating women's desire for relationality. When a woman is raped by a stray man from earth and when an animal is caught in a trap, these events are met with incredulity and horror, showing up by contrast their everyday nature in the world in which we live. Feminist science fiction, though it has mushroomed in recent years, is not a new phenomenon. In 1915, in the midst of war, Perkins Gilman produced in serialized form her novel *Herland*.[46] In what is a fascinating glimpse into the social relations of the time, three American males land in Herland (populated only by women) in an aeroplane. They get themselves into hot water through their mistaken assumptions. In its sequel *With Her in Ourland*, set back in America where one of the men has taken his wife from Herland, American society is shown up for what it is through her naive questions.

The work of Mary Daly may also be said to be eschatalogical. Daly is a visionary. Her work meets what I would take to be the criterion of utopian writing: she thinks in terms of a disjuncture between what she would propose and that which currently we know. Thus Daly:

> Together with Virginia Woolf, feminists moan: 'As a woman I have no country.' And together with her we may add: 'As a woman I want no country. As a woman my country is the whole world.' But there is something poignant about this brave assertion, for 'the whole world' is groaning under phallic rule. It must be, then, that it is in some other dimension that 'the whole world' is the country, the homeland of the Race of Women. This is not to say that a woman should cease struggling for survival within, or rather, on the boundary of, phallocracy. But that struggle is inadequate without Pure Lust, the active longing that propels a woman into her own 'country', that is, into the Realms of Elemental Reality, of ontological depth.[47]

I believe Daly's work to be effective politically (and not a cop-out as some have suggested), through the very fact that she creates a vision. All radical movements have needed their vision if they were to understand themselves. Without a vision the feminist movement will die – or be assimilated. It has been well said, of the radical feminist movement, that it performs the function of being the 'conscience' of the movement as a whole.

The radical feminist movement has manifested a tendency towards separatism. In Britain there are small radical feminist communes, and the permanent peace camp at Greenham has also been separatist. Much radical feminism, and utopian writing, is of course lesbian. This may be of its essence. The lesbianism is often 'political lesbianism' on the part of women some of whom were previously married. Women have come to believe that the male world is so corrupt that they wish to separate themselves from it on every level. Political and personal agendas become interwoven. Separatism is often read as anti-men. It may of course be that. But it is more than that; it is an attempt to create something new in the midst of the old. If one is to operate according to a different ideology – for example a radical equality – it may be necessary to put a certain distance between yourselves and society. Separatism is not necessarily permanent. Many a woman of recent years has found it to be extraordinarily powerful, and healing, to be for a limited period of time in a consciously all-women's group.

In her mythical work *Les Guérillères* (*The Warriors*) (1969) the French feminist writer Monique Wittig says, in words which have become well known among feminist thinkers: 'There was a time when you were not a slave, remember that.... You say there are no words to describe this time, you say it does not exist. But remember. Make an effort to remember. Or, failing that, invent.' If it could be said of the Goddess movement that it represents an attempt to 'remember', to go back behind a patriarchy to a pristine state of affairs, it might be said of the creation of utopias that they are an attempt to invent.[48] Feminism has at this point become a total vision, involving different ethics, a different politics, a different ecology, and not least a different spirituality. In the light of the current predicament of our world, who can say that this is far-fetched?

In what then in a word does the feminist vision consist? How should we bring together the threads of this chapter? If I were to choose one word I should say that it is a vision of connectedness. Of feminism Eleanor Haney writes that it 'offers us individually and collectively the possibility of making connections with ourselves, one another, the earth, and all that is and can be'.[49] As we have seen, the problem with the concept of sin as pride is that it does not fit women's predicament. It assumes an isolated individual. Salvation for a woman may be to come into her own; finding the right relationship to herself and to others, and so healing. Women may well, on a political level, see sin as a break in connectedness, and salvation as a reweaving of the web of life. Creation, or the relationship to nature, is a theme in feminist writing because feminist women want to elevate the profound connectedness between humankind and the rest of nature. It may be because women live, to a greater extent than do many men, in a web of relations with others that *Angst* may not be such a dominant theme in their lives. While the fear of death is not in the same way caused by a desire to retain an individuated self through all eternity. In their drawing of the vision as to what humanity might become, women create a relationality between people, and between people and the earth. Haney adds: 'Indeed, humanity literally yearns for what feminism intends.'[50]

NOTES

1. *In a Different Voice: Psychological Theory and Women's Development* (Cambridge, MA: Harvard University Press, 1982).
2. *Toward a New Psychology of Women* (Boston, MA: Beacon Press, 1986) (1976).
3. 'Preaching the Word', in *The Journey is Home* (Boston, MA: Beacon Press, 1985), p. 55 (1974).

4 *The Reproduction of Mothering: Psychoanalysis and the Sociology of Gender* (Berkeley, CA: University of California Press, 1978).

5 'A Different Reality: Feminist Ontology', in C. Gould (ed.), *Beyond Domination: New Perspectives on Women and Philosophy* (Totowa, NJ: Rowman & Allenheld, 1984).

6 See pp. 153–6.

7 *The Nature and Destiny of Man* (New York: Charles Scribner's Sons, 1964) (1941). On sin see vol. I, *Human Nature*, chs 7 and 8.

8 'The Human Situation: A Feminine View', in C. P. Christ and J. Plaskow (eds), *Womanspirit Rising: A Feminist Reader in Religion* (New York and San Francisco: Harper & Row, 1979), pp. 35, 36, 37 (1960).

9 *The Sickness Unto Death*, ed. and tr. H. V. and E. H. Hong (Princeton, NJ: Princeton University Press, 1980), pp. 49–50. Cf. my discussion 'Reinhold Niebuhr on Sin: A Critique', in R. Harries (ed.), *Reinhold Niebuhr and the Issues of Our Time* (London: Mowbrays, 1986; Grand Rapids, MI: William Eerdmans, 1986), pp. 47–9, 53.

10 *Sex, Sin and Grace: Women's Experience and the Theologies of Reinhold Niebuhr and Paul Tillich* (Washington, DC: University Press of America, 1980), p. 3.

11 *Sociality, Ethics and Social Change: A Critical Appraisal of Reinhold Niebuhr's Ethics in the Light of Rosemary Radford Ruether's Works* (Lanham, MD: University Press of America, 1983).

12 See p. 29.

13 *Sociality, Ethics and Social Change*, p. 79.

14 *The Irony of American History* (New York: Charles Scribner's Sons, 1952), p. 139; cited by Vaughan, *Sociality, Ethics and Social Change*, p. 124.

15 *A Different Heaven and Earth* (Valley Forge, PA: Judson Press, 1974), pp. 157–8.

16 *Nature and Destiny*, vol. I, p. 192.

17 *Different Heaven*, pp. 155–6.

18 'Some Things I Have Learned', *Saturday Review*, 6 Nov. 1965, p. 22; (mis)quoted by Vaughan, *Sociality, Ethics and Social Change*, p. 117.

19 *The Nature and Destiny of Man*, vol. II, *Human Destiny*, pp. 108–10.

20 'Feminism, Contractualism, and Community', unpublished paper given to the St Andrews University Women's Group, May 1987.

21 *Beyond God the Father: Toward a Philosophy of Women's Liberation* (Boston, MA: Beacon Press, 1973; London: The Women's Press, 1986), p. 25.

22 *Feminine Soul: The Fate of an Ideal* (Boston, MA: Beacon Press, 1985), p. 186.

23 The argument of *Three Guineas* (New York: Harcourt Brace Jovanovich, 1966) (1938).

24 *Pure Lust: Elemental Feminist Philosophy* (Boston, MA: Beacon Press, 1984; London: The Women's Press, 1984), preface p. vii.

25 *Woman and Nature: The Roaring Inside Her* (New York: Harper & Row, 1978; London: The Women's Press, 1984), p. xvi.

26 *Pornography and Silence* (New York: Harper & Row, 1981; London: The Women's Press, 1981), p. 260.

27 'Finitude, Death and Reverence for Life', in *Laughter of Aphrodite: Reflections on a Journey to the Goddess* (San Francisco: Harper & Row, 1987), p. 221.

28 Ibid. p. 215.

29 *Dreaming the Dark: Magic, Sex and Politics* (Boston, MA: Beacon Press, 1982), p. 9.

30 Ibid. p. 4.

31 Ibid. p. 11.

32 'Anarchism, Buddhism, and Political Economy', lecture, San Francisco, 1984, quoted by Spretnak, 'The Spiritual Dimension of Green Politics', in C. Spretnak and F. Capra (eds), *Green Politics*, appendix C (London: Paladin, 1985), p. 238.

33 *Dreaming the Dark*, pp. 16, 17.

34 Frankie Armstrong. Title line 'Shall there be Womanly Times or Shall We Die?' courtesy of Ian McEwan.

35 After a song by Holly Near.

36 Peggy Seeger.

37 'Between Autonomy and Sociality', *Cultural Hermeneutics*, 1 (April 1973), p. 22.

38 *His Religion and Hers: A Study of the Faith of Our Fathers and the Work of Our Mothers* (Westport, CT: Hyperion, 1976), pp. 46–7 (1923).

39 *The Redemption of God: A Theology of Mutual Relation* (Washington, DC: University Press of America, 1982), p. 69.

40 Cf. Sheila Collins' interesting discussion of anthropological material here, *Different Heaven*, pp. 202–5.

41 *Women's Reality: An Emerging Female System in the White Male Society* (Minneapolis, MN: Winston Press, 1981), pp. 142–3.

42 *Laughter of Aphrodite*, pp. 213, 215, 221, 222.

43 *Metaphorical Theology: Models of God in Religious Language* (Philadelphia, PA: Fortress Press, 1982; London: SCM Press, 1983), p. 163.

44 *Women's Review*, 3 (January 1986), p. 12.

45 *The Wanderground* (Boston, MA: Alyson Publications, 1984; London: The Women's Press, 1985).

46 *Herland* (New York: Pantheon Books, 1979; London: The Women's Press, 1979).

47 *Pure Lust*, p. 6.

48 *Les Guérillères*, tr. D. Le Vay (London: The Women's Press, 1979; Boston, MA: Beacon Press, 1985), p. 89.

49 'What is Feminist Ethics? A Proposal for Continuing Discussion', *Journal of Religious Ethics*, 8 (1980), p. 124.

50 Ibid. p. 124.

CHAPTER 5

Theology

THE TASK OF FEMINIST THEOLOGY

In this chapter I shall be concerned with the conceptualization of God. The claim will be made that the conceptualization which we have known is in large part the projection of a masculinist construal of reality. Once one sees this to be the case the question opens up as to what a conceptualization would look like which conformed to feminist values and women's sense of reality. These are large questions on which to embark. In this concluding chapter I can do no more than consider some of the work which has been done and indicate my own position. It is here that my interests in theology lie.

Less work has been undertaken by feminists on the conceptualization of God than for example in the field of what I have called theological anthropology. This is not surprising. Feminists working in theology tend to be interested in the understanding of the human person and in human relationships. Many bring to theology a political agenda: they then become interested for example in liberation theology. Moreover, it must be said that for women wishing to work within the Christian tradition (and the majority of feminists working in theology wish to be Christian) it is less dangerous, and probably comes more naturally, to reformulate subsidiary questions within the tradition than to reconceive God. Thus more work has been done within biblical scholarship, or researching the history of the Christian tradition, than in systematic theology.

The revolution which I at least would like to see take place in theology thus lies ahead. I believe that we need to reconceive the notion of God in such a way that it will become tenable in this day and age (as I do not believe the Christian notion to be). I think that such a reconceptualization will in fact conform closely to feminist paradigms. Indeed I believe that feminist thought provides a context within which such a rethinking of the notion of God may fruitfully be undertaken. A different conception of God is implicit in much feminist theology; it remains for the implications of that theology for the understanding of God to be spelled out. (It must in addition be said that women who employ the notion of 'the Goddess' are working with symbolism greatly at variance with the tradition, though it is unclear that they are theistic, believing Her to exist.)

It is important for feminists (and others who would reconceive the notion of God) to come to see how far the conceptualization of God in the major tradition as we have known it has been the product of patriarchy. Indeed I would want to say that not only is it a conceptualization which has arisen within patriarchy and reflects patriarchal values, but that it has been a masculinist conception which has been a reflection of what is often a male way of conceiving the relationship of the self to others. When people understand the conceptualization of God which we have known to reflect a social context, it becomes less sacrosanct. It ceases to be the only way in which one could conceive God – as though God were by definition to be equated with the God which we have inherited. The possibility that a major shift should take place arises. The theological imagination of human beings is called upon as they seek to articulate an understanding of God which is true both to their experience of God and to their values. Thus I shall in the second section of this chapter consider 'The Christian God', asking how the conceptualization of God in the west has conformed to a patriarchal and masculinist understanding of reality.

There are two levels at which the feminist critique and reconstruction of the notion of God can take place, though they are not entirely to be separated from one another. In the first place the language and metaphors which have been used for God may be criticized, and language which is female or which has female connotations substituted. I shall call the attempt to do this the 'renaming' of God. But to rename God is already to embark on reconceiving God, inasmuch as different language or metaphors carry different connotations. There is also a second and more fundamental level of critique and reconstruction possible: what I shall call the 'reshaping' of the notion of God. Now one does not simply give female names to a male God, or replace a God conceived as male with one conceived as female, but articulates differently and non-anthropomorphically what one means by God. Such a non-anthropomorphic understanding of God, in which God is not conceived as a discrete entity of which a personal pronoun could be used, is I believe the more fundamental revolution. Of course in order to put forward such a conceptualization one does not need to move quite outside the western tradition. Although the major western conception has been that of an anthropomorphically conceived God, there have always been other strands present. Feminists may well want to build on these. I shall accordingly devote the third and fourth sections of this chapter to the project of 'renaming God' and to the question of 'the shape of God'.

In the final section I shall explore my own thought. I espouse a religious position, within the western tradition, founded upon human experience of God. My position is based on the efficacy of prayer and the awareness of God. In particular, a certain centredness in oneself and a concentrated attentiveness to the world in which one is set are crucial to me. I shall accordingly call this section 'perceptivity'. If one does not believe as I do not (and as I have discussed in connection with how a post-Christian position functions methodologically)[1] that there can be a particular revelation in a certain age, such that that revelation and tradition become normative for all others, then methodologically the place where theology arises must be out of our own experience of God. This is not of course to say that one does not draw on the thought of others, either living today or in past ages. But theology is predicated upon our perception of God, not on revelation, and the act of perceiving becomes crucial. I believe our own ethical integrity to be fundamental to the possibility of such perception, and so also to construing the world religiously.

The task of feminists working in theology is (as I conceive it) to formulate a conceptualization of God which is true both to what we may in the late twentieth century think the world to be, and moreover to the norms and values which feminists hold. I am not, then, saying that God is a human projection. I believe the word God to refer, and that moreover some theologies may better fit what we may believe to be the case than others. What seemed credible in one age no longer seems credible today. Furthermore it is not the case that ethically there is nothing to choose between different conceptualizations of God. Feminists claim that their way of conceiving reality, their way of understanding the self in relation to others, is ethically superior to the oppositional stance of male thought and behaviour. They may then well also believe that a conceptualization of God which embodies such an ethic and is commensurate with such a sense of relationality will both reflect and also tend to legitimate a social order which they would promote.

THE CHRISTIAN GOD

The basic conceptualization of God in the west has been that of monotheism. God has been seen as transcendent above humankind, as
having a will and all-powerful, so that 'He' is an agent who can act on
the world. He has been appropriately, and not surprisingly, described using masculine metaphors. For many people God is a kind of
spiritual being, separate from the world, yet its creator and able to
intervene in it at will. Of course God is also thought to be related to
the world, but an understanding of God as immanent has taken a
second place to the transcendent God. What interests me here is not
monotheism per se (there could be a monotheism which conceived
God as spirit, interrelated with all), but the particular connotations
which have been given to the monotheistic conception of God. It
would seem that a certain social paradigm and a particular understanding of the human being have been built into the understanding
of God.

Thus God is seen as all-powerful. He does not need to consult. His
will is what is right – by definition. He may appear to humans to be
arbitrary, but the fact that He is God is justification enough for what
He chooses to do. Perhaps even more significant, He is said to be self-
sufficient. He has aseity: He is a se, entire unto himself. He did not
have to create the world, for He is complete in himself. Nor was He in
any way limited by any reality other than Himself. As I recently
heard one who is a liberal churchman say: 'When God created, He
had to take into account nothing else whatsoever.' There is but one
God, and He will allow no competition. Pseudo-gods are to be named
idols. Of course I have portrayed God at His worst, but these properties are indeed predicated of the western God. His power, freedom
and self-sufficiency know no bounds. Is He, one wonders, the reflection
of what have been many a man's wildest dreams?

Feminists naturally have taken issue with such a conceptualization of God. The Christian feminist and Anglican priest Carter
Heyward writes as follows:

> It is in the nature of our idol to be intolerant of ambiguity. His first and
> only love is Himself. He is an impassive unflappable character who
> represents the headship of a universal family in which men are best
> and women least. He is the keeper of an ethical scorecard on which
> 'reason' gets good marks and 'relation' fails. He is a master plan-maker
> who maps out and, by remote-control, directs our journeys before we

have learned to walk. His narcissism is unquenchable. He demands
that he be loved. This cold deity is the legitimating construct of the
patriarchal desire to dominate and control the world. He is the eternal
King, the Chairman of the board, the President of the institution, the
Guru of the youth, the Husband of the wife, the General of the army,
the Judge of the court, the Master of the universe, the Father of the
church. He resides above us all. He is our superior, never our friend.
He is a rapist, never a lover, of women and of anyone else beneath Him.
He is the first and final *icon of evil* in history.[2]

As one woman remarked to me after a seminar, when she had become clear how far the western conception of God was modelled after
characteristics which she disliked when she found them in human
beings: '*Now* I understand why I have no use for such a God!'
    Christians are wont to say that their understanding of God differs
greatly from this what they take to be 'old testament' understanding
of God. That may be true. Jesus taught his followers to call God
'Father' and they may so conceive of God. One must however be
careful here. The God of the Hebrew scriptures is also a God of compassion, and that of the Christian scriptures also one of wrath. If
what is being said is that people in the western tradition, Christians
and Jews alike, have had an understanding of God as compassionate,
merciful and loving, that need not be doubted. The Hebrew God is not
necessarily less acceptable than that of the Christian scriptures. The
question however which I am raising here is not that of whether the
monotheistic, transcendent God is seen to behave well, but that of
the conceptualization of God which there has been. God – whether
benevolent or indifferent – is conceived to have freedom, power and
independence. These attributes apparently belong to the definition
of what it is to be God.
    Such a conceptualization of God affects also the way in which
human beings are understood. For human beings are conceived in
relationship to God as one pole in a di-polar construal of reality. Thus
human beings are seen as weak for God is strong, as sinful in comparison with God's goodness. It is not in the first place said of
humans that, God being one with them, they are filled with God's
goodness and so transformed. Humans are understood as the opposite to what God is conceived to be. Moreover, as we have noted, these
patterns tend to repeat themselves in relations between human
beings: man is held to be superior to and the opposite of woman.
Indeed 'man' may be held to represent God in relation to humanity,
while 'woman' is conceived to represent humankind in relation to

God. It may then well be that monotheism tends to reinforce hierarchy, for it creates a chain of command. In this it embodies a structuring of reality and an ethic at odds with the dominant trend of post-Enlightenment thought. For the past two hundred years human beings have wanted to put the realization of persons at the centre of the stage.

Certainly feminists are operating according to very different paradigms. They are interested in self-actualization, equality and the empowerment of others. A transcendent monotheism would seem to fit singularly ill with the feminist vision. Rather do feminists want to create conditions which allow for difference, multiplicity and plurality. Catherine Keller, in the context of an exploration of the relational nature of feminist thought, writes interestingly in criticism of the radical monotheism of H. Richard Niebuhr, the brother of Reinhold Niebuhr. Having spoken so hopefully of a self which finds identity in reciprocal dialogue with another, Niebuhr, when he turns to the understanding of God, reverts to the singularity of monotheism. In his monotheism, she writes, Niebuhr 'defeats his own pluralism: ... that is, he construes ... multiplicity more as threat and temptation than as an ambiguous plenum of relations.' She, by contrast, wants to say of women that they 'sense ... that precisely such assertion of a one against the cosmic many is an androcentric principle'. Keller concludes: 'Philosophically and theologically, a radical monism or monotheism too easily tempts us away from a truly multiple integrity.'[3]

It is indeed the honouring of pluralism, rather than seeing the nature of reality as unitary, which has been fundamental to those who have joined the pagan movement. This becomes very clear in the critique of monotheism brought forward by Margot Adler. Monotheism is said to be dualistic, and to foster hierarchy.[4] Emily Culpepper, in an article which she designates a 'sympathetic critique' of contemporary Goddess theology (the term is often used for thought about the Goddess, in contrast with theology, which concerns the male God) is of like opinion. She writes: 'There is too much wonderful diversity, contrast and movement in the world – what de Beauvoir has called "the plurality of the concrete" – for the One to function positively as our major symbol. We need symbols for unity, but the unity of the many is very different from a collapse of all diversity into a static One.... Starkly put, The One is basically a hostile term for feminists.'[5] Speaking from such a perspective, she finds herself critical of those within the Goddess movement who would seem to

replace the monotheistic male God with a similar, but female, Goddess. Rather would she have us seek out images which reflect plurality.

But Christianity is not simply a religion of monotheism, the monotheism of a transcendent, all-powerful God. There are other themes
present. The characteristic attributes of monotheism may be said to
be mitigated both through the doctrine of the trinity, which embodies
relationality, and through the doctrine of the incarnation, which
speaks of a giving up of power in favour of powerlessness. I want to
suggest however that, although it may indeed be the case that these
themes serve as a partial corrective to the primary way in which God
is envisaged, they are not particularly useful to feminists. Moreover,
I believe it to be the case that specifically feminist values and
paradigms do not find expression in the basic structuring of the
Christian religion.

The doctrine of the trinity is indeed an understanding of God as
relational. But it is this only in a limited way. The persons of the
trinity are said to be alike save in their mutual relations: namely, the
Son is held to be dependent on the Father. (The very use of the
metaphors of 'Father' and 'Son' convey to the mind's eye a particular
kind of relation, which is not one of equality.) Many people however
(as I earlier indicated) appear to have given up all understanding of
God as relational, their religion consisting rather in a polytheism of
two (perhaps three) gods. But – given that we take the classical
understanding of the trinity, which sees God in God's self as relational – it must still be said that the relation concerned is that of a
Father and a Son. The trinity does not as a symbol embody equality
between male and female.

Nor does the doctrine of the trinity imply that, unlike what is the
case in a transcendent monotheism, God is conceived as one with humankind, or as promoting equality between human beings. It is classically held that, through the taking on of humanity by the second
person of the trinity in the incarnation, humanity is taken into God.
But this is humanity taken into God: humanity is still not the
primary focus of our attention. God moreover, even though in Himself trinity, is still held to have aseity. He is the creator of humans,
and their saviour. This is scarcely a paradigm which embodies
reciprocity. Nor is it the case that one whose theology is deeply
trinitarian necessarily espouses equal relationships between woman
and man. Barth, one might think, has every opportunity to expound
the relation between woman and man as paralleling the relation

between Son and Father. But in fact when he turns to the relation of God to humanity, Barth speaks in terms of hierarchy, both between God and humans and, within humanity, between man and woman.

The transcendent monotheism of an all-powerful God is also clearly mitigated within Christianity by the particular way in which incarnation has often been understood. Following Paul in Philippians chapter 2, there is said to have been a *kenosis* or voluntary self-emptying on the part of the second person of the trinity. It is however difficult, one suspects, for more radical Christians to take this up as a model for God, as they tend not to think in terms of incarnation. Rosemary Ruether, while not speaking of incarnation, points to the fact that Jesus' conduct as a person offers a challenge to patriarchy. She writes:

> Jesus as the Christ ... manifests the *kenosis of patriarchy*, the announcement of the new humanity through a lifestyle that discards hierarchical caste privilege and speaks on behalf of the lowly. ... [The] system [of patriarchal privilege] is unmasked and shown to have no connection with favor with God. Jesus, the homeless Jewish prophet, and the marginalized women and men who respond to him represent the overthrow of the present world system and the sign of a dawning new age in which God's will is done on earth.[6]

But if Jesus is not directly said to be God, then this cannot (except in so far as Jesus may be said to show us what God is like) influence our understanding of God.

Moreover, it is far from clear that the theme of *kenosis* is the way in which monotheism would need to be qualified in order to bring the understanding of God more into line with feminist values. Clearly *kenosis* is indeed a critique of patriarchy. That it should have featured prominently in Christian thought is perhaps an indication of the fact that men have understood what the male problem, in thinking of terms of hierarchy and domination, has been. It may well be a model which men need to appropriate and which may helpfully be built into the male understanding of God. But, as we have said in our discussion of what salvation might be for women, the theme of self-emptying and self-abnegation is far from helpful as a paradigm. *Kenosis* is a counter-theme within male thought. It does not build what might be said to be specifically feminist values into our understanding of God. Such feminist themes as that for example of the mutual empowerment of persons would seem to be absent from the symbolism of Christian theology.[7]

RENAMING GOD

I come then to a consideration of the attempt by feminists of recent years to use different, and specifically female, language for God. Nothing would seem to indicate better the incompatibility between feminism and Christianity than the difficulty in naming God in a female way within that tradition. Yet that they should see God in their own image, and not in the image of the opposite sex, has become fundamental to many women. Christian feminists try to introduce female language into the Christian religion. Matriarchalists, on account of what they believe to be the insuperable nature of the problem, have moved outside the religion. Of course it is not simply a case of using different language. Female metaphors carry other resonances and convey a different sense of God or of the divine.

The opposition with which the use of female language for God is met by many Christians provides a good indication of how fundamental it has been to Christianity that God is conceived as male. In Scotland when Anne Hepburn, closing the opening devotions of the Woman's Guild as its President, used the words 'Dear Mother God' this did not pass unnoticed. The church set up a commission to study the question of the theological implications of the 'Motherhood' of God, both representatives of the Woman's Guild and of the church's Panel on Doctrine being invited to serve. The matter rapidly became a matter of heated national debate. The commission in its report considered all aspects of the question, concluding (of the biblical material) that while God is never addressed directly as mother there are present female metaphors for God.[8] When the report was placed before the 1984 General Assembly, Hepburn, who presented it, was met with jeers and sarcasm, and the behaviour of certain ministers and elders was such that – in an almost unprecedented occurrence – the Moderator was moved to rebuke the Assembly for its rudeness. Having conducted no proper debate on the report's contents, the Assembly proceeded to vote 'to depart from the matter'.[9]

There is indeed a very real problem here. The Jewish and Christian traditions overwhelmingly make use of male metaphors in describing God, and unfailingly address God in words that, in the society in which they came to be used of God, referred exclusively to males. It is not clear what the justification can be for introducing female language for God. That some Christians have become concerned not to be exclusive of women, and that many women have come to feel strongly about inclusive language, is another matter.

Often feminist women will simply proceed to use such language, whether or not it is biblical or there is any warrant in the tradition for such a naming of God. Christian feminism then becomes frankly syncretistic, women saying that they will draw on the biblical language in so far as this is useful, and supplement what is perceived to be a deficiency in the Jewish and Christian traditions by drawing on other sources.

Thus Rosemary Ruether has edited a collection of texts intended to 'provide a resource for the doing of feminist theology', *Woman-guides*.[10] Feminist theology, she says 'must create a new textual base, a new canon; ... [it] cannot be done from the existing base of the Christian Bible'.[11] The collection consists of prose and pictures, from 'the ... cultural matrix that has shaped Western Christianity: the ancient Near East, the Hebrews, the Greeks, the New Testament, and the marginated communities at the edges of Judaism and Christianity'.[12] The texts and illustrations range variously from a picture of the Goddess Isis leading Queen Nefertari by the hand, to a psalm addressed to the great Goddess of Babylonia; from the Holy Spirit conceived as Mother in Syriac Christianity, to the Father/Mother God of Christian Science; from the Rabbinic tradition of Lilith, to the medieval understanding of Christ as mother; and from stories of women in the Christian gospels to those of courageous women in the nineteenth century. The aim is 'to make women's experience visible'.[13] Both through the symbolization of the female in mythology and through the stories of the lives of actual women, women are to be given a sense of their tradition.

I find myself sceptical. I fail to see how this can be named 'our' experience? Women know so little about women in ancient Egypt that they have to be told about it. Why indeed should women particularly want to associate with women in the remote past, in a wholly different society? Under the picture showing the Goddess Isis with Queen Nefertari we find the caption: 'Hand in hand, women guide each other as they claim their buried past and journey to the place of the death of patriarchy and the beginning of new possibilities for womanbeing.' Can this possibly be meaningful? I doubt it in modern Europe. Perhaps, in the different cultural atmosphere of the United States, it is. Women can scarcely use these images, can they, as vehicles through which to reach God? Again, I find myself unclear how it can be that 'the texts provide norms for judging good and evil, truth and falsehood, for judging what is of God/ess and what is spurious and demonic'.[14] It is presumably intended that such a collection shall provide material for use in women's base communities, such as those which Ruether advocates in her book *Women-Church*.[15] There 'women-church' is described as a 'feminist exodus community', one which, while remaining within the church, has a different centre. Though for the present a separatist movement of women, the hope is expressed that it will become possible to have 'a new cohumanity of men and women liberated from patriarchy'.[16] Why, however, is this to be designated 'church'? It would appear to be a community which celebrates women's experience; it is not clear how it is that it centres upon God.

The most sophisticated attempt that has been made to rename God, and to rewrite systematic theology around this renaming, is Sallie McFague's book *Models of God*.[17] McFague starts out from the question as to what kinds of metaphor are pragmatically useful to us in this our 'ecological' 'nuclear' age? What metaphors, she asks, will best convey the Christian faith? She suggests, firstly, that the world be conceived as 'God's body', taking up an ancient motif which fell by the wayside; secondly, that God be conceived as mother, as lover and as friend. The metaphor of the world as God's body suggests God's integral connection with the world, if also God's transcendence to it, as are we to our bodies. God as mother allows us to conceive that God is intimately and impartially concerned for the world; God as lover tells of God's passion for the world and of God's suffering with it; while God as friend suggests that God sustains the world, working in a reciprocal relationship with us. The skill of McFague's discussion lies in the fact that she does not simply substitute female images for male. Through the use of different and suggestive metaphors – which she concedes are only metaphors – she gives us a whole different sense of what God may be.

If I admire this book (though McFague does not conceive God in the kind of way in which I myself wish to do so), I must also raise basic questions about it. My problem with it is that it tries to straddle a fence; and in the process I think masks a basic confusion. Is it Christian? In the course of the book – after what was, in my case, considerable bafflement – we become clear that, according to the definition of Christian which I suggested,[18] it could not be counted such. Jesus is not unique. He is a 'paradigmatic person'. And in this he is not alone. He is simply, for Christians, their 'foundational figure'.[19] If this is the case – and Jesus is a very fine human being, but not God – then there are passages which are confusing. Jesus, in his life and death, she tells us, 'manifests ... that the heart of the universe is unqualified love.... This we never would have guessed.'[20] This sounds more like revelation? Again, she speaks of God's 'incarnation – ... in paradigmatic individuals, most notably, Jesus of Nazareth'.[21] What can that mean? If Jesus is one among others, it would seem unlikely that he can be so exceptional. She more than once implies (or does not contradict the idea) that Jesus could heal. (I do not doubt myself that he had healing powers; but then there are those who have this capacity today.) She, however, suggests this of none other.

Given that hers is, according to my definition, not a Christian position, then of course she may construct whatever models for God she may wish. These models need have nothing in common with past models, though past models may also be taken up if they seem helpful. Has she chosen well? I think that for many people these models may indeed be useful: they are more impressive as she develops them than one might imagine to be the case from the bald statement that God is to be described as mother, lover and friend; or that the world is to be conceived as God's body – with the slightly odd imagery that that conjures up. Yet – as one who is in the position of being a post-Christian – I have moved considerably further from classical models for God. I find myself asking then whether such a highly anthropomorphic conceptualization of God as these metaphors convey is really credible today? Consider some examples of the way in which McFague speaks. She conceives of God's 'loving attention';[22] of God as creator; of God as participating in the pain of the world. Again, she says that God needs us. What kind of an agent is this? What kind of an anthropomorphic being? One understands why Christians should have an anthropomorphic model of God: anthropomorphism is basic both to the biblical texts and to the tradition. As a post-Christian however, free to conceptualize God as one will, should one not move further out?

But of course McFague wishes to be Christian. Indeed, in concluding her book she comments that it is no coincidence that she has advocated three models for God, and that they '[fall] into the categories of creator, savior and sustainer', replacing the trinitarian model. Her project constitutes 'a deliberate attempt to unseat those names as descriptions of God which will allow no supplements or alternatives'.[23] So then I have a different question. How can the Christian church make use of her models, how can they mesh with the models which it already has? For it can hardly be that her models will replace the former models. As long as Christians read the Hebrew and Christian scriptures, or address God through the Lord's prayer (which they will presumably continue to do), they will conceive God in a different way, using different metaphors, from those which she advocates. The way of speaking of God present in the bible and in the church is (as she sees) highly authoritarian. All power, whether (in her words) of 'domination or benevolence', is God's.[24] We shall have a different religion if, of God's relation to the world, we may say of her that she is related to the world as to her body. It is as though the cuckoo has used the nest to lay its egg and ousted the previous chicks.

Indeed the more I ponder this book, the less clear I become how it is that it is theistic. The definition which she gives of being Christian is that it is 'to believe that the universe is neither malevolent nor indifferent but is on the side of life and its fulfillment'.[25] But how is it that this is not simply humanism? Atheists may dare to have faith (and she speaks as though Christianity is an attitude of faith) that at the heart of things lies goodness rather than evil, may they not? I would agree that it is prerequisite to holding a religious outlook to espouse such a stance. But that is not to say that everyone who espouses such a stance is thereby Christian, perhaps not even theistic. I become all the more unclear how it is that this is a theistic model (in the commonly understood sense of the term) when I hear that there is no unmediated divine presence, that we are to relate to God through relating to the world, and that God loves not individuals but the world as a whole.[26] What reason has she for speaking of God, such that her position is indeed theistic? Theologians surely construct models for God either because they believe in particular revelation (which she does not), in which case their models in some way presumably follow the biblical pattern; or because they believe (as she does not) that we can speak of personal religious experience. That is to say, the construction of models for God is predicated upon what one construes to be evidence for belief in God; which one then wants to capture in a model. Her work lacks talk of such evidence.

I turn then to the position of those who hold that there is no genuine place for female symbols within the Christian religion: that women, if they are to come into their own, must needs move outside it and espouse rather the symbol of the Goddess. The case for this has been made forcefully by Carol P. Christ, most notably in her article 'Why Women Need the Goddess'.[27] 'Symbol systems', Christ argues, 'cannot simply be rejected, they must be replaced. Where there is not any replacement, the mind will revert to familiar structures at times of crisis, bafflement, or defeat.'[28] It will not do, she contends, to name the divine 'It'; rather should we say 'She'. Christ writes:

> The more radical proposal that female language be used in addressing God is more adequate, I believe, than the proposal that sex-linked language for God be avoided. I do not believe the hold of the male image of God on the Western mind will be broken or that women will fully recognize themselves in the image of God until female God language counters the traditional symbols.[29]

Religions centred on the worship of a male God, Christ argues, keep women in a state of 'psychological dependence' on men. A woman 'can never have the experience that is freely available to every man and boy in her culture, of having her full sexual identity affirmed as being in the image and likeness of God'.[30]

Clearly this is a powerful argument. One can, as a woman who grew up within the western tradition, scarcely conceive what it would be like to be of the same gender as the personal pronoun used for God. People may be dismissive of the idea that the gender attributed to God is of any import, informing us that God is 'beyond' sex. But such thinking should not be granted. Symbols are effective at a subconscious and pre-rational level. Hence the point made by the joke about the person who came back from the dead and, asked what God is like, replied 'She's black'. The fact that we are brought up short shows us how deep are our presuppositions. I well remember the quiet smile which crept across my face – and I am no Conservative – when in the early days the BBC would report 'the Prime Minister, ... she'. It did me a world of good at a time when, on account of my sex, I had been denied ordination to the diaconate. We should not, then, underestimate the impact which it may make on us, even though we know the word to be a symbol, of naming the divine 'She'.

The problem with the use of female language for God is that it is difficult to avoid its conjuring up a feminine understanding of God – just as indeed male language has always carried with it a masculine image, as masculine has in our society been conceived. Talk of God as 'mother' or as 'nurturative' may well imply (and serve to reinforce) a certain understanding of women. If the divine, no less, as female, has this essential nature, then these traits and characteristics (it will be thought) must surely belong to some essential nature of woman. Many women, not least those who are feminists, would surely be worried by this. Sallie McFague tries hard to avoid such a pitfall, insisting that she is using female metaphors, not suggesting a supposedly 'feminine' understanding, one which would seem to limit women in what they can be or do. Much Christian feminism is, one would think, less careful here.

Finally, it must be said that the use of both personal pronouns together for God, cannot but cause a certain confusion, not necessarily helpful in worship. It is frequently held that, in theology, we need the richness that only the clustering of a variety of images, which capture different aspects of God, can supply. But 'he' and 'she' are mutually exclusive. I want to know how I could direct my attention to one whom, with Rosemary Ruether, I named 'God/ess'. Again a sentence like Sallie McFague's 'God as lover finds all species of flora and fauna ... attractive, she finds ...; God as lover finds himself ...' leaves me baffled.[31]

Carol Christ suggests that if we do not replace the naming of God as 'he' by 'she', we shall in time of crisis turn again to a male God. I know the temptation; when I first attempted to move beyond Christianity I would frequently revert to calling God 'Father' – as I had all my life. But, as my understanding of God has evolved, it would simply no longer make sense to me to name God explicitly anthropomorphically. If I need to name God, it is better for me to say simply 'God'. (In lecturing I repeat the word God, as for example 'God in God's self ...' rather than use a personal pronoun, and my students adopt the habit.) I do not believe that the word God any longer has deeply anthropomorphic or male connotations for me. But then I am not a Christian and do not hear it used in church in conjunction with anthropomorphic language about God, nor read a bible in which God is described in masculine terms. I have found it the easiest transition to make. Moreover it does not have the problems associated with either anthropomorphic naming, or specifically female naming. It is the best that I can do.

THE SHAPE OF GOD

An observant friend once remarked that whereas Christian feminists want to change the actors in the play, what I want is a different kind of play. It is true that Christian feminists, wishing to stay within the Christian tradition, have on the whole experimented with renaming God: in order, that is, to continue the analogy, to have different actors. Of course referring to God as Mother rather than as

Father does give one a different sense of God. But it continues to be in effect the Christian God, placed within the Christian story. God is an agent, an actor on the scene, conceived anthropomorphically, if now named by female names. Some feminists however, myself included, have wanted to reconceive what the term 'God' connotes. I think it must be true of all of them that in doing this they have moved outside the Christian tradition. They want a different kind of play. Of course that is not to say that elements of this play are not to be found within the Christian tradition of the west. God is not there conceived wholly anthropomorphically.

I want here to consider one example of a transformation in the understanding of what one might mean by God, an example which has caught the feminist imagination. I refer to Alice Walker's discussion in the central chapter, the chapter which gives the novel its title, of *The Color Purple*.[32] The chapter contains in short compass, and in inimitable language, discussion of many of the themes of this present book. There is consideration of theodicy. The central character, Celie, finds that she has to divest herself of her previous understanding of God because He has, given the circumstances of her life, become incredible. Yet trying to do without Him is a strain; something which must be familiar to many a feminist who was earlier immersed within the Christian tradition. To go through the shift which she undertakes, Celie needs the help of a friend. In this discussion of the nature of God, the novel is really about the feminist imagination, the possibility of thinking new thoughts. In other respects too the book concerns themes which have been central to this present book. It is within the community of a group of women that Celie comes to heal. Indeed it might well be said to be a novel about 'salvation' if salvation be defined as healing.

The plot of this novel will be well known to many of my readers. Celie, poor and Black, grows up in the rural American south in the early part of this century. She is raped by the man whom she takes to be her father, by whom she has two children. Celie is then married off to a man who treats her with considerable bestiality, whom she refers to simply as Mr _____. Celie's two children have gone to Africa with Nettie, her much loved sister, whom she never expects to see again. Meanwhile Celie has developed a ripening friendship with Shug, short for Sugar, which is transforming her life. The book takes the form of letters. Celie at first, from age fourteen, writes to 'God'. Later she and Nettie have made contact and Celie writes to her.

Central to the book I believe is Celie's reconception of what she understands by God. As long as she had simply to reject the earlier 'God' she had known, there was a hole in her life. The reshaping of her understanding of God, so that that understanding now fits the rest of what may be called her life-philosophy, allows her to gain a certain completeness. In the final letter of the book she can again address herself to God, a God now associated with her love of the world and of other people. She perceives God – to employ the language I shall use in the final section of this book – in and with her perception of all else. She writes: 'Dear God. Dear stars, dear trees, dear sky, dear peoples. Dear God.'[33]

I turn then to a consideration of the chapter in which she reports the shift in her conceptualization of God.[34] Celie writes of a conversation with Shug, the starting-point of which was that her previous 'God' has been thrown out and become wholly superfluous to her life. The relationship to other women – symbolized by the fact that she now writes to Nettie, not God – appears to have replaced the need for such a God. Celie writes to Nettie as follows.

> I don't write to God no more, I write to you.
>   What happen to God? ast Shug.
>   Who that? I say.
>   She look at me serious.
>   Big a devil as you is, I say, you not worried bout no God, surely.
>   She say, Wait a minute. Hold on just a minute here. Just because I don't harass it like some peoples us know don't mean I ain't got religion.
>   What God do for me? I ast.
>   She say, Celie! Like she shock. He gave you life, good health, and a good woman that love you to death.
>   Yeah, I say, and he give me a lynched daddy, a crazy mama, a low-down dog of a step pa and a sister I probably won't ever see again. Anyhow, I say, the God I been praying and writing to is a man. And act just like all the other mens I know. Trifling, forgitful and lowdown.

Though she may be angry, and the God of Christianity has become an impossibility to her, Celie has nothing else to which to turn. 'She', in what follows, is Shug.

> She talk and she talk, trying to budge me way from blasphemy. But I blaspheme much as I want to.
>   All my life I never care what people thought bout nothing I did, I say. But deep in my heart I care about God. What he going to think. And come to find out, he don't think. Just sit up there glorying in being deef,

I reckon. But it ain't easy, trying to do without God. Even if you know
he ain't there, trying to do without him is a strain.

In a lovely turn, Shug proceeds to find out how Celie has conceived
this God whom she has rejected. As she discovers, 'He' is in the image
of the people who have damaged Celie's life, white and male.

I decide to stick up for him, just to see what Shug say.
Okay, I say. He big and old and tall and graybearded and white. He
wear white robes and go barefooted.
Blue eyes? she ast.
Sort of bluish-gray. Cool. Big though. White lashes, I say.
She laugh.

It takes Celie an effort to understand that 'God' is not, as she had
supposed, a given, but that in a white, patriarchal, society 'God' has
been shaped in the image of those who have created Him. Shug tells
her: 'If you wait to find God in church, Celie, ... that's who is bound to
show up, cause that's where he live.' Celie is incensed: 'God wrote the
bible, white folks had nothing to do with it.' How then, asks Shug,
who had gone through her own revolution, that the God of the bible
looks like white folks. Shug comments: 'When I found out I thought
God was white, and a man, I lost interest.' The penny drops for Celie.
The image of God, as she has known Him, becomes for her relativized, the product of the people who have conceived Him.
But Shug is not living in a religious wilderness. She has been able
to develop what she earlier knew of God within Christianity and
arrive at a conception which is vital, encompassing and intrinsic to
human beings. Shug has earlier said to Celie that 'any God I ever felt
in church I brought in with me'; that people 'come to church to share
God not to find God'. Celie reports to Nettie: 'Here's the thing, say
Shug. The thing I believe. God is inside you and inside everybody
else.' God comes to be seen to be available and present through all
that is. It is not pantheism: God is not equated with the world. But
God may be perceived in all beauty and in human relationships.
Shug tells Celie:

You come into the world with God. But only them that search for it
inside find it.
And sometimes it just manifest itself even if you not looking, or don't
know what you looking for....
It? I ast.

Yeah, It. God ain't a he or a she, but a It.

But what do it look like? I ast.

Don't look like nothing, she say. It ain't a picture show. It ain't something you can look at apart from anything else, including yourself. I believe God is everything, say Shug. Everything that is or ever was or ever will be. And when you can feel that, and be happy to feel that, you've found it.

Shug tells Celie of the quiet revolution through which she herself had gone: 'She say, my first step from the old white man was trees. Then air. Then birds. Then other people.' The sense of God is for Shug vitally bound up with a sense of connectedness. 'One day when I was sitting quiet and feeling like a motherless child, which I was, it come to me: that feeling of being part of everything, not separate at all.' This is a new world, in which God is not conceived as an 'other' in apposition to humankind, but is part of the one reality of all that is.

Celie begins to breathe again, to become a religious person. She sees that she has been so obsessed with the God she now turns her back on, so angry with the God who gloried in being deaf, that she has failed to have eyes for the manifestation of God in the world around her. Shug declares: 'I think it pisses God off if you walk by the color purple in a field somewhere and don't notice it.' Her new insight has for Celie the quality of a revelation: 'I been so busy thinking bout him I never truly notice nothing God make. Not a blade of corn (how it do that?) not the color purple (where it come from?). Not the little wildflowers. Nothing.'

The theodicy problem is not cured. It is not that evil no longer exists. But the evil which has been meted out to her no longer has the power to overwhelm her. 'Now that my eyes opening, I feels like a fool. Next to any little scrub of a bush in my yard, Mr ____'s evil sort of shrink. But not altogether.' The real salvation lies in the fact that she has come into her own, so that the world of men is not to be allowed to dominate her. In her new situation, male behaviour will no longer be able to obscure God for her. 'Still, it is like Shug say, You have to git man off your eyeball, before you can see anything a'tall.' She reports to Nettie: 'Man corrupt everything, say Shug. He on your box of grits, in your head, and all over the radio. He try to make you think he everywhere. Soon as you think he everywhere, you think he God. But he ain't.' She has come to have her own estimate of things, an estimate reinforced by a society of women which she has entered, rather than being in a situation where ideologically the image of God reinforced the hierarchical and exploitive world she had known.

The real difficulty – as many feminists have surely found – is actually coming to credit, emotionally and at the level of the imagination, the transition which with one's intellect one may be ready to make. 'Us talk and talk bout God, but I'm still adrift. Trying to chase that old white man out of my head.' The problem is the most acute, and the transition the least easily made (as I shall come to consider below) in the realm of addressing God in prayer. Celie writes to Nettie: 'Whenever you trying to pray, and man plop himself on the other end of it, tell him to git lost, say Shug. Conjure up flowers, wind, water, a big rock. But this hard work, let me tell you. He been there so long, he don't want to budge.'

Taking as her example the dialogue in *The Color Purple* which I have just considered, Mary Daly suggests that the naming of what she calls 'deep Reality' by the term 'It', or even 'God', male term though that be, may actually be more revolutionary if taken to denote a different reality, than is the naming of the male God-as-ever-was, 'She'. The meaning of a word must be understood in the context of what it is that it is intended to convey. 'It', a more neutral term, Daly contends, may be preferable to the *'apparently* more radical choice of female pronouns and nouns for divinity'. She writes:

> The use of the feminine forms merely suggests that the christian divinity ... is so superior and magnanimous that he can contain all female values. ... The christian god can arrogantly announce that he is also a 'she' (during alternative services) and doesn't mind occasionally being referred to as 'the Goddess' (whose history and force he has vampirized, contained, and reversed for millennia). ... In contrast to this, the apparently neuter 'It' and even 'God,' as these function in the context of Shug Avery and Other Crones, work as instruments of Other-centered intuition and communication. ... Shape-shifting, then, is contextual. The occasional appearance of old words, such as 'God' and 'It' to Name deep Reality, can serve as a reminder to examine the atmosphere in which words are spoken. Such jarring of the radical imagination can work for [feminists] as a safeguard against using and accepting Hag-identified [viz. women-identified] new words as taken-for-granted labels, converting them into mere foreground terms.[35]

By foreground terms Daly evidently means that, while it appears that much has changed, for now female imagery is being used, the change is but superficial in that the same God is conveyed. Meanwhile, as she says, the God of the tradition, now female, has absorbed women's reality into the tradition of western theological thought, thus hiding what in fact the fate of God conceived as female has been within the western tradition.

What of Daly's own position? There has been development, even since she explicitly defined herself as postchristian.[36] The last chapter of *Beyond God the Father* still retains what have been Christian sensibilities, though now converted into another and feminist mode.[37] Thus she conceives there to be some kind of a *telos* or goal, some concerted movement towards a better world. The goal, it should be noted, is not however the static goal of Christian theology, but the goal of human fulfilment. The Aristotelian 'final cause' now becomes the cause of women, that movement which lies behind all genuine movement. She is very interested in process, in becoming. The sacred she conceives as manifesting itself, not once but once and again. Daly has not developed these themes, and has moved beyond any explicitly religious language. She no longer refers to herself as postchristian. Still to say that her work was not 'religious' in a wider sense of the word would, I think, be to misunderstand it. Fundamental to her outlook is a sense of the goodness and beauty of what is, of the possibilities of creation. A sense of wonder pervades her writing – and lies behind her outrage at the annihilative forces of patriarchy.

I think that the real question for those who, like myself, wish to have no anthropomorphically conceived God, yet a theistic sensibility, is the question of the possibility of prayer. Prayer, one might think, is almost by definition a turning to one conceived as a 'thou', one who in our imagination stands over-against us as a kind of entity. Certainly this is the dominant form that prayer has taken in the west; which is why indeed God has been conceived using anthropomorphic vocabulary. Conversely it may be that it is the use of such vocabulary, coupled with the understanding of God as an agent able to act upon the world, which has promoted such prayer. Rita Gross, herself Jewish, at an earlier stage of her spiritual journey (for she is now Buddhist) captures this well:

> I am convinced that Judaism is theistic through and through and that theism – the view that the absolute can be imaged as a person entering into relationships of love and responsibility with humans – requires anthropomorphism. ... The Jewish religious enterprise involves talking ... *to* God. ... Anthropomorphism can be exorcised from theology to some degree; but it is the inevitable concomitant of theism and prayer.[38]

What may we say of the attempt to pray when one has moved beyond such a conceptualization of God? Maybe there will always be times when humans, because of what they are, need to turn to 'God' as to a very real 'other'. As human beings we only know of relations with other persons which are inter-personal – and we naturally model God upon such relationships. We should hold in mind however that because we picture God in this way, it does not necessarily follow that God is in fact a kind of anthropomorphic agent, able to intervene in the world, or indeed a spiritual entity, complete in God's self, and independent of the world. Nor should one limit the possibility of prayer to a situation conceived as dialogue between an I and a thou. As one's intellectual understanding of what the word God connotes changes, so too may one's practice. It may well become more natural (perhaps building on sensibilities which were earlier present in one's prayer but not dominant) to speak of resting in God. One may think of oneself as being open and present to what one conceives to be a greater reality than one's self, knowing oneself as loved and upheld. I should not now want to speak of worship of God, which has hierarchical connotations. I tend not to think of God as a 'thou'. But I should have no difficulty in saying, with Julian of Norwich, of God, that God is one 'in whom my soul standeth'. Furthermore I am – as a feminist interested in coming into my own – excited by the possibility of taking up the daring words which Catherine of Siena is reputed to have uttered: 'My real me is God.'

PERCEPTIVITY

Our consciousness of God arises I believe through our perceptivity. I use this term both for our response to God in the world and for a more direct awareness of God, as for example when someone prays for us and we are helped. The starting-point for theology is our openness to that which we then name God. Theology is a second-order discipline. It is because our experience is what it is, that we undertake the task of theology. That is not of course to say that our theological formulation is without effect on the quality of our experience and the interpretation which we give to it. But the experience is prior, and our attempt to conceptualize what it may imply, predicated upon it. The task of theology is to understand as best we may what it is that is the case, such that our experience is what it is.

I am very clear then that for me the word 'God' refers. It is not simply a construct in language; however profoundly our conceptualization of God be shaped by the linguistic and cultural tradition to which we belong. Nor is using religious language for me simply a way of naming the world, a way of affirming (for example) that I will have faith that there is an underlying goodness. (Though such a faith may indeed be prerequisite to construing the world religiously.) To affirm that the word 'God' refers is however not necessarily to believe that the word refers to a kind of entity, one which could be distinguished from all else that is. It has always been recognized in theology that there is a necessary problem in naming God – and mystics have deliberately chosen negative language, saying what God is not, rather than falsely confine our sense of God through inadequate vocabulary. The word God names what one concludes must be the case, the other level of reality which one believes to exist. If it were not that prayer is effective, I cannot see what grounds there could be for using the word God.

What strikes me then about much modern theology – and this is not least true of feminist theology – is how profoundly secular it is. It is as though theology has lost its moorings. In the case of feminist theology, what seems to have replaced talk of God is largely talk of women's experience. It is not even women's experience of God: it is simply women's experience. Thus Elisabeth Schüssler Fiorenza tells us of the community of women in the early church, celebrating their courage in adversity and their egalitarian politics. Rosemary Ruether looks to alternative traditions within the Christian heritage, suggesting that here we may find communities, the knowledge of which will empower us. Mary Daly advocates the self-realization of women and the overcoming of oppression in a new age. Catherine Keller weaves together an understanding of the person as relational, but – except for a few glances sideways – fails to draw out what the implications of such a construal of reality might be for an understanding of God. Sallie McFague does indeed consider what metaphors we should use for God. But when all is said and done it is unclear to me whether she is in fact speaking of God, or rather of an attitude to life. In all this, what I miss is 'theology': talk of God.

Of course the problem which a position such as mine that rests on experience encounters is that experience is so personal that it is difficult to convey to another. (And certainly embarrassing to write about in a book!) Moreover experience at second hand is easy to dismiss. It must – we surmise – have resulted from social conditioning, or the peculiar state of mind in which our friend found herself. (Besides which – a feminist will say - is it not pietistic, and individualistic?) It is however the case that some kind of evidence can be collected. The material assembled in recent years by Sir Alister Hardy and his team of researchers at the Oxford Religious Experience Research Unit is I believe impressive.[39] It must be significant that so many should be prepared to answer in the affirmative the basic question which the Unit asks: 'Have you ever been aware of or influenced by a presence or power, whether you call it God or not, which is different from your everyday self?'[40] I should have thought that what convinces many is that, as they are open and receptive, they find that they are helped in ways of which they could not have conceived, or made aware of what they could not otherwise have known to be the case. Hardy reports, for example, of a woman who implores her husband to take her home at once, arriving just in time to rescue her baby from a burning house[41] – and many others have had such experiences, if not so dramatic. To be religious may be to choose to view the world a certain way. But it is to choose to view the world a certain way in response to what we find to be the case.

Given such a world of experience, the theological question arises as to how we shall interpret it. There is no need, necessarily, to think that God exists apart from humankind. We lack any way of determining the answer to such questions as whether God would exist if human beings did not, or whether God existed before the advent of human beings. It is fully comprehensible that people should have envisaged God as a kind of spiritual entity, one who exists apart from humankind. At times one does sense the presence of God so deeply that it makes sense to speak of God as though God were a 'person'. Presence is for human beings always personal, so no wonder we personalize God. But what in fact God is in God's self is another question. It seems to me to be far from axiomatic that it makes the most sense today to conceive God in traditional terms as a kind of agent, separate from the world, who can act upon it. Much in science (and contemporary thought forms) suggests that all power, all reality, is in some way in flow and interconnected. May 'God' not be a dimension of all that is?

What I believe we need to do then is to find a way to conceptualize God which is independent of the Christian myth, a myth which is neither tenable nor ethical. We must find a way to capture our experience of God in the language of our day. In doing this we shall be doing no more than did others in their time, drawing on the cultural milieu in which they lived. There is nothing to prevent our taking up past conceptualizations of God if we wish. But we are not constrained to do so if new thought forms appear more persuasive. We may believe that there is (if one takes what I have called a post-Christian stance) no privileged age, such that our understanding has to conform to the understanding of that past age. We shall need language and metaphor. But that we shall need a highly articulated mythology and symbolism, such as Christianity employs, would seem to be unlikely. It can hardly be that we require a comprehensive myth about creation, fall and salvation in order to speak of religious awareness. Nor do we necessarily, as I have suggested, need concrete and anthropomorphic images for God.

It is not the case – even if we want to think as radically as this – that there is nothing in the past on which we can draw. God has been conceived not simply as though God were an anthropomorphic spiritual object, but also as that which is through all, which upholds all and is the basis of all. There are various thinkers to whom one might turn. I find the thought of Friedrich Schleiermacher, the great theologian of the early nineteenth century, sometimes designated the founder of modern theology, to be an inspiration. For Schleiermacher opened up the possibility of conceiving that it is through our knowing of ourselves that we come to a perception of God. God is not to be known apart from ourselves, though God is more than are we. Methodologically it becomes possible to speak of God without dependence on particular revelation. (Though Schleiermacher himself, as a Christian, wanted subsequently to draw in revelation.) His work may well be open to a certain kind of reductionism. We live, as he did not, the other side of Feuerbach and of Freud, and ask the inevitable question as to how he can guard himself against the possibility that he may be deluded. I myself would want to bring forward much more empirical evidence for belief that there is a dimension of existence which we should name God than he ever adduces. But his conceptualization is fruitful. Thus one remains in dialogue with the tradition.

Christianity, it seems to me, has often short-changed people when it comes to developing their own religious awareness. Particularly is this true of Christianity in its Protestant form. To be religious – through the fact that Christianity has had a highly developed myth and structure of doctrine – has become a case of believing this system to be objectively true. (Dare I say that there may be something peculiarly male about this striving for distance and objectivity, rather than looking to one's own experience and possibility of receptivity?) It has in these circumstances been difficult for people to develop their own religious sensibilities. I have had occasion in recent years to witness people's reaction to me when I defined myself as religious, but not Christian. In Protestant circles this is often received with incomprehension. I remember one occasion on which an entire audience, the person in the chair and the other speaker, unitedly went for me. I admit to having been slightly shaken, but kept my cool. I was also observing (like a fly on the wall) the uproar. (Some members of the audience later apologized to me.) What struck me was that someone who proclaimed herself not to believe the revelation was deeply threatening; for, were there no revelation, the rug would have been pulled out from under the feet of those present. There seemed to be no deeper level at which they were religious persons.

Whether the quality of women's experience tends to be different, such that they may want to speak of God in other ways than do men, it must be difficult to know. There is possibly some evidence that women tend to conceptualize what God may be differently. But we have no test case: we have not been in a situation where women were free to name God as they would. Women have thought their thoughts within the context of a patriarchal society, dominated by a patriarchal religion. What I think we can say is that some of the thought forms which have developed, not least within feminism, in recent years, may be peculiarly suited to expressing what we mean by God. Thus a realization of relationality and of connectedness may well allow us the better to conceive how it is that prayer for another is effective. The interest which feminists have shown in the relationship of the self to its world may enable us to think in subtle and complex ways about that relationship between what we mean by self and what we mean by God. Feminist development of the ethical importance of the concept of attention to, or acute perception of, another, may allow us to think about receptivity to the presence of God in our world.

Feminist women will then find themselves to be at the forefront of theological thought. Many a woman – in a way in which this has not on the whole been true of men – has had to turn her back upon the religion within which she grew up. It simply became impossible. For any woman apprised of what the history of women has been, the question of theodicy raised by the previous conception of God has made that conception of God unthinkable. That God, moreover, was most clearly not made in her image, and became superfluous as she came to herself and acquired a feminist consciousness. In this situation there is, among those women who wish to find a way to be in some sense religious, a desire to find a way forward. What would seem to be crucial is the question as to whether we can learn to perceive, and to find new ways to conceive, the presence of God in our world. It is here that I believe that feminist paradigms may prove peculiarly useful. But that must be the subject of another book.

NOTES

1 See pp. 7–9, 41–4.
2 *The Redemption of God: A Theology of Mutual Relation* (Washington, DC: University Press of America, 1982), p. 156.
3 *From a Broken Web: Separation, Sexism, and Self* (Boston, MA: Beacon Press, 1986), p. 181.
4 *Drawing Down the Moon: Witches, Druids, Goddess-Worshippers, and Other Pagans in America Today* (New York: Viking Press, 1979), pp. 14–38.
5 'Contemporary Goddess Thealogy: A Sympathetic Critique', in C. Atkinson, C. Buchanan and M. Miles (eds), *Shaping New Vision: Gender and Values in American Culture* (Ann Arbor, MI: UMI Research Press, 1987), p. 65.
6 *Sexism and God-Talk: Toward a Feminist Theology* (Boston, MA: Beacon Press, 1983; London: SCM Press, 1983), pp. 137–8.
7 I pursue this theme in my 'On Power and Gender', *Modern Theology*, 4, no. 3 (April 1988).
8 A. Lewis (ed.), *The Motherhood of God: A Report by a Study Group appointed by the Woman's Guild and the Panel on Doctrine on the invitation of the General Assembly of the Church of Scotland* (Edinburgh: The Saint Andrew Press, 1984).
9 'Deliverances', *The Church of Scotland: General Assembly*, 1984, p. 7.
10 *Womanguides: Readings Toward a Feminist Theology* (Boston, MA: Beacon Press, 1985).
11 Ibid. p ix.
12 Ibid. p. xi.
13 Ibid. p. x.
14 Ibid. p. ix.
15 *Women-Church: Theology and Practice of Feminist Liturgical Communities* (San Francisco: Harper & Row, 1985).
16 Ibid. p. 61.
17 *Models of God: Theology for an Ecological, Nuclear Age* (Philadelphia, PA: Fortress Press, 1987; London: SCM Press, 1987).
18 See p. 50.
19 *Models of God*, p. 136.
20 Ibid. p. 55.
21 Ibid. p. 183.
22 Ibid. p. 72.
23 Ibid. p. 181.
24 Ibid. p. 64.
25 Ibid. p. 152.
26 Cf. ibid. pp. 60, 184–5, 86.
27 'Why Women Need the Goddess', in C. P. Christ and J. Plaskow (eds), *Womanspirit Rising: A Feminist Reader in Religion* (New York and San

Ruether

Ruether

Francisco: Harper & Row, 1979); and in *Laughter of Aphrodite: Reflections on a Journey to the Goddess* (San Francisco: Harper & Row, 1987).

28 'Why Women Need the Goddess', in *Womanspirit Rising*, p. 275.

29 'The New Feminist Theology: A Review of the Literature', *Religious Studies Review*, 3, no. 4 (October 1977), p. 207.

30 'Why Women Need the Goddess', in *Womanspirit Rising*, p. 275.

31 *Models of God*, p. 135.

32 *The Color Purple* (New York: Harcourt Brace Jovanovich, 1982; London: The Women's Press, 1983).

33 Ibid. p. 242.

34 Ibid. pp. 164–8.

35 *Pure Lust: Elemental Feminist Philosophy* (Boston, MA: Beacon Press, 1984; London: The Women's Press, 1984), pp. 403–4.

36 Daly, who invented the term, writes it thus.

37 *Beyond God the Father: Toward a Philosophy of Women's Liberation* (Boston, MA: Beacon Press, 1973; London: The Women's Press, 1986), pp. 180–93.

38 'Female God Language in a Jewish Context', in Christ and Plaskow (eds), *Womanspirit Rising*, pp. 168, 172.

39 Cf. Alister Hardy, *The Spiritual Nature of Man* (Oxford: Clarendon Press, 1979) and writings by other members of the Unit.

40 Ibid. pp. 125, 126. See also p. 18.

41 Ibid. p. 46.

SELECT BIBLIOGRAPHY

GENERAL COLLECTIONS

C. P. Christ and J. Plaskow (eds), *Womanspirit Rising: A Feminist Reader in Religion* (New York and San Francisco: Harper & Row,1979).
—— *Weaving the Visions: New Patterns in Feminist Spirituality* (New York and San Francisco: Harper & Row,1989).
Loades, A. (ed.) Feminist Theology: A Reader (London: SPCK, 1990 forthcoming; Louisville, KY: Westminster/John Knox Press, 1990 forthcoming).

FEMINIST LITERARY CRITICISM OF BIBLICAL TEXTS

Fuchs, Esther, 'The Literary Characterization of Mothers and Sexual Politics in the Hebrew Bible', in A. Yarbro Collins (ed.), *Feminist Perspectives on Biblical Scholarship* (Society of Biblical Literature, Centennial Publications; Chico, CA: Scholars Press, 1985).
—— 'Who Is Hiding the Truth? Deceptive Women and Biblical Androcentrism', in Yarbro Collins (ed.), *Feminist Perspectives.*
Furman, Nelly, 'His Story versus Her Story: Male Genealogy and Female Strategy in the Jacob Cycle', in Yarbro Collins (ed.), *Feminist Perspectives.*
Setel, Drorah, 'Prophets and Pornography: Female Sexual Imagery in Hosea', in L. Russell (ed.), *Feminist Interpretation of the Bible* (Philadelphia, PA: Westminster Press, 1985; Oxford: Basil Blackwell, 1985).
Trible, Phyllis, 'Depatriarchalizing in Biblical Interpretation', *JAAR*, 41, no. 1 (March 1973), pp. 30–48.
—— 'Eve and Adam: Genesis 2–3 Reread', in Christ and Plaskow (eds), *Womanspirit Rising. (Andover Newton Quarterly*, 13, March 1973.)
—— *God and the Rhetoric of Sexuality* (Philadelphia, PA: Fortress Press, 1978).
—— 'A Meditation in Mourning: The Sacrifice of the Daughter of Jephthah', *Union Seminary Quarterly Review*, 36, Supplementary Issue, 1981, pp. 59–73.

—— *Texts of Terror: Literary and Feminist Readings of Biblical Narratives* (Philadelphia, PA: Fortress Press, 1984).

WOMEN IN THE ANCIENT WORLD, NEW TESTAMENT, EARLY CHURCH AND MIDDLE AGES

Anselm: *The Prayers and Meditations of St. Anselm*, tr. B. Ward (Harmondsworth: Penguin Classics, 1973).

Aquinas, Thomas: A relevant selection from the *Summa Theologica* together with commentary is found in E. Clark and H. Richardson (eds), *Women and Religion: A Feminist Sourcebook of Christian Thought* (New York and San Francisco: Harper & Row, 1977).

Børresen, Kari, *Subordination and Equivalence: The Nature and Role of Women in Augustine and Thomas Aquinas*, tr. C. H. Talbot (Washington, DC: University Press of America, 1981).

Brooten, Bernadette, '"Junia ... Outstanding Among the Apostles" (Romans 16.17)', in L. Swidler and A. Swidler (eds), *Women Priests: A Catholic Commentary on the Vatican Declaration* (New York: Paulist Press, 1977).

—— 'Early Christian Women and Their Cultural Context: Issues of Method in Historical Reconstruction', in A. Yarbro Collins (ed.), *Feminist Perspectives on Biblical Scholarship* (Society of Biblical Literature, Centennial Publications; Chico, CA: Scholars Press,1985).

—— 'Paul's Views on the Nature of Woman and Female Homoeroticism', in C. Atkinson, C. Buchanan and M. Miles (eds), *Immaculate and Powerful: The Female in Sacred Image and Social Reality* (The Harvard Women's Studies in Religion Series; Boston, MA: Beacon Press, 1985).

Bynum, Caroline, *Jesus as Mother: Studies in the Spirituality of the High Middle Ages* (Berkeley, CA: University of California Press, 1982).

Cardman, Francine, 'The Medieval Question of Women and Orders', *The Thomist*, 42 (October 1978), pp. 582–99.

Julian of Norwich: *Revelations of Divine Love*, tr. C. Wolters (Harmondsworth: Penguin Classics, 1966).

McLaughlin, Eleanor, 'Equality of Souls, Inequality of Sexes: Woman in Medieval Theology', in R. Ruether (ed.), *Religion and Sexism: Images of Woman in the Jewish and Christian Traditions* (New York: Simon & Schuster, 1974).

—— '"Christ my Mother": Feminine Naming and Metaphor in Medieval Spirituality', *Nashotah Review*, 15, no. 3 (Fall 1975), pp. 366–86.

Ochshorn, Judith, *The Female Experience and the Nature of the Divine* (Bloomington, IN: Indiana University Press, 1981). A shorter version of her position is to be found in J. Kalven and M. Buckley (eds), *Women's Spirit Bonding* (New York: Pilgrim Press, 1984).

Pagels, Elaine, *The Gnostic Gospels* (New York: Random House, 1979).

Patterson, Lloyd, 'Women in the Early Church: A Problem of Perspective', in Marianne Micks (ed.), *Toward a New Theology of Ordination* (Somerville, MA: Greeno, Hadden. Copyright Virginia Theological Seminary, 1976).

Ruether, Rosemary, 'Misogynism and Virginal Feminism in the Fathers of the Church', in R. Ruether (ed.), *Religion and Sexism*.

Schüssler Fiorenza, Elisabeth, *In Memory of Her: A Feminist Theological Reconstruction of Christian Origins* (New York: Crossroad Publishing, 1983; London: SCM Press, 1983).

—— *Bread Not Stone: The Challenge of Feminist Biblical Interpretation* (Boston, MA: Beacon Press, 1984).

Swidler, Leonard, *Biblical Affirmations of Woman* (Philadelphia, PA: Westminster Press, 1979).

Tolbert, Mary Ann, 'Defining the Problem: The Bible and Feminist Hermeneutics', *Semeia*, 28 (Chico, CA: Scholars Press, 1983).

CHRISTOLOGY AND FEMINIST LIBERATION THEOLOGY

Heyward, Carter, *The Redemption of God: A Theology of Mutual Relation* (Washington, DC: University Press of America, 1982).

—— *Our Passion for Justice: Images of Power, Sexuality, and Liberation* (New York: Pilgrim Press, 1984).

Ruether, Rosemary, *New Woman, New Earth: Sexist Ideologies and Human Liberation* (New York: Seabury Press, 1975).

—— *To Change the World: Christology and Cultural Criticism* (New York: Crossroad Publishing, 1981; London: SCM, 1981).

—— *Women-Church: Theology and Practice of Feminist Liturgical Communities* (San Francisco: Harper & Row, 1985).

—— 'The Liberation of Christology from Patriarchy', *New Blackfriars*, 66, nos 781/782 (July, August 1985), pp. 324–33.

Russell, Letty, *Human Liberation in a Feminist Perspective* (Philadelphia, PA: Westminster Press, 1974).

Wilson-Kastner, Patricia, *Faith, Feminism and the Christ* (Philadelphia, PA: Fortress Press, 1983).

THE CONSERVATIVE CATHOLIC AND ORTHODOX RESPONSE

Demant, V. A. (Anglican), 'Why the Christian Priesthood is Male', *Women and Holy Orders: Report of the Archbishops' Commission*, appendix C (London: Church Information Office, 1966).

Hopko, Thomas (Orthodox), 'On the Male Character of Christian Priesthood', in T. Hopko (ed.), *Women and the Priesthood* (Crestwood, NY: St Vladimir's Seminary Press, 1983).

'Inter Insigniores: Declaration on the Question of the Admission of Women to the Ministerial Priesthood' (Roman) (Publications Service, Canadian

Conference of Catholic Bishops, Ottawa, Canada). Also given in L. Swidler and A. Swidler (eds), *Women Priests: A Catholic Commentary on the Vatican Declaration* (New York: Paulist Press, 1977).

Leonard, Graham (Anglican), 'The Ordination of Women: Theological and Biblical Issues', *Epworth Review*, 11, no. 1 (January 1984).

Lewis, C. S. (Anglican), 'Priestesses in the Church?', in W. Hooper (ed.), *God in the Dock: Essays on Theology and Ethics* (Grand Rapids, MI: William Eerdmans, 1970), and in Hooper (ed.), *Undeceptions: Essays on Theology and Ethics* (London: Geoffrey Bles, 1971) (1948).

Mascall, Eric (Anglican), 'Women Priests?' (pamphlet) (London: Church Literature Association, 1972 and 1977).

Moore, P. (ed.) (Ecumenical), *Man, Woman and Priesthood* (London: SPCK, 1978).

'The Ordination of Women: Official Commentary from the Sacred Congregation for the Doctrine of the Faith on its declaration *Inter Insigniores*: "Women and the Priesthood" of 15th October 1976' (Roman) (pamphlet) (London: Catholic Truth Society, undated).

THE CONSERVATIVE PROTESTANT RESPONSE

Barth, Karl, *Church Dogmatics*, vol. I.2, *The Doctrine of the Word of God* (E.T. Edinburgh: T. & T. Clark, 1956), pp. 190-3 (on Mary); *Church Dogmatics*, vol. III.1, *The Doctrine of Creation* (E.T. Edinburgh: T. & T. Clark, 1958), pp. 298–307 (on the relation of woman to man); vol. III.4, *The Doctrine of Creation* (E.T. Edinburgh: T. & T. Clark, 1961), pp. 162–81 (on the super-ordination and sub-ordination of man and woman). (Extracts from Barth, III.4, and a summary of his position, is given in E. Clark and H. Richardson (eds), *Women and Religion: A Feminist Sourcebook of Christian Thought*, New York and San Francisco: Harper & Row, 1977.)

For criticism of Barth from within a conservative Protestant perspective, see Paul Jewett, *Man as Male and Female* (Grand Rapids, MI: William Eerdmans, 1976). For feminist criticism see Joan Arnold Romero, 'The Protestant Principle: A Woman's-Eye View of Barth and Tillich', in R. Ruether (ed.), *Religion and Sexism: Images of Woman in the Jewish and Christian Traditions* (New York: Simon & Schuster, 1974).

Stott, John, *Issues Facing Christians Today* (Basingstoke: Marshall Morgan & Scott, 1984).

Wenham, Gordon, 'The Ordination of Women: why is it so divisive?', *Churchman*, 92, no. 4 (1978), pp. 310–19.

THEOLOGICAL ARGUMENTS FOR THE ORDINATION OF WOMEN

Baker, John Austin, 'The Right Time' (pamphlet) (London: Movement for the Ordination of Women, 1981).

Hampson, Daphne, 'Let Us Think About Women' (pamphlet) (The Group for the Ministry of Women in the Scottish Episcopal Church, 1979).

Jewett, Paul, *The Ordination of Women: An Essay on the Office of Christian Ministry* (Grand Rapids, MI: William Eerdmans, 1980).

Kiesling, Christopher, 'Aquinas on Persons' Representation in Sacraments', in Swidler and Swidler (eds), *Women Priests* (see below).

Miller, Jeremy, 'A Note on Aquinas and the Ordination of Women', *New Blackfriars*, 61, no. 719 (April 1980), pp. 185–90.

Norris, Richard, 'The Ordination of Women and the "Maleness" of Christ', *Anglican Theological Review*, Supplementary Series, 6 (June 1976), pp. 69–80. Reprinted in M. Furlong (ed.), *Feminine in the Church* (London: SPCK, 1984).

Riches, John, 'The Case for the Ordination of Women to the Priesthood', unpublished paper (London: Anglican Consultative Council AO/JDD 185).

Stendahl, Krister, 'The Bible and the Role of Women' (pamphlet) (Philadelphia, PA: Fortress Press, Facet Books, Biblical Series 15, 1966).

Swidler, L. and Swidler, A. (eds), *Women Priests: A Catholic Commentary on the Vatican Declaration* (New York: Paulist Press, 1977).

Wijngaards, John, *Did Christ Rule Out Women Priests?* (Great Wakering, Essex: Mayhew-McCrimmon, 1977, revised edn 1986).

LANGUAGE, IMAGERY AND SYMBOLISM

Daly, Mary, *Beyond God the Father: Toward a Philosophy of Women's Liberation* (Boston, MA: Beacon Press, 1973; London: The Women's Press, 1986).

Hamerton-Kelly, Robert, 'God the Father in the Bible and in the Experience of Jesus: The State of the Question', in J.-B. Metz and E. Schillebeeckx (eds), *God as Father?*, *Concilium* no. 143 (Edinburgh: T. & T. Clark, 1981; New York: Seabury Press, 1981).

Lewis, A. (ed.), *The Motherhood of God: A Report by a Study Group appointed by the Woman's Guild and the Panel on Doctrine on the invitation of the General Assembly of the Church of Scotland* (Edinburgh: The Saint Andrew Press, 1984).

McFague, Sallie, *Models of God: Theology for an Ecological, Nuclear Age* (Philadelphia, PA: Fortress Press, 1987; London: SCM Press, 1987).

Moltmann, Jürgen, 'The Motherly Father: Is Trinitarian Patripassionism Replacing Theological Patriarchalism?', in Metz and Schillebeeckx (eds), *God as Father?*

—— *The Trinity and the Kingdom of God* (E.T. London: SCM Press, 1981; New York, Harper & Row, 1981).

Plaskow, Judith and others, 'The Coming of Lilith', in R. Ruether (ed.), *Religion and Sexism: Images of Woman in the Jewish and Christian Traditions* (New York: Simon & Schuster, 1974).

Ruether, Rosemary, *Womanguides: Readings Toward a Feminist Theology* (Boston, MA: Beacon Press, 1985).

Slee, Nicola, 'Parables and Women's Experience', *The Modern Churchman*, 26, no. 2 (1984), pp. 20–31. Reprinted in Loades, A. (ed.), *Feminist Theology: A Reader* (London: SPCK, 1990 forthcoming; Louisville, KY: Westminster/John Knox Press, 1990 forthcoming).

Warner, Marina, *Alone of All Her Sex: The Myth and the Cult of the Virgin Mary* (New York: Alfred A. Knopf, 1976; London: Weidenfeld & Nicolson, 1976).

Weber, H.-R. (ed.), *On A Friday Noon* (London: SPCK, 1979; Geneva: WCC, 1979).

THE GODDESS AND WOMEN'S SPIRITUALITY

Adler, Margot, *Drawing Down the Moon: Witches, Druids, Goddess-Worshippers, and Other Pagans in America Today* (New York: Viking Press, 1979; Boston, MA: Beacon Press, revised edn 1986).

Christ, Carol P., 'Why Women Need the Goddess: Phenomenological, Psychological, and Political Reflections', in C. P. Christ & J. Plaskow (eds), *Womanspirit Rising: A Feminist Reader in Religion* (New York and San Francisco: Harper & Row, 1979), and in Christ, *Laughter of Aphrodite* (see below).

—— *Laughter of Aphrodite: Reflections on a Journey to the Goddess* (San Francisco: Harper & Row, 1987).

Culpepper, Emily, 'Contemporary Goddess Thealogy: A Sympathetic Critique', in C. Atkinson, C. Buchanan and M. Miles (eds), *Shaping New Vision: Gender and Values in American Culture* (Ann Arbor, MI: UMI Research Press, 1987).

Goldenberg, Naomi, *Changing of the Gods: Feminism and the End of Traditional Religions* (Boston, MA: Beacon Press, 1979).

Spretnak, C. (ed.), *The Politics of Women's Spirituality: Essays on the Rise of Spiritual Power within the Feminist Movement* (Garden City, NY: Anchor Doubleday, 1982).

Starhawk, *The Spiral Dance: A Rebirth of the Ancient Religion of the Great Goddess* (San Francisco: Harper & Row, 1979).

—— *Dreaming the Dark: Magic, Sex and Politics* (Boston, MA: Beacon Press, 1982).

WOMEN AND THE FUTURE, UTOPIA, ECOLOGY

Daly, Mary, *Pure Lust: Elemental Feminist Philosophy* (Boston, MA: Beacon Press, 1984; London: The Women's Press, 1984).

Gearhart, Sally, *The Wanderground* (Boston, MA: Alyson Publications, 1984; London: The Women's Press, 1985).

Gilman, Charlotte Perkins, *Herland* (New York: Pantheon Books, 1979; London: The Women's Press, 1979) (1915).

Griffin, Susan, *Woman and Nature: The Roaring Inside Her* (New York: Harper & Row, 1978; London: The Women's Press, 1984).

Wittig, Monique, *Les Guérillères*, tr. D. Le Vay (London: The Women's Press, 1979; Boston, MA: Beacon Press, 1985) (1969).

SIN AND SALVATION IN MEN AND WOMEN

Hampson, Daphne, 'Reinhold Niebuhr on Sin: A Critique', in R. Harries (ed.), *Reinhold Niebuhr and the Issues of Our Time* (London: Mowbrays, 1986; Grand Rapids, MI: William Eerdmans, 1986).

Kierkegaard, Søren, *The Sickness Unto Death*, ed. and tr. H. V. and E. H. Hong (Princeton, NJ: Princeton University Press, 1980) (1849).

Niebuhr, Reinhold, *The Nature and Destiny of Man*, vol. I, *Human Nature*, vol. II, *Human Destiny* (New York: Charles Scribner's Sons, 1964) (1941).

Plaskow, Judith, *Sex, Sin and Grace: Women's Experience and the Theologies of Reinhold Niebuhr and Paul Tillich* (Washington, DC: University Press of America, 1980).

Saiving, Valerie, 'The Human Situation: A Feminine View', *Journal of Religion*, 40 (April 1960), pp. 100-12, reprinted in C. P. Christ and J. Plaskow (eds), *Womanspirit Rising: A Feminist Reader in Religion* (New York and San Francisco: Harper & Row, 1979).

Vaughan, Judith, *Sociality, Ethics and Social Change: A Critical Appraisal of Reinhold Niebuhr's Ethics in the Light of Rosemary Radford Ruether's Works* (Lanham, MD: University of America Press, 1983).

THEOLOGY

Christ, Carol P., 'Feminist Liberation Theology and Yahweh as Holy Warrior: An Analysis of Symbol', in J. Kalven and M. Buckley (eds), *Women's Spirit Bonding* (New York: Pilgrim Press, 1984).

Coakley, Sarah, '"Femininity" and the Holy Spirit?', in M. Furlong (ed.), *Mirror to the Church* (London: SPCK, 1988).

Collins, Sheila, *A Different Heaven and Earth* (Valley Forge, PA: Judson Press, 1974).

Daly, Mary, *Beyond God the Father: Toward a Philosophy of Women's Liberation* (Boston, MA: Beacon Press, 1973; London: The Women's Press, 1986).

—— 'Feminist Postchristian Introduction', *The Church and the Second Sex* (New York and San Francisco: Harper & Row, 1975; Boston, MA: Beacon Press, 1985).

Hampson, Daphne, 'On Power and Gender', *Modern Theology*, 4, no. 3 (April 1988), pp. 234–50.

Hampson, Daphne and Ruether, Rosemary, 'Is There a Place for Feminists in a Christian Church?', *New Blackfriars*, 68, no. 801 (January 1987). (Available as a pamphlet from WIT Publications, 15 Moorland Road, Boxmoor, Hemel Hempstead HP1 1NH, price £1.25 or $3.00 including postage.)

Keller, Catherine, *From a Broken Web: Separation, Sexism, and Self* (Boston, MA: Beacon Press, 1986).

—— 'Walls, Women and Intimations of Interconnection', in U. King (ed.), *Women in the World's Religions, Past and Present* (New York: Paragon House, 1987).

Ruether, Rosemary, *Sexism and God-Talk: Toward a Feminist Theology* (Boston, MA: Beacon Press, 1983; London: SCM Press, 1983).

Walker, Alice, *The Color Purple* (New York: Harcourt Brace Jovanovich, 1982; London: The Women's Press, 1983).

FEMINIST ETHICS AND PSYCHOLOGY

Chodorow, Nancy, *The Reproduction of Mothering: Psychoanalysis and the Sociology of Gender* (Berkeley: University of California Press, 1978).

Daly, Mary, *Gyn/Ecology: The Metaethics of Radical Feminism* (Boston, MA: Beacon Press, 1978; London: The Women's Press, 1979).

Gilligan, Carol, *In a Different Voice: Psychological Theory and Women's Development* (Cambridge, MA: Harvard University Press, 1982).

Haney, Eleanor, 'What is Feminist Ethics? A Proposal for Continuing Discussion', *Journal of Religious Ethics*, 8 (1980), pp. 115–24.

Massey, Marilyn Chapin, *Feminine Soul: The Fate of an Ideal* (Boston, MA: Beacon Press, 1985.)

Miller, Jean Baker, *Toward a New Psychology of Women* (Boston, MA: Beacon Press, 1976; second edn, Boston, MA: Beacon Press, 1986; Harmondsworth: Penguin Books, 1988).

Schaef, Anne Wilson, *Women's Reality: An Emerging Female System in the White Male Society* (Minneapolis, MN: Winston Press, 1981).

Whitbeck, Caroline, 'A Different Reality: Feminist Ontology', in C. Gould (ed.), *Beyond Domination: New Perspectives on Women and Philosophy* (Totowa, NJ: Rowman & Allenheld, 1984).

INDEX